D1243176

Annals of the American Society for Adolescent Psychiatry

ADOLESCENT PSYCHIATRY

DEVELOPMENTAL AND CLINICAL STUDIES

VOLUME 22

Annals of the American Society for Adolescent Psychiatry

ADOLESCENT PSYCHIATRY

DEVELOPMENTAL AND CLINICAL STUDIES

VOLUME 22

AARON H. ESMAN
Editor in Chief

LOIS T. FLAHERTY
HARVEY A. HOROWITZ
Associate Editors

THE ANALYTIC PRESS
1998   Hillsdale, NJ   London

©1998 by The Analytic Press, Inc.

Published by The Analytic Press, Inc.
Editorial Offices: 101 West Street, Hillsdale, NJ 07642

ISBN: 0-88163-196-5
ISSN: 0-226-24064-9

Printed in the United States of America
10 9 8 7 6 5 4 3 2 1

CONTENTS

PART III. ADOLESCENCE AND SOCIAL CRISIS

EDITOR'S INTRODUCTION

AARON H. ESMAN

It is with mingled feelings of sorrow and enthusiasm that, with this volume, I take up the reins as Editor-in-Chief of *Adolescent Psychiatry*. Sorrow because, having barely recovered from the untimely death of my predecessor, Richard Marohn, we have been devastated by the loss of our beloved Editor Emeritus, Sherman Feinstein. Sherman was the life blood of the annals for 20 years, and his wisdom, judgment, experience, and encouragement will be irreplaceable. A memorial tribute by his old friend and colleague Bertram Slaff appears in this volume.

But despite our grievous losses, we are determined to carry on in the tradition our late leaders have established, and to this task we direct ourselves with vigor and enthusiasm. With the help of Lois Flaherty and Harvey Horowitz, who stepped into the breach to complete Volume 21, and with the support of our editorial board, we have mustered our resources and have contrived to carry forward the task of producing an annual compilation of the best statements of current thinking about adolescence from multiple perspectives.

Every editor brings to his task a particular experience and a particular point of view. At the same time, it is his responsibility to be receptive to other points of view and other sorts of experience. My background has been that of a clinician and educator, working primarily within a psychoanalytic frame of reference in both a community agency and a psychiatric hospital, as well as in private practice. Simultaneously, I have been interested in the application of psychoanalytic ideas to the products of culture. All of these interests will be reflected in this volume.

At the same time I am acutely aware of the growing role of empirical research into both developmental and clinical issues in adolescence, and its importance in the changing structure of today's medicine and contemporary psychiatry in particular. I am also sensible of the profound impact of cultural change and cultural variation on the phenomenology of normal and deviant adolescence. All of these matters will also receive appropriate attention in these pages.

It is our hope and expectation to maintain the standards of quality established by the pioneers in this venture. We shall depend upon the help of our colleagues and readers to keep us alert and responsive and, above all, to provide us with the kind of material that will enable us to continue the compilation of an annual volume that preserves those standards and serves the needs of the professional and scholarly communities.

To the question, "Another Society! Why?" Sherman and I responded, "The essential function of an adolescent psychiatry society is to provide a forum for the encouragement and discussion of the psychiatric needs of youth. Teenagers are treated by child psychiatrists and adult psychiatrists as well as by those who limit their work to this age group. Therapists' conceptualizations and approaches vary greatly, depending on their training opportunities and experiences. The forum approach encourages communication in a specific area among psychiatrists of diverse backgrounds."

In 1971 Sherman led a group of us to Buenos Aires, Argentina, to a joint meeting of the Sociedad Argentina de Psiquiatría y Psicología de la Infancia y de la Adolescencia and ASAP. The co-presidents of the meeting were Eduardo Kalina and Sherman Feinstein. Incidentally, Sherman showed his additional talents as tour manager during this adventure. His intelligence and diplomatic skills in negotiating with our Latin American colleagues led to the formation of the Panamerican Forum for the Study of Adolescence, which held well-attended meetings in Brazil, Mexico, and the United States during the decade of the 70s.

Nineteen seventy one also marked the advent of the annual volume *Adolescent Psychiatry*—under the co-editorship of Sherman Feinstein, Peter L. Giovacchini, and Arthur A. Miller. After Miller died, shortly after the book appeared, Feinstein and Giovacchini co-edited the next six volumes. Over the years, Sherman, together with various co-editors, published 19 volumes, the last six as editor-in-chief. This series of volumes has maintained a very high standard, acknowledged by authorities in the field. Developmental issues, psychopathology, the relationship between disorders within the adolescent community and the cultural-political scene at large, treatment issues and, more recently, the effects of managed care on the delivery of therapeutic services to teenagers have all been covered in depth.

As a contributor to several volumes of *Adolescent Psychiatry*, I can testify to Sherman's editing skills, his kindliness in suggesting improvements, his tact, and his recognition of the vulnerability that many writers feel about their work.

In 1973 Sherman held a World Health Organization Travel-Study Fellowship, with the goal of providing a study of community child and adolescent mental health programs in France. There he became acquainted with Serge Lebovici, a prominent child-adolescent psychoanalyst, and Daniel Douady, then head of psychiatric services to the French University student population.

This experience led Sherman and Sara into a new realm, that of organizing and attending child and adolescent psychiatry meetings around the world. In 1976 Sherman was program chairman for the International Forum on Adolescence meeting in Jerusalem, Israel, and in Edinburgh, Scotland. In 1982 he was Adolescent Psychiatry Program Chairman at the Dublin, Ireland, Congress of the International Association of Child and Adolescent Psychiatry and Allied Professions (IACAPAP), and at that meeting he was designated as Chairman of the Organizing Committee for the International Society for Adolescent Psychiatry. That society was formed in Paris in 1985, with Sherman Feinstein elected as its first president. Additional meetings took place in Geneva in 1988, Chicago in 1992, and Athens in 1995.

Sherman's published papers indicate the wide range of his interests and accomplishments. Topics include anorexia nervosa in the male child, an integrated adolescent care program in a general psychiatric hospital, training issues in adolescent psychiatry, juvenile manic–depressive illness, adolescent depression, adolescent psychosis, psychotherapy with adolescents, the cult phenomenon, and assimilating Piaget: cognitive structures and depressive reaction to loss.

During all these years of more than full-time activity as therapist, consultant, editor, organization leader, politician, and provocateur, Sherman maintained a deep and abiding commitment to his family. With Sara he shared almost 50 years of mutual devotion and support. To his sons, Joel and Paul, he was a kind and generous father, sharing his interests with them, listening to their ideas, scuba diving, playing chess, playing tennis, going to sports events. The printing press in their home is an expression of the family hobby, reminding one of the Hogarth Press of Leonard and Virginia Woolf. Joel has become a pediatrician who does child abuse research; he and his wife, Joan, have eight children and one grandchild. Paul is a domestic relations attorney. He and his wife, Andrea, have one son.

Sherman's final illness was a four-month siege; he was comforted by a large and loving family and many friends. We applaud his vast achievement.

IN MEMORIAM
PETER BLOS, Ph. D.

AARON H. ESMAN

Peter Blos died in his 94th year on June 12, 1997 at his home in Holderness, New Hampshire. He is survived by his wife, Betsy Thomas Blos, his son, Peter Blos, Jr., M. D., his daughter, Lillemor Beenhouwer, four grandchildren, and three great-grandchildren.

The customary biographical data—his birth in Karlsrühe, Germany; his teaching diploma from the University of Heidelberg; his Ph. D. in biology from Vienna; his emigration to the United States in 1934; his years of teaching and guidance work in New Orleans and New York— evoke some of the flavor of his restless, inquiring mind and his devotion to education and psychological service to the young. But the heart of his professional life and the organizing core of his work derived from those years in Vienna when he became a part of the psychoanalytic circle, began his psychoanalytic studies, and served as director of the now legendary Experimental School, in collaboration with Anna Freud, August Aichorn, Dorothy Burlingham, and his childhood friend Erik Erikson. Out of this experience grew his commitment to the welfare of the young, a commitment from which he never wavered and to which he brought the full measure of his creative energy.

My first encounter with him occurred at the Jewish Board of Guardians in New York, where, as a newly-appointed junior psychiatric consultant, I was given the privilege of attending his staff training seminars on adolescence. It was there that he developed and refined his ideas about assessment and adolescent development that were elaborated in his now classic book, *On Adolescence* (1962). There he proposed his (by now canonical) classification of developmental substages, as well as formulating the process of ego development in adolescence and the crucial influence of sociocultural factors on that process.

On Adolescence established Peter as the founding father of the modern understanding of adolescent development and psychopathology. His later work, much of it published in these *Annals*, served to deepen and consolidate this position. Drawing on the work of Margaret Mahler, he set forth in 1967 the concept of the "second individuation process," in which he described the oscillation between progressive and regressive trends that, in his view, were indispensable for normal developmental progression. Still later, he propounded in a series of papers and in his book *Sons and Fathers* (1985) the view that the consolidation of psychic structure and character development in late adolescence (particularly in males) is contingent on the resolution of the preoedipal dyadic attachment to the same-sex parent and its reactivation during the oedipal period and in early adolescence.

True to his early interest in education, Peter was a dedicated and gifted teacher. After he was (somewhat belatedly) granted a Special Membership in the New York Psychoanalytic Society in 1965, he was appointed the following year as a Supervisor and Instructor in the Child Analysis program at the New York Psychoanalytic Institute. In that role, he served as a mentor and model to generations of students and candidates in Child and Adolescent Analysis. Subsequently, in 1967 he was appointed lecturer, and taught the course in adolescent development in that and the following year. A few years later, in 1972, he introduced a course in the analysis of the late adolescent, which he continued to offer until his retirement from active teaching in 1977. He also lent his talents as teacher and supervisor to other training facilities, notably to the Columbia Psychoanalytic Center, where he was a founding member of their Child Analysis program.

As we both aged, we came to see each other less, mostly at meetings, occasionally at parties. But Peter was unfailingly generous in responding to appeals for advice, opinions, and ideas. It is a source of pride and pleasure to me that he proposed me as discussant for papers that he and others presented at various meetings, and he was invariably gracious and complimentary in his responses to these discussions.

Peter was, in that overused phrase, a Renaissance man—scholar, therapist, musician, craftsman, poet. He was, in truth, a towering figure in the scientific and intellectual life of our time, one of the last of a great generation of clinical scholars whose work formed the foundations of psychoanalysis and of adolescent psychiatry as we have come to know them. His contributions to the understanding and, therefore, the welfare of young people everywhere are boundless and of lasting value. He will be missed and mourned by all who knew him and were touched by his wisdom, his good humor, his enthusiasm, and his generosity of spirit. My own debt to him can never be repaid.

Annals of the American Society for Adolescent Psychiatry

ADOLESCENT PSYCHIATRY

DEVELOPMENTAL AND CLINICAL STUDIES

VOLUME 22

PART I

ADOLESCENCE: GENERAL CONSIDERATIONS

Adolescence has long been favored ground for the literary imagination. Despite the concerns of many clinicians about the poverty of adult recollections of adolescent experience, autobiographies and fictional treatments of this period of life abound, ranging from St. Augustine's and, later, Rousseau's *Confessions* to the novels of development so characteristic of the Romantic period and, indeed, of our own. In his essay Milton Horowitz relates this effusion to the upsurge and fluidity of daydream in the adolescent years, the very fount, he believes, of the creative imagination. In my own chapter, I find remarkable evocations of contemporary adolescence in Shakespeare's treatment of his youthful characters, suggesting that little has changed in the behavior patterns of teenagers over the centuries. Vivian Rakoff shows how the dominant conception of adolescence in the psychoanalytic literature (and, I might add, in the popular imagination) is rooted in the Nietzschean vision of the storm, strife, and conflict that dominated the central European milieu in which those who formulated this point of view had their intellectual origins.

1 ADOLESCENT DAYDREAMS AND CREATIVE IMPULSE

MILTON H. HOROWITZ

All of us are dreamers but few of us are poets. Yet in adolescence the daydream is a theater of the mind, starring oneself and often rich in plot and characterizations. Consciously wished-for or sometimes seemingly unbidden, the daydream achieves a structural architecture and heads toward a goal. Attended by powerful sexual and ambitious aims, daydreams serve purposes of gratification, control, consolation, reward, revenge, and reinvention of oneself and the world. Though the life of fantasy persists as long as we live, the adolescent daydream seems specific to that period. We enter adolescence with all the remnants of the unfinished business of childhood, now inhabiting a newly bulky, changed body with violently intensified sexual and aggressive needs and wishes. With bewildering rapidity we enter a new world with upheavals in family relationships, new inner demands, heights and depths of passions and intensifications of excitement, joy, anxiety, depression, guilt, and shame. New choices of friends, imagined sexual partners, new interests in learning, music, literature, movies, television, art, sport, power, and money crowd in upon the adolescent. Adolescent daydreaming, now the counterpart of childhood play, gives shape and form to this panoply of desire. Moreover, the daydream often has its immediate translation into creative acts: love letters, love poetry, diaries and journals filled with hope, longing, and despair, music, sport, and challenging deeds of prowess. Mountains are climbed, inventions are constructed, skills developed, and business schemes hatched. The daydream is often the preparation for a life of work and love but as frequently it is the repository of old hopes and lost hopes, paralyzed intentions, and the psychology of regret.

Psychoanalysis, with its roots in the biology of human development and its methodology based upon the disciplines of history and literature,

3

shifted its philosophical ground from the experimental methods of natural science to the observational methods of the poets, novelists, and historians. Sigmund Freud, trained as a neuropathologist, was himself taken aback as he realized his case histories read like novels. But we should not be surprised by this trajectory of Freud's career. Observe, for example, the most striking remnant of his adolescence. Ernest Jones (1955) tells us of an experience that Freud shared with Jones. I quote the episode in its entirety:

In 1906, on the occasion of his fiftieth birthday, the little group of adherents in Vienna presented him with a medallion, designed by a well-known sculptor, Karl Maria Schwerdtner, having on the obverse his side-portrait in bas-relief and on the reverse a Greek design of Oedipus answering the Sphinx. Around it is a line from Sophocles' *Oedipus Tyrannus*. ὃς τὰ κλεὶν' αἰνὶγματ' ἤσει καὶ κράτιστος ἦν ἀνήρ. ("Who divined the famed riddle and was a man most mighty.")

When he showed it to me a few years later I asked him to translate the passage, my Greek having rusted considerably, but he modestly said I must ask someone else to do it. Thanks to Dr. Hitschmann's kindness I am happy to possess a duplicate of this medallion.

At the presentation of the medallion there was a curious incident. When Freud read the inscription he became pale and agitated and in a strangled voice demanded to know who had thought of it. He behaved as if he had encountered a *revenant*, and so he had. After Federn told him it was he who had chosen the inscription, Freud disclosed that as a young student at the University of Vienna he used to stroll around the great arcaded court inspecting the busts of former famous professors of the institution. He then had the fantasy, not merely of seeing his own bust there in the future, which would not have been anything remarkable in an ambitious student, but of it actually being inscribed with the *identical* words he now saw on the medallion.

Not long ago I was able to fulfill his youthful wish by presenting to the University of Vienna, for erection in the court, the bust of Freud made by the sculptor Königsberger in 1921, and the line from Sophocles was added. It was unveiled at a ceremony on February 4, 1955. It is a very rare example of such a daydream of adolescence coming true in every detail, even if it took eighty years to do so [pp. 13–14].

Freud's daydream and its ambitious goal was a commonplace, grandiose in outlook and almost poignant for a member of a despised minority born in provincial Moravia. Identified with the tragic hero-king, Freud set about his own solution to the riddle of the Sphinx: how to understand the stages of human life by observation and inquiry. Despite endless individual variations and gaps of culture and circumstance, Freud saw that the developmental tasks bore some remarkable similarities in individuals. In a set of creative works, beginning with the observations that all human infants are helpless, and must mature and develop only with the help of others, he and a few colleagues created psychoanalysis. The childhood need for nurture and help is the basis for what was called transference. Viewing human behavior through its conflictual vicissitudes, psychoanalysis became an observational method, a therapeutic modality, and a set of explanatory hypotheses about the operation of the mind throughout the life cycle. A mixture of scientist and poet, Freud created something new which has proved durable despite endless attacks and frequent premature notices of its demise.

It has been my very great privilege over many years of psychoanalytic practice to have known and treated many creative artists, people who have often been more intelligent and more capable than I was. Creative artists—authors, poets, playwrights, painters, composers, and scientists—seek analysis for the same reasons as others less talented. Troubled in love or work, beset by anxiety and depression, they seek relief of pain. They agonize over the ubiquitous inhibitions in their creativity. Initially, none have ever presented issues of their adolescent daydreams and fantasies as having any special importance. Yet in almost every instance, those fantasies were crucial in understanding their subsequent careers. Was the content of those fantasies remarkably different from those of other adolescents? What seemed so striking to me was that the content was commonplace. Thus we may ask the question, what makes all of us dreamers but only some of us poets? Here I think that much of what has been written psychoanalytically about art has foundered because of focussing on the content of fantasies. Most artists I have known do not recognize themselves in conventional psychoanalytic formulations that seem to them to be farfetched and speculative. What seems recognizable to them is that they had to find shapes or forms for the expression of their artistic choices. The day-to-day work of the artist is often in the making of a choice even when the ideas seem to come unbidden, even when the procedure seems either arbitrary or aleatory, whether the work proceeds from spontaneous gesture or measured event. The work may document the creative process as well as present content representing a variety of sources: wishes, needs, observations of people or nature, terrors and horrors, rhythms and sounds, words, music, color, and light. Of talent, we can say little other than about special sensitivities that began in early childhood, and that is very little. Of craft, we can say much and of inhibition we can say even more. Central to all creative work are identifications with parents, admired figures from present or past, other artists, and the higher concept of art itself. It is those identifications that both fuel the works and give rise to the ubiquitous fears of plagiarism that have haunted every artist I have known.

The need for confidentiality has restrained me, and almost every other analyst, from reporting upon the only specific information that would convey to an audience any sense of conviction that we have something to say about creativity. The method I have chosen is to try to convey some of my observations through a series of disguises, a masked ball of the beaux arts. This was a method used by Phyllis Greenacre (1958) in her paper on "The Family Romance of the Artist," but will be put to some different uses here.

I will try to present material from the writings and the biographies of Anthony Trollope, Leo Tolstoy, St. Augustine, Jean-Jacques Rousseau, Nicolas-Edmé Restif de la Bretonne, Napoleon Bonaparte, Elizabeth Gaskell, Charlotte Brontë, and Virginia Woolf. I have chosen examples from these authors because I have in them pieces of documented information they are close to observations that my patients have shared with me. Each of the authors is a mask for issues encountered in real patients. Though the content used was derived from public sources, the psychoanalytic experiences are real and vivid and private. The patients' experiences are theirs alone and though your conviction may be incomplete, we may approach the task knowing that the crucial issues are real and only the method of exposition contrived.

Anthony Trollope, one of the most readable of Victorian novelists, had his literary career undergo an eclipse with his posthumously published autobiography. In it, Trollope (1883) had described a method of writing his 47 novels, five volumes of short stories, biographies, and travel books as well as a translation from the Latin. Trollope assaulted the sensibilities of those with pre formed notions of the travail of cre-

6

ativity by reporting that he had assigned himself the task of writing a certain number of words, instantly *ready for publication*, every morning. His mother Frances had been a much-published writer who had abandoned him for a crucial period of his childhood, leaving him with his half-mad father. The pinnacle of Trollope's success was in his two sequences of multiple novels: the Barsetshire novels and the Palliser political novels. Here is a remarkable excerpt from *An Autobiography* (please understand that this book was not written for publication; it was given as a memoir to his son Henry in 1876 and was published by him seven years later, only after Trollope was dead):

I will mention here another habit which had grown upon me from still earlier years—which I myself often regarded with dismay when I thought of the hours devoted to it, but which, I suppose, must have tended to make me what I have been. As a boy, even as a child, I was thrown much upon myself. I have explained, when speaking of my school-days, how it came to pass that other boys would not play with me. I was therefore alone, and had to form my plays within myself. Play of some kind was necessary to me then, as it has always been. Study was not my bent, and I could not please myself by being all idle. Thus it came to pass that I was always going about with some castle in the air firmly built within my mind. Nor were these efforts in architecture spasmodic, or subject to constant change from day to day. For weeks, for months, if I remember rightly, from year to year, I would carry on the same tale, binding myself down to certain laws, to certain proportions, and proprieties, and unities. Nothing impossible was ever introduced,—nor even anything which, from outward circumstances, would seem to be violently improbable. I myself was of course my own hero. Such is a necessity of castle-building. But I never became a king, or a duke,—much less when my height and personal appearance were fixed could I be an Antinous, or six feet high. I never was a learned man, nor even a philosopher. But I was a very clever person, and beautiful young women used to be fond of me. And I strove to be kind of heart, and open of hand, and noble in thought, despising mean things; and altogether I was a very much better fellow than I have ever succeeded in being since. This had been the occupation of my life for six or seven years before I went to the Post Office, and was by no means abandoned when I commenced my work. There can, I imagine, hardly be a

7

more dangerous mental practice; but I have often doubted whether, had it not been my practice, I should ever have written a novel. I learned in this way to maintain an interest in a fictitious story, to dwell on a work created by my own imagination, and to live in a world altogether outside the world of my own material life. In after years I have done the same,—with this difference, that I have discarded the hero of my early dreams, and have been able to lay my own identity aside (pp. 36–37).

Here, Trollope touches on a theme repeated in the memoirs of many artists, his tendency to give an extended, ongoing, and continuous shape to his thought-productions. This shaping helped him achieve what some composers refer to as his "own voice," the unique signature of sound and style. Trollope described his trajectory into being an artist.

It is important in understanding creative experience that we not try to interpolate our own biases and expectations. Much psychoanalytic writing about art has the flavor of "what the artist must have thought, what the artist might have referred to, what childhood experience should have contributed" and so on. We should always keep in mind an aphorism of Ludwig Wittgenstein: "Of that which nothing is known, nothing can be said."

Virginia Woolf provides us with yet another example of achieving form in relation to memory as well as daydream. In a *Sketch of the Past* Woolf (1957) says: "I find that scene-making is my natural way of marking the past." For Woolf, memory and fantasy could be woven into "scenes" providing much of her writing with a gorgeous visual vividness; she invites us to "see" along with her. Adolescence heightens the ability to create such "scene-like" imagery and to attach it to a narrative that offers vividness, excitement, and continuity. It is an ability described by playwrights and directors of film and stage. For some the scene is not just visual but a mix of sight, sound, and word, not just a theater of the mind but the mind as a recording device that mixes perception, memory, and invention. Old events are recalled in entirety to give vividness to the new work. Saul Bellow reminded us recently that a writer's productions were not autobiographical jottings but were the product of imaginative invention. He noted that the words uttered by a character in a novel did not necessarily reflect the mind of the artist but of a personality *invented* by the writer. Woolf was adept at such imaginative invention in the creation of characters derived from memories. However, Woolf's invitation to the reader to join her in the scenes is not so specific as to limit the audience's participation. A genius for ambiguity, as demonstrated in *Orlando* (Woolf, 1993), allows time to be kaleidoscoped and sexual identity to be transformed. Here too is a commonplace of adolescent daydream: ambiguity of time and sexual identity. Peter Blos, many years ago, alerted us to the frequency with which preadolescent and adolescent boys consciously fantasize themselves as women imagined to be powerful, and Robert Bak, Otto Fenichel, and Bertram Lewin all described patients' fantasies of a woman with a penis, anatomically ambiguous. Ambiguity can also mask hidden precision (Kris, 1953).

Now one of the contrasts between my actual clinical experience and the written memoirs of artists is that written memoirs tend to be sanitized, that is, they tend to be either totally or partially stripped of their sexual and aggressive intensities. Many, if not most, adolescent fantasies and daydreams have some connection to masturbation and sexual excitement.

We might pause for a moment for some thought about the terms "fantasy" and "daydream." I do not think that there is always a clear distinction. Psychoanalysis has tended to view fantasy as having unconscious roots reaching up into consciousness in a derivative form, much like the distinction we make in studying dreams between a manifest content and latent dream thoughts. In the psychology of dream formation, as distinct from the physiology of dream formation, we have been much concerned with the manner in which dream images arise through the entrepreneurial use of remnants of perceptions while awake, the so-called day-residue. So too we recognize that the conscious daydream has latent thoughts derived from old memory, unconscious wishes (i.e., fantasy) and a day-residue that gives it form. In common English usage, the daydream as described in the *Oxford English Dictionary* is "a dream indulged in while awake, especially one of happiness or gratified hope or ambition, a reverie, a castle in air." Its first quoted use, by Dryden in 1685 (*Lucretia*): ". . . and when awake, thy soul but nods at best, Day-dreams and sickly thoughts revolving in thy breast." Steele (1711) wrote: *Spectator essay #167*: ". . . the gay Phantoms that dance before my waking Eyes and compose my Day-Dreams" place the spectator in a passive position observing the dancing phantoms. Accompanied by a mild alteration in consciousness, the daydream is experienced sometimes passively as if unbidden and sometimes as an active conjuring-up of a created event. The daydream is a triumph of the synthetic, integrating and organizing functions of the ego.

To return to the edited and sanitized versions as depicted in memoirs, as contrasted to excited masturbatory adolescent memories frequently described by patients, we must remember that this editorial process may not have been merely for purposes of respectable publication. Anna Freud had noted that in a manner analogous to the amnesia for events experienced by patients trying to recall early childhood, there is a related amnesia of adolescence. This is usually not about events but about the emotional *intensities* of that period. Many of us have forgotten the emotional roller-coaster of our adolescent years. Racked with love, rage, shame, and despair, high on joy, thrilled by love, oscillating between fickleness and promises of endless fidelity, adolescence usually gives way to a calmer period. The driven intensity of sexual feeling and aggressive impulse is partially replaced by something less driven. What is later sanitized for the press is also seen in this amnesia for the adolescent peaks of emotionality as observed in older patients. However, the direct connection of daydream and intense sexuality may be seen in the work of Nicolas-Edmé Restif de la Bretonne. Restif was born in 1735 and wrote many novels of blatant sexuality. In *Monsieur Nicolas*, an autobiography subtitled *The Human Heart Unveiled*, Restif reports numerous daydreams and conscious fantasies. Restif, who kept diaries and journals throughout his life, recorded all his sexual adventures in a manner comparable to the memoirs of Casanova. Whether real or invented, these lists bid fair to rival Don Giovanni's "1003" in Spain. Restif was known in French literary circles as "Le Rousseau du ruisseau," the "Rousseau of the Gutter," and Restif viewed the two great confessions of St. Augustine and Rousseau simply as apologias. Restif (1930–31) records the following daydream of 1748, age 13:

I thought of Jeannette and imagined that I was ten years older, and had worked and won a position, and become an advantageous match for her, and that I presented myself to ask for her in marriage. I won her. But my fantasies about her were never such as I sometimes wove about other girls—for in my frequent lapses into despair of ever obtaining Jeannette, I used to fall back on others such as Marianne Taboué, the pink-cheeked Nolin, a certain Adine, young Bourdillat; and I even imagined Mme. Chevrier a widow and I her husband. All these fantasies ended in marriage; but although they were not without a certain sweetness, they left a trail of lassitude, disgust and remorse; whereas, when Jeannette was the heroine they only grew more exquisite after marriage [Vol. 1, pp. 307 ff].

He then goes on to spin a narrative into old age, with children married, the daughters-in-law chosen from "the children of those who most attracted me after Jeannette." The "pure" Jeannette and the others who gave rise to guilty disgust describe a splitting of the images of women analogous to his own splitting of himself into a saint of truthfulness and a confessed sinner. Restif was a shoe fetishist of whom Grand-Carteret said, "If Restif was a fetishist, the whole eighteenth century was fetishist with him." Restif's autobiographical confessions and novels had great influence. They are said to have "modelled the soul" of the writer Gérard de Nerval. Furthermore, Schiller called Goethe's attention to *Monsieur Nicolas* as of "incalculable value." The daydream and the sexually explicit confessions of Rousseau and Restif leaped into the romanticism of the 19th century. Schiller's *The Robbers* (1780) and its extolling of revenge, Goethe's *Werther* and its picture of hopeless love and romanticized suicide, Berlioz's Symphonie Fantastique, and the explosion of "Wagnerism" were the high-water marks of this trend, and psychoanalysis with its emphasis on emotion was an important romantic spin-off into the twentieth century. Young love, young revenge, young poetry leaped on to the stage. Shelley, Keats, Byron, Coleridge, Wordsworth—what a cast, extolling youth and passion. The Gothic novel (Shelley wrote two) sent shivers up young spines; Mrs. Radcliffe's *Mysteries of Udolpho* was a bestseller, Walpole's *Castle of Otranto* titillated numerous English readers and Jane Austen and Thomas Love Peacock laughed at them all with mockeries of overblown horror.

Now everyone has *some* masturbatory fantasies, everyone has had frightening dreams, but only artists give them specific ongoing form and give them a quality related to what has been styled by the secondary revision of dreams. The ideas and sensations must be placed in communicable extended forms, a process I have chosen to call *thematic elaboration* and *thematic transformations*. The essence of romanticism was thematic elaboration. Thematic variations add richness to the tapestry of creative work in which inner conflicts could be represented in many forms, and repeated patterns; multiple meanings served as a further invitation to the audience to participate. This too helps us to understand the difference between the private thought of many adolescents that tends to be repetitively stereotyped and limited, and the richness of elaboration and the need for communication that characterizes the future artist even where that artist has some elements of stereotypy in the daydream. The daydream is close to the wish for

11

immediate gratification, but the construction of a work of art usually (though not always) is a form of delayed gratification (Kris, 1953).

For a few moments I would like to turn your attention to the man about whom more has been written than about anyone who ever lived, not excepting Jesus. That man was Napoleon Bonaparte. Napoleon wrote fiction, though that is a surprise to many, and though he aped Rousseau in the attempt to write romances, he was a failed artist. Napoleon could not elaborate. He wrote in a condensed manner some rather puerile and soupy attempts at explications of love when he was an adolescent cadet and young officer. In an 1802 conversation with Claire de Remussat he said, ". . . I often let myself dream in order that I might afterwards measure my dreams by the compass of my reason." He told her how he contrived his youthful novels, using, without credit, Rousseau's description of how *La Nouvelle Héloïse* was written. Napoleon's *Clisson et Eugenie*, a caricature of Rousseau, is a bare-bones outline of a romance without any meat on its flesh. Napoleon had a passion for condensation and summary. The late 18th century was no time for minimalist art. When reading works of history he crossed out ruthlessly what he considered excess verbiage in his attempt to distil essences. Finally, on the voyage to conquer Egypt, having carried a library aboard, he upbraided his secretary Bourienne for reading *Paul et Virginie* and Berthier for reading Goethe's *Werther*. He commented: "Books for lady's maids; only give them history books. Men should read nothing else." He had turned from his attempts at being a man of sensibilities, a replica of Rousseau, and was now wholly a man of action, identified with Paoli, the hero of Corsican resistance against the French. Having confided in Bourienne, his military schoolmate since age eight, he revealed his wishes and daydreams: "I will do these French all the mischief I can . . . but you do not ridicule me, you like me." He reported daydreams of the liberation of Corsica, the heroism of Paoli and a glorification of his own father as Paoli's adjutant. His daydreams became less personal and more political; he wrote about the overthrow of kings *before* the Revolution and about ideas of revenge in the *New Corsica*. The theme of revenge thereafter occupied his life. Its consequence was fateful for the world. His most profound creation was himself, a reinvention of a four-foot eleven-inch outcast into the Emperor Napoleon, now identified with Caesar. His revenge on the French was complete on June 18, 1815 at Waterloo. Napoleon destroyed himself and France in a disastrous and helpless campaign.

Daydreams of revenge are commonplace in adolescence and though few become Napoleons many become sadomasochists, and many become criminals. A few creative artists express their needs for revenge in creative work; rarely is revenge the actual theme of the work; more often revenge fuels ambition. They desire to "get back" at someone or something, to "show" someone. It is in these circumstances that one can witness the reinvention of the self as an act of creation. Changing one's name, immersion in family romances, grandiose new identifications—sometimes with another artist—spring forth and fuel the reinvention. I have seen this more in performers than in creators. A recent biography of the singer Josephine Baker documents such a reinvention: a poor and despised black child who transformed herself into a heroine of the French resistance as well as a renowned sexual figure, sought after by both men and women, successful and a failure in rapid cycles.

The acts of vengeance for the hurts of the past have some resemblance to a commonplace childhood fantasy: "When I am big, and you are little, I will spank you," where a wished-for reversal of positions is the modality of revenge.

Loneliness has often been central to the young lives of many artists, sometimes persisting throughout the life cycle. In a scientific era when a tendency of psychiatric diagnosis is to pare the wide range of human affects down to only two—anxiety and depression—loneliness seems to get short shrift by professionals. But loneliness is one of the most painful of emotions and an important aspect of the life of most adolescents. It is the spur to daydreams, and the invention of stories. Nowhere in the history of art is this more poignant than in the history of the Brontë sisters, especially Charlotte. What a piece of good fortune it was for the world of literature that Charlotte Brontë's biography was written by her friend, the skilled novelist Elizabeth Gaskell (1919). In my view it remains one of the best biographies ever written, though little read now. Mrs. Gaskell, an acute observer of the psychology of women and an early champion of women's rights, especially the rights of poor women, had the deepest sympathetic response to the plight of the Brontë sisters as lonely children. And she deeply understood the relationship of loneliness to daydreaming. This from the biography:

Life in an isolated village, or a lonely country house, presents many little occurrences which sink into the mind of childhood, there to be brooded over. No other event may have happened, or be likely to happen, for days, to push one of these aside before it

13

has assumed a vague and mysterious importance. Thus, children leading a secluded life are often thoughtful and dreamy: the impressions made upon them by the world without—the unusual sights of earth and sky—the accidental meetings with strange faces and figures (rare occurrences in those out-of-the-way places)—are sometimes magnified by them into things so deeply significant as to be almost supernatural [p. 71].

This view is repeatedly confirmed in Charlotte Brontë's novels, especially in the masterpiece, *Jane Eyre*. Loneliness led to daydreaming, invention, story-telling, and the playing of rôles. It was not only true that women had enormous difficulty gaining access to publishers, leading them to frequently adopt men's names: Currer Bell, George Eliot, George Sand, but that the weakness of the girls, compared to what Charlotte termed her "August Father," led her to extolling hero men and identifying with them in adolescence. Central to this attitude was the extolling of the Duke of Wellington; almost all Charlotte's *juvenilia* were said by her to have been written by a "Lord Charles Wellesly" (the Duke's family name). The manuscript for *Jane Eyre* was submitted with the author's name "Currer Bell" and it probably would not have been published if sent by someone named Charlotte. But realistic and practical matters were not all that was involved. Charlotte wrestled with issues of masculinity and femininity for much of her early life. She saw literature as a path with which to express this conflict and the poetic gift as a mode of compromise resolution. She writes to G.H. Lewes on January 18, 1848: "It is *poetry*, as I comprehend the word, which elevates that masculine George Sand, and makes out of something coarse, something Godlike." The letter is signed Currer Bell. When she finally met Lewes in 1850 she again knit together masculine and feminine. In a letter to a friend, she says: "I have seen Lewes too . . . I could not feel otherwise to him than half-sadly, half-tenderly—a queer word that last, but I use it because the aspect of Lewes's face almost moves me to tears; it is so wonderfully like Emily—her eyes, the features, the very nose . . . even at moments the expression" (p. 356). (Lewes later became George Eliot's husband.)

All hopes in the Brontë family had been centered by the father upon his ne'er-do-well son, Patrick, who died of alcoholism. Charlotte commented, "My poor father naturally thought more of his *only* son than of his daughters." She married late to her father's curate, an event which had been her father's wish, and died following childbirth. She had spent a lonely childhood, beset by losses, always trying to please her overidealized father and his glorious imagined counterpart: the Duke of Wellington. Her lonely daydreams and her adolescent writings, especially her poetry, culminated in the masterpiece *Jane Eyre*. She had combined her conflicting adolescent masculine and feminine images and emerged one of the greater writers of the last century.

The multiple deaths and losses in Charlotte Brontë's life are not uncommon in the life of artists. In fact there is considerable evidence in my own psychoanalytic experience that loss and the need to replace that loss in an act of new creation is a powerful motive for some artists. This seems especially intense when the losses occur in early childhood.

I will introduce in my masked-ball of artists the figure of Leo Tolstoy. Tolstoy (1930) was remarkable in his need for truthfulness and in his recording of his childhood and adolescent daydreams in very slight fictional disguise in his short novellas, *Childhood, Boyhood* and *Youth*. His letters, now translated into English, reinforce our awareness of his commitment to historical truth much colored by his deep guilt and his moral needs. Tolstoy's mother died when he was two, his father when he was eight. He was raised by someone he styled as his "Aunt Tatyana." He records the following in *Youth*:

I am convinced that there is no human being and no age devoid of this benign, consoling capacity to dream. But except for a general characteristic of impossibility and fairy-likeness, the dreams of each man and each period of life have their own distinctive characteristics. At that period, which I regard as the end of boyhood and beginning of youth, my dreams were based on four feelings: love of *her*, the imaginary woman of whom I always dreamt in one and the same way and whom I expected at any moment to meet somewhere. *She* was a little of Sónya, a little of Másha, Vasili's wife, when washing linen in the wash-tub, and a little of a woman with pearls round her white neck whom I had seen long ago at the theatre in the box next to ours. The second feeling was the love of being loved. I wanted everybody to know me and love me. I wanted to tell my name—and for everybody to be struck by this information, to surround me, and thank me for something. The third feeling was hope of some unusual, vain-glorious good fortune, and was so strong and firm that it verged on insanity. I was so convinced that I should very soon by some extraordinary occurrence suddenly become the richest and most distinguished person in the world, that I was continually in a perturbed state of expectation of some magic happiness. I kept expecting that it would now begin and I should attain all that man can desire, and I was always in a hurry, imagining that it was already *beginning* somewhere where I was not. The fourth and chief feeling was self-disgust and repentance, but repentance so mingled with hope of happiness that it had nothing sad about it. It seemed to me so easy and natural to tear oneself away from all the past, to alter and forget all that had been, and to begin one's life with all its relations completely anew, in such a way that the past would not oppress or bind me. I even revelled in my reputation for the past, and tried to see it blacker than it really was. The blacker the circle of my recollections of the past, the clearer and brighter stood out the clear, bright point of the present, and the fairer streamed the rainbow colors of the future. That voice of repentance and passionate desire for perfection was the main new sensation of my soul at this period of my development, and it was this that laid a new foundation for my views of myself, of mankind, and of God's universe [p. 230].

Tolstoy daydreamed throughout his life, always full of wishes, always full of guilt. He recognized that the content of daydreams shifted with the developmental epochs, and he recorded his daydreams as he documented his memories. The act of remembering, fused with acts of invention, were his working methods. They were attempts at the mastery of loss. (The creation of "memories" had a restitutive effect.)

A letter, in French, to his "Aunt" Tatyana tells a daydream when he was 24. He is on his way to the Caucasus and writes:

This is how I picture it to myself . . . I am at Yasnaya . . . you still live at Yasnaya too. You have aged a little, but are still fresh and in good health . . . I work in the morning, but we see each other almost the whole day; we have dinner; in the evening I read you something that doesn't bore you; then we talk . . . you talk to me of your memories—of my father and mother. We recall the people who were dear to us and who are no more; you will weep, I will do the same; but these tears will be sweet . . . You know that perhaps my only good quality is my sensibility [p. 23].

War and Peace with its depiction of Tolstoy's family, member by member, set against the then antique backdrop of the Napoleonic wars, is the artistic outcome of this daydream and the culmination of this sensibility. Tolstoy recreated his own lost world in a glorious novel and its stunning essays on how little one can know about history even if one is an eye-witness observer. But the deepest poignancy is in the last line before the second epilogue when the little Prince Nicholas, after the death of his father Prince Andrew, daydreams of doing "something with which even *he* would be satisfied." *War and Peace* was that "something." The wish to have someone proud of you is one of the great motivating factors of adolescence and a momentous union of self, parents, and conscience. It has been an important factor in the life of every artist I have known, even if unconscious at the outset of the analysis. The one who is to be proud is the unseen audience whose love is needed.

The hunger for the dead parent, especially the dead mother, never goes away. Tolstoy, who died at 82 wrote this two years before that event which he believed would rejoin them: "I walk in the garden and I think of my mother, of Maman; I do not remember her, but she has always been an ideal of saintliness for me. I have never heard a single disparaging remark about her" And also:

Felt dull and sad all day. Toward evening the mood changed into a desire for caresses, for tenderness. I wanted, as when I was a child, to nestle against some tender and compassionate being and weep with love and be consoled . . . become a tiny boy, close to my mother, the way I imagine her. Yes, yes, my Maman, whom I was never able to call that because I did not know how to talk when she died. She is my highest image of love—not cold, divine love, but warm, earthly love, maternal. . . . Maman, hold me, baby me! . . . All that is madness, but it is all true.

Here is the need to create memory. All of this confirmed by my experience with a patient who wears Tolstoy's mask at our *Ballo in Maschera*.

Turn now to just a few words about conscience, guilt, shame, and exhibitionism in the creative. The two great confessions dominated by guilt, shame and explosive exhibitionism were those of St. Augustine and Rousseau. Both writers were seeking to exculpate themselves from sins of which they felt horribly guilty—sins of the flesh, rejection of God and morality, excesses leading to shame, but all continuing while the breast was being beaten. Augustine (1961) says of his youth, addressing God: "Give me chastity and continence, but not just now" (p. 7). His memory of himself as a whoring, thieving pagan adolescent was linked to his pagan father and distant from his saintly Christian mother.

It is one of the characteristics of adolescent remorse over masturbation that however many times it is abjured, it is repeated. Religious and moral daydreams, and their promissory counterparts—religious and moral vows—are there to be broken and repudiated, only to be renewed again. Confessional literature, novels, and poetry of sin and expiation seem to bear a special relationship to exhibitionism traceable to specific experiences of adolescence. Religious and quasi-religious political conversions are often presented with great fanfare. The need for punishment *and* forgiveness is so great at that period of stormy and imperious sexual need that it must be trumpeted as an aspect of those needs and a derivative of them. It is a forerunner of the exhibitionistic need to declare oneself a good and kind person—a variety of reaction formation. But to cast one's ideas as a confession has an enormous appeal and a ready audience. Everyone likes to hear about the crimes of others. Millions of people read murder mysteries in order to find the bad culprit and hold themselves blameless of wishes to murder. So too there is a ready audience for sexual confessions. At the same time, they are stimulating and also offer distance from the described events. The observer may be titillated but free of guilt, as with the murder mystery. The shape and form of the *Confessions* of Augustine and of Rousseau are not only derived from the periods in which they were written but also reflect the emotional position of their authors: Augustine, now a disciplined churchman, identified with his mother, Santa Monica, and with St. Ambrose; Rousseau, feeling freed of restraints, patterned himself upon the fictional Robinson Crusoe. The model of the confession has as its backdrop the need for an audience to participate, be excited, and be forgiving. It is the model derived from both wishing that one's incestuous and murderous masturbatory wishes be fulfilled and simultaneously being relieved of guilt. Its motto is: "Give me expiation, but not yet." (What awaits my further study are those confessions about one's family which lead to greater guilt and to inhibition about telling more.)

I have presented to you a variety of experiences derived from the analyses of creative people in which their adolescent daydreams, and the special shapes and forms which mediated their talents, seem to have had some influence upon later works. To do this I have taken you to a masked ball populated by the famous and the dead where you may have access to their published works, and no one's privacy has been compromised.

18

MILTON H. HOROWITZ

The Place of Adolescence in Psychoanalytic Theory and Practice

Creative artists are not a race apart. The content of their fantasies from childhood onward are no different from the content of similar fantasies of almost all people. It has been speculated by some that there is a higher incidence of depressive illness among artists; that has not been my experience in the analytic treatment of artists and the many more that I have seen in consultation. It was once speculated that there was a higher incidence of family romance fantasies in artists. Some artists have family romance fantasies but so does one-third of the population at large. In their personality structure, artists are much more similar to the general population than they are different. They come to consult analysts for the same reasons others seek our help. They suffer. They experience anxiety, depression, guilt, shame, phobias, sexual problems, and love problems, but for them work problems, especially inhibition, seem to loom larger than do others. The work of the artist, the making of art, seems to occupy a greater rôle in the picture of oneself and the regulation of self-esteem than is common. That is not to say that work is not central to the identity of most of our patients. It is that the artist's products are always under scrutiny and judgment: his or her own, the opinions of other artists, the rôle of critics, the opinions of publishers, gallery owners, museums, collectors, producers, directors, and ticket buyers. In fact, everyone is a critic, everyone has what is considered "taste" and all have a judgment. They may not know much about art but they know what they like. (Most critics and some psychoanalysts are failed artists; oscillating between awed admiration and bloody-minded envy they can write much that is puzzling. We expect insight in psychoanalysts, and are astonished to find that insight in the critic.) Few of us are under constant scrutiny with such diverse possibilities of success or failure except in school. Though there are some differences between the "popular" arts such as theater and film requiring instant audience approval and other art forms as the novel, poetry, painting, and sculpture, criticism is ubiquitous. (For example, a book might sit on a shelf for later appreciation, but a closed play or musical has no audience.)

And of course it is the emphasis on product that has occupied us in our masked ball. How one became an artist as an adult is in my view the special consequence of whatever constitutes innate talent and intelligence *and* the special circumstances of adolescence. Now adolescence serves that same function in everyone. What has been there in earlier development now either comes together or falls apart. Adolescence is a time both of burgeoning development and rapid regression, sometimes in cycles. I have given particular emphasis to daydreams because they are so accessible in the analysis of adults. I have often been impressed by the relative absence of information about adolescence in psychoanalytic case reports and in the psychoanalytic literature in general. I have rarely seen a candidate in supervision who had a clear picture of the patient's adolescence, information that was almost immediately accessible. Rather, endless speculations are offered about "what must have happened" in the earliest childhood where no memory is available and the only evidence is in questionable interpretations of actions observed in the transference situation. This tendency to bypass the accessible and seek to search out earlier and earlier etiologic formulas now seems endless. Anna Freud once attempted an explanation of this trend. She said that once her father was able to trace the origins of adult sexuality back to the earliest infancy, the issues of adolescence seemed to recede into the background. Those analysts whose roots were in education never relegated adolescence to a secondary position: Anna Freud, Berta Bornstein, Peter Blos, Erik Homburger Erikson, and August Aichhorn. When Siegfried Bernfeld demonstrated to us in 1938 that adolescence offered a glimpse of recapitulation of all the earlier phases of development we should have been alerted more intensely. But even the wheel needs to be rediscovered periodically. The exploration of adolescence is the potential gold-mine of every adult analysis. Evidences of all the earliest object relations reemerge, all the old impulses, all the old desires and all the old fears, and, some new ones. Defenses change and consolidate; conscience, standards, and moral issues shift and structuralize as never before; object-choice and gender identity emerge in new form and both work and love take on new meaning. Central to this study is the rôle of conflict, which achieves new importance both in its intensity and in the methods of conflict resolution. It is the exploration of a remembered adolescence that then allows us a better chance of understanding a forgotten childhood and infancy. It is certainly, in my experience, not the other way round. There was some wisdom in an old analytic idea that we should analyze from the surface to the depth; this is slightly facetious since all experience is interfolded, but we cannot ignore the accessible in favor of the speculative.

Some few adolescents will grow into future artists, some potential future artists will have their talents wither if not encouraged either from within or without. (Gray's country churchyard: where "some mute inglorious Milton here may rest.") But all of us emerge into adulthood with a somewhat new personality, a new identity; few Tolstoys or Napoleons, but many of us with new self-inventions, to be known not by our products but by our personalities.

After the Ball

I attended my first Freud Lecture in 1952, and I reacted to it with a sense of wonder and astonishment. It was given by Ernst Kris and was titled "Psychoanalysis and the Study of Creative Imagination." I had just applied for admission to the New York Psychoanalytic Institute and what I knew about psychoanalysis was very little, and that was linked to issues of psychiatric pathology. Kris's lecture was a revelation. I was suddenly aware that psychoanalysis was about the life of humankind, about its long history, the capacity to create art as the one really durable product of human endeavor, and that traces of creativity were within each of us though few of us were artists. All were dreamers, all daydreamers, all living in various levels of conflict. The creative imagination was at work in all, tending toward problem-solving and the emergence from conflict. Most important for me, I could envision the "creative imagination" as essential to psychoanalytic work, part of the art of psychoanalysis, a link to the poets, albeit a tenuous link.

For those that have read *Winnie-the-Pooh*, I knew then what Tigger likes best. I wanted to learn from artists what went into their work and I could do that by offering help with their suffering. I knew I would have to be knowledgeable about development. Eventually I became in charge of the adolescent service at Bellevue Hospital in New York, an experience for which I am forever grateful. I also discovered that I learned more about the inner workings of adolescence from my adult patients than from my adolescent patients, much as I tried. Real adolescence is full of emergencies that require instant attention, and exploration of inner life is so difficult that it was clear to me that adult memories of adolescence were actually a much richer mine. How order is created out of chaos seemed to me a worthy study, how art emerges from conflict, how a good interpretation arises out of a welter of associations, how insight develops out of pain all impressed me in conceptualizing psychoanalysis as an art. Psychoanalysis is not a lonely endeavor, but the making of great art is. Psychoanalysis is a *joint* collaboration. I am always *with* the patient, and psychoanalysis *is* a conversation, though peculiar in its structure. Moreover, the long apprenticeship aspect of analytic education with exposure to many teachers and supervisors, students and colleagues makes for an awesome richness of identifications and new learning. Sometimes it seems like work done by a committee.

That richness of background is an ever-present part of the work supporting the imaginative equipment of the analyst. Many of our identifications, beginning with our link to Freud himself, have developed in our adolescent and early adult life, whatever the earlier models were. All contribute to how we work, sometimes styled as the "technique of analysis." I soon found that in each analysis, there were two techniques of working, mine and that of the patient's, each based on myriad antecedents and each subtly containing complex—often unconscious—identifications with persons of the past. All hinged upon the capacity for creative imagination in both participants, both undergoing various levels of access to that imagination, some of it depending upon a capacity for a kind of self-observant irony. Analysis, like daydreaming, bears some relation to play, and its relation to play, practice, and mastery has been very evident in many patients, but may be more accentuated in the creative. By play, I do not mean fun; play is dark and weighty and, as Kris (1953) demonstrated, *insight* might emerge from darkness. A "good" interpretation is an aspect of a sort of play—it is not that it is right or wrong—it is that it stimulates both participants to further thought, new combinations and, as in art, finding the right images and words to make order out of chaos.

I leave you with my own confession—I am an inveterate day dreamer. But, John Dryden (1985) could say it better:

> I strongly wish for what I faintly hope:
> Like the daydreams of melancholy men,
> I think and think on things impossible,
> Yet love to wander in that golden maze.
> [from *The Rival Ladies*, p. 293]

REFERENCES

Abel, E. (1989), *Virginia Woolf and the Fictions of Psychoanalysis*. Chicago: University of Chicago Press.
St. Augustine (1961), *Confessions*, trans. R.S. Pine-Coffin. London: Penguin.
Blos, P. (1962), *On Adolescence*. New York: Free Press.

Bonaparte, N. (1972), Clisson et Eugenie. In: *Napoleon Wrote Fiction* ed. C. Frayling. New York: St. Martin's Press.

Dryden, J. (1685), Plays and poems including *Lucretia* and *The Rival Ladies*.

Freud, A. (1958), Adolescence. In: *The Psychoanalytic Study of the Child*, Vol. 13, New York: International Universities Press.

Freud, S. (1908), Creative writers and day-dreaming. *Standard Edition*, 9:141–153. London: Hogarth Press, 1961.

Gaskell, E. (1919), *The Life of Charlotte Brontë*. London: Oxford Press.

Greenacre, P. (1958), The family romance of the artist. In: *Emotional Growth*, Vol. 2. New York: International Universities Press, 1971, pp. 505–532.

Jones, E. (1955), *Sigmund Freud: Life and Work, Vol. 2*. London: Hogarth Press.

Kris, E. (1953), Psychoanalysis and the study of creative imagination. *Bull. NY Acad. Med.*.

Maude, A. (1910), *Life of Tolstoy*. New York: Dodd Mead.

Restif de la Bretonne, N.-E. (1930–31), *Monsieur Nicolas*, trans R. Crowdy Mathers. London: J. Rodker, 1930–1931.

Rousseau, Jean-Jacques, (1992), *Confessions*. New York: Everyman Edition.

Steele, R. (1711), *The Spectator*. London: J. M. Dent, 1907.

Trollope, A. (1883), *An Autobiography*. London: Oxford University Press, 1953.

Tolstoy, L. (1930), *Childhood, Boyhood, Youth*. London: Oxford Press.

——— *War and Peace*. London: Oxford Press, 1930.

Woolf, V. (1957), "Sketch of the Past," "A Room of One's Own." New York: Harcourt, Brace, 1957.

——— *Orlando*. London: Penguin, 1993.

2 SHAKESPEARE'S ADOLESCENTS

AARON H. ESMAN

Adolescent psychiatry is essentially a clinical discipline. Most of what we know, or think we know, about adolescent development and psychopathology (not to mention the treatment of adolescent disorders) derives from the clinical practice of our sages, mentors, and ourselves. True, in recent years much has been learned from empirical studies, mostly in the realm of epidemiology and social science, but the bulk of our theory building and our technical methods is the fruit of a century of clinical experience beginning with Freud's epochal, if abortive study of Dora almost 100 years ago (Freud, 1905).

There is, however, another substantial body of information that, for some of us at least, has proved to be both enlightening and entertaining. I refer, of course, to the rich trove of imaginative literature about adolescence, carefully assembled into an annotated bibliography some years ago by Norman Keill (1959)—his *The Adolescent Through Fiction*. The *bildungsroman*, or novel of development, has been a staple of Euro-American literature since Goethe, with masterpieces ranging from Turgenev's *First Love* through Joyce's magnificent *Portrait of the Artist as a Young Man* to McCullers' *Member of the Wedding* and Salinger's *Catcher in the Rye*. Generally autobiographic in large measure, they provide insightful views of adolescent experience as filtered through the consciousness of great creative artists.

Of these, the greatest is certainly William Shakespeare. The eminent theater critic Robert Brustein (1996) cites a number of Shakespearean scholars, including the formidable Harold Bloom, in support of his contention that "Shakespeare valued personality above any other element in his drama . . . character was the supreme dramatic element in Shakespearean drama" (p. 27). We know virtually nothing about his adolescence, but in his plays he limned a number of portraits that, if they do not offer us new insights, certainly serve to enrich and reinforce

25

some of the insights we have and, in the process, inform us about perceptions of adolescent behaviors in his time, just 400 years ago. The French social historian Philippe Aries (1962) contended that, before the eighteenth century, no conception of adolescence as a distinct developmental period existed in Europe, and that the language held no term for it. Yet the shepherd in *The Winter's Tale* complains, "I would there were no age between ten and three-and-twenty, or that youth would sleep out the rest, for there is nothing in the between but getting wenches with child, wronging the ancientry, stealing, fighting." Not much seems to have changed between the days of Elizabeth I and Elizabeth II except that now we have a name for it.

It must be remembered, too, that in Shakespeare's theater all roles, including those of adolescent girls, were played by male actors. As Peter Quennell (1963) puts it,

Little is recorded of those gifted adolescents—how they were engaged and trained or the kind of personal lives they led. . . . Presumably both looks and talent were required; boy actors must fit naturally into the parts of pretty well-bred girls, have waistlines that would suit a stomacher, and sufficient agility and grace to manage the cumbersome skirts of an Elizabethan farthingale. The boy actor must cut a fashionable figure, too, in doublet, cloak and trunk-hose; girls travestied as boys were always immensely popular with an Elizabethan audience, and Shakespeare not only allowed his comic heroines frequent excuses to put on masculine apparel but gave their mentality and speech a slightly ambiguous, hermaphroditic cast. With their strange mixture of innocence and experience, romantic feeling and sharpspoken candor, masculine bravado and feminine nervosity, they tread a delicate line between the sexes. None of them is a completely mature woman; they belong to a period of human existence when the mildest girl is sometimes tomboyish and even the most energetic boy may now and then shed girlish tears [pp. 180–181].

Could one want a better description of early adolescence than that?

The best-known of Shakespeare's teen-agers are, of course, Romeo and Juliet. Endless quantities of ink have been spilled, and endless variations on the theme have been attempted, about these "star-crossed lovers," and I shall return to them myself later on. But perhaps the most radiant example of all is that of Miranda, Prospero's nubile 15-year-old daughter in *The Tempest*. You will recall that, since she was exiled at age three along with her father, he has kept her closely sheltered on his little island, knowing only Prospero, the monstrous Caliban and the fairy-sprite Ariel. The wise magician has educated her but kept her innocent—a nice description of a latency child.

Suddenly the arrival of Prospero's shipwrecked enemies shatters this protected childhood—and Miranda discovers the world of men and, in particular, the handsome young Ferdinand, son of Prospero's old foe. Miranda's reaction—"Oh wonder! How many goodly creatures are there here! How beauteous mankind is! Oh brave new world that has such people in it!"—is a magnificent metaphor for the adolescent awakening of sexuality and the emergence from the enclosed world of the family to the wider world beyond it. Or, as Prospero dryly responds to her, "Tis new to thee!"

Shakespeare's acute sensibility is shown in the wonderful scene in which Prospero finds the young lovers in his cave—playing chess! Twenty years after the frenetic romantic ardors of Romeo and Juliet, Shakespeare has apparently learned how the fires of pubertal passion may be banked by the screen of intellectualization. Ferdinand's and Miranda's youthful amorousness burns brightly, marked by its characteristic idealization, the mutual projection of their infantile narcissism and the longing for the ideal parent of early childhood. Thus Ferdinand's "You, oh you, so perfect and so peerless, are created of every creature's best," and Miranda's "I would not wish any companion in the world but you; nor can imagination form a shape, besides yours, to like of." But, in response to Prospero's admonition to Ferdinand—"If thou dost break her virgin knot before all sanctimonious ceremonies may with full and holy rite be ministered . . . barren hate, sour-eyed disdain and discord shall bestrew the union of your bed with weeds so loathly that you shall hate it both"—the young lovers, unlike Romeo and Juliet, curb their lusts and confine their entanglement, for the duration of the play, at least, to the chessboard.

Shakespeare was, it would seem, no stranger himself to youthful passion. He was married, at age 18, to Anne Hathaway, eight years his senior, who bore their first child only six months later. It is as though, at 29, he is in Romeo and Juliet "looking back on youth with affection and compassion and regret," as Quennell (1963) put it (p. 149). It is no news that in this play Shakespeare captured much of the essence of adolescence for all time; Leonard Bernstein and Steven Sondheim did not have to do great violence to the original in their musical updating in

27

West Side Story. Not only did he distill the essence of adolescent romantic ardor into his central couple, but even in his subsidiary characters he caught aspects of what, at least in a particular milieu, survives as "teen" behavior four centuries later.

Take, for example, Mercutio. He is the prototype of youthful braggadocio and exhibitionistic machismo—as Romeo describes him, "A gentleman that loves to hear himself talk, and will speak more in a minute than he will stand to in a month." He is, in short, intoxicated with language, and with the new found ability to play with words as symbols, as abstractions, as implements, much in the manner of that more modern adolescent wordsmith Holden Caulfield. We are familiar with the developmental tendency to exploit to the fullest a newly-acquired capability. Much like the toddler's "love affair with the world," Mercutio has a "love affair with the word," shaped in part by the capacity for formal operational thought that comes, Piaget (1969) tells us, with pubescence. Thus we have Mercutio's great "Queen Mab" speech:

"She is the fairies' midwife, and she comes / In shape no bigger than an agate-stone / On the forefinger of an alderman / Drawn with a team of little atomies / Athwart men's noses as they lie asleep: / Her waggon-spokes made of long spinners' legs; / The cover, of the wings of grasshoppers; / The traces, of the smallest spider's web; / The collars, of the moonshine's watery beams; / Her whip, of cricket's bone; the lash, of film . . ."

and so on for another 32 lines until Romeo interrupts with "Peace, peace, Mercutio, peace! Thou talks of nothing!"

But if Mercutio is intoxicated by words, Romeo is drunk on love. Remember that when he first espies Juliet while he is crashing the Capulet ball, Romeo is on the rebound from his unrequited passion for the chaste Rosaline—suffering, as he says, "from being out of her favor where I am in love."

And, as 15 year-old lovers will, he idealizes his beloved; to Benvolio he declaims, "Show me a mistress that is passing fair / What doth her beauty serve but as a note / Where I may read who pass'd that passing fair." Until, that is, he spots Juliet; in a trice the fickle boy forgets his Rosaline. "Did my heart love till now? Forswear it, sight / for I ne'er saw true beauty till this night," It makes glorious poetry, but to the prosaic mind of the psychoanalyst it smacks of the projection of a narcissistic ego ideal of perfection so typical of the intense crushes of the young adolescent in the throes of early object removal.

And what of Juliet? She has been the beneficiary of an extended study by Katherine Dalsimer (1988), to whom I am indebted. Dalsimer places Juliet in the subphase of mid-adolescence, and it is true that in some ways this fits. But it is necessary to remember (and Shakespeare repeatedly reminds us) that Juliet is only 13 years old. We know— again, Shakespeare informs us—that she has passed her menarche; in his rage at her refusal to marry the County Paris her father addresses her as "green-sickness carrion" and "tallowface"—implying the condition of "chlorosis", or microcytic iron-deficiency anemia common in young menstruating women in premodern times. Still, at 13 she was expected not only to marry but to be prepared to bear children. Lady Capulet is quite explicit about this: "Younger than you / here in Verona, ladies of esteem / are made already mothers; by my count / I was your mother much upon these years that you are now a maid." Here Shakespeare tells us something about the times of which, and perhaps in which, he was writing; apparently his audience would not have thought such expectations of a 13-year-old girl unusual or outrageous.

Yet, although viewed by the adults in her world as a social and biological woman, she is, at least initially, very much a compliant, latency-like child; when her mother summons her to talk of marriage, Juliet replies, without irony, "Madam, I am here, what is your will?" As her mother proposes that she consider Paris as a potential husband, she submissively responds, "I'll look to like, if looking liking move, / But no more deep will I endart my eye / Than your consent gives strength to make it fly." In short, we see her as a model preadolescent girl, demure, willing, obedient.

Passion, however, transforms her. As her encounter at the ball with Romeo inflames her nascent libido, she is flung headlong into adolescence. The process of object removal is instantaneous; her loyalty and devotion to her parents and to her entire family are swept away, supplanted by her newfound attachment to her once-"loathed enemy"— "Oh, Romeo, Romeo, wherefore art thou Romeo? / Deny thy father and refuse thy name, / Or if thou wilt not, be but sworn my love / And I'll no longer be a Capulet!" Not only does she become rebellious, she becomes devious and deceptive, lying to her mother, defying her father, equivocating to them both. They believe she is mourning the death of her cousin Tybalt when in fact she is in despair about the banishment of her lover Romeo who has killed him.

Juliet's sexual awakening, in the end, thrusts her abruptly into adolescence and, inexorably, to her death. Like many of the young women we see in our emergency rooms, the loss of her lover drives her to an impulsive, self-destructive act. It is as though her sense of self and of security, only recently dependent on her attachment to her parents, her clan, and now on her union with her once-alien lover, was so shattered by her loss that her only refuge becomes the fantasy of reunion or merger in death. This fantasy is made explicit by Romeo himself when, believing Juliet to be dead, he exclaims, "I still will stay with thee / And never from this palace of dim night / Depart again: here, here will I remain / With worms that are thy chambermaids / O! here will I set up my everlasting rest."

Romeo and Juliet's pre-Romantic *liebestod* gives voice to yet another of the fantasies of the adolescent suicide—or parasuicide; the fantasy that the grownups, the parents, those left behind, will be shocked into remorseful reflection and moved to mend their ways ("They'll be sorry when I'm dead"). Thus Montague and Capulet resolve to end their blood feud, Montague promises to raise a statue to Juliet "in pure gold," and Capulet, not to be outdone, pledges to do the same in Romeo's memory. By their self-sacrifice, the children teach the parents about love, peace and harmony. A story that, especially since the 60s, we have all heard more than once, I am sure.

In the cases we have considered so far—Miranda, Romeo, and Juliet—Shakespeare does not carry us beyond the trials, triumphs, and tragedies of early adolescence. Matters are quite different in the case of young Henry Monmouth, who first appears in absentia in *Richard II*, commands our attention as Prince Hal in *Henry IV*, and dominates the stage and history as *Henry V*. Prince Hal has not escaped the attention of psychoanalytic scholars; Ernst Kris (1948) addressed his "conflict" in a characteristically rich and scholarly paper, and Alexander Aarons (1970) cited him as a paradigmatic case of "sowing one's oats" in adolescence. Peter Blos (1974) addressed the process of ego-ideal formation in the vicissitudes of Hal's relations with his father and with Falstaff. My bent has been to see Prince Hal in an Eriksonian framework, to observe his development through the substages of adolescence and the consolidation of his identity at its close.

Our first sense of the young prince occurs at the end of *Richard II*, when the usurper Henry Bolingbroke, newly crowned as Henry IV, expostulates,

Can no man tell me of my unthrifty son? / 'Tis full three months
since I did see him last / . . . Inquire at London, 'mongst the tav-
erns there / for there, they say, he daily doth frequent / With unre-
strained loose companions, / Even such, they say, as stand in
narrow lanes / And beat our watch and rob our passengers, / While
he, young wanton and effeminate boy / Takes on the point of
honor to support / So dissolute a crew.

Sure enough, in *Henry IV, Part I* we find Prince Hal consorting with
the crew of drunkards and cutpurses led by Sir John Falstaff, one of
Shakespeare's greatest creations. Although Hal's father evidently
thinks him a gross delinquent at best, Shakespeare, ever mindful of his
political p's and q's, carefully assures us that Hal is merely an observer,
never a participant in the criminal acts of Falstaff's gang. Thus when
Falstaff tries to induce Hal to join him in an incident of highway robbery, Hal responds, "Who, I rob? I a thief? Not I, by my faith." Indeed,
Shakespeare has Hal put us on notice about his intentions in Act 1,
Scene 2: addressing the absent Poins he soliloquizes:

I know you all, and will awhile / uphold the unyok'd humor of
your idleness . . . So, when this loose behavior I throw off, / And
pay the debt I never promised / By how much better than my word
I am / By so much shall I falsify men's hopes; / And like bright
metal on a sullen ground, / My reformation, glittering o'er my
fault, / Shall show more goodly and attract more eyes / Than that
which hath no foil to set it off.

Nonetheless, Hal later induces Poins to join him in an elaborate
scam, in which they in turn rob Falstaff of his ill-gotten gains, only later
to humiliate the old man for his cowardice and boastfulness. The scene
ends with Hal, off to the civil wars, assuring us that "The money shall
be paid back" to the original victims, "with advantage."

A classic father-son confrontation then ensues; the king berates Hal
for his "inordinate and low desires / such poor, such bare, such lewd,
such mean attempts / Such barren pleasures, rude society," complains of
his "vile participation; not an eye / but is weary of thy common sight /
Save mine, which hath desired to see thee more." Or, in other words,
"You're always out with your low-life friends; we never see you at home
any more." He then contrasts Hal with Harry Percy—"Hotspur," brave,

warlike, noble. Speaking of Hotspur's father, he intones, "Oh, that it could be prov'd / That some night-tripping fairy had exchang'd / In cradle clothes our children where they lay / And called mine Percy, his Plantagenet / Then would I have his Harry, and he mine." Unfortunately this same Hotspur is now leading a rebellion against King Henry; Hal, promising to reform, pledges to vindicate himself by besting Hotspur on the field of battle, thus redeeming himself in his father's eyes. By the end of Part I, he succeeds; at Shrewsbury he defeats Hotspur in single combat, thus suppressing the rebellion and saving his father's throne.

But there is more to come! By the fourth act of Part 2, the rebellion is crushed; and Hal, like many another errant adolescent, is back to his old tricks, hanging out with Poins and Falstaff, to his father's despair and dismay. "Most subject is the fattest soil to weeds, / And he, the noble image of my youth / Is overspread with them; therefore my grief." He is not reassured when his advisor Warwick tells him that "The prince but studies his companions like a strange tongue, wherein to gain the language / . . . The prince will in the perfectness of time cast off his followers." The king replies "Tis seldom, when the bee doth leave her comb / in the dead carrion." Or, in other words, "The leopard doesn't change his spots."

The conflict reaches its apogee when Hal, believing his sick father to have died, picks the crown off his pillow and proceeds to try it on himself. Waking from a deep sleep, the king finds both prince and crown missing, and learns that Hal has taken the symbol of his power. Hal, returning, defends himself: "I never thought to hear you speak again." "Thy wish was father, Harry, to that thought," says the king; "I stay too long by thee, I weary thee. Dost thou so hunger for my empty chair / That thou wilt needs invest thee with mine honors / Before thy hour be ripe?" King Henry makes, that is, an Oedipal interpretation to his son; "Thy life did manifest that thou loved'st me not / And thou will have me die assured of it." Hal responds with a lengthy denial and rather sanctimonious rationalization which his father, moved by his countertransference, eagerly accepts.

The resolution comes soon enough. King Henry dies, and Hal becomes the rightful Henry V. Falstaff greets the news with joy, anticipating preferment from his erstwhile follower and playfellow. But in a scene replete with drama and pathos, Hal, newly crowned, repudiates him. Falstaff: "My king, my Jove! I speak to thee, my heart!" King Henry V: "I know thee not, old man: fall to thy prayers; / How ill white hairs become a fool and jester . . . Presume not that I am the thing I was,

/ For God doth know, so shall the world perceive / That I have turned away my former self / So will I those that kept me company."

Shakespeare gives us here the very model of the Eriksonian concept of identity formation in adolescence. Hal, enjoying the royal prerogative of a "moratorium of choice," has spent his midadolescence rebelliously experimenting with what Erikson (1968) called a negative identity—values and conduct in direct opposition to those of his father, his family, his class and his calling. He has even adopted a negative father-surrogate in Falstaff, with whom he partially identifies, and, at a critical moment, he acts out his patricidal Oedipal fantasy.

Yet, when called upon by fate and the needs of the state, he abruptly—at least for dramatic purposes—assumes both the mantle and the identity of king, casting off the trial and partial identifications with which he had toyed during his moratorium, consolidating his identification with his father and becoming, like him, every inch a true, late-medieval warrior-king. Both his private and his public faces are transformed, and his former comrades, who had not read Erikson, are bewildered, discomfited and dejected by his seeming metamorphosis.

It is striking that, throughout, Hal lives in an exclusively male world. Where Hotspur, doubtless a few years older, has both wife and mother, there is no mention of a mother to Prince Hal or queen to his father the king; the only women with whom Hal has any contact at all are in Falstaff's crew—Mistress Quickly, his landlady, and Doll Tearsheet, his bawd. In fact, Hal's mother, Mary Bohun, died in 1394 when Hal was but seven years old; Henry IV did not remarry until 1403, the year of the battle of Shrewsbury, when Hal was 16 and already engaged in the events recorded in Part I.

It is interesting to note how Shakespeare transforms history for dramatic purposes; one could not know from the texts of the plays that 10 years elapsed between the events at Shrewsbury (1403) and Hal's accession to the throne (1413). Actually, Hal had begun to play an active role in government in 1409, and was thus fully prepared to ascend the throne on his father's death. What historically occurred as a gradual process during Hal's late adolescence and early adulthood is condensed by Shakespeare into a brief span, accelerating and accentuating (happily, for our purposes) the transition from boy to man, from Prince to King, from unruly adolescent to royal adult.

One might even conjecture, if one dared at almost 600 years' remove, that Hal's motherless state served to intensify the relationship—and thus the conflict—between Hal and his father. Following the line of

Peter Blos (1987) one could imagine that it heightened Hal's negative oedipal longings toward his father for affection and nurturance, against which he had to defend himself through his rebelliousness and which he displaced onto Falstaff. Thus not only oedipal, but preoedipal conflicts were involved in Hal's "sowing his wild oats" in adolescence, and were worked through in the prolonged crisis of identity formation that was resolved by his coronation. Hal, warrior-king that he became, did not himself marry until he was 33, and then as much for reasons of state as for love, as Shakespeare clearly shows us in the delightful scene of courtship between Henry V and Princess Catherine of Valois.

What, then, have we learned from this brief exercise? We have learned, at least, that despite Aries' insistence that no such phase as adolescence was recognized in pre-18th century Europe, the phenomenology of adolescence as we know it was well enough understood that the greatest dramatist of the age could represent it in terms that we can readily recognize today. It may have had no name, but it surely had a face. Of course, true to the conventions of his time, Shakespeare tells us mostly of the lives of the royals, the nobles, the aristocrats, who presumably had the wealth and leisure to allow for an adolescent moratorium akin to the one we know; of the lower orders he tells us less. Still, we know from other sources of riotous apprentices, and the previously quoted shepherd of *Winter's Tale* was, in all likelihood, complaining as much about the young of his class as about the nobility. And, after all, even Aristotle had described the gilded youth of his time in terms that are strikingly modern in tone. So although historical evidence seems pretty clear that it was not until the industrial revolution that adolescence became demarcated as a phase distinct from childhood on the one hand and maturity on the other, "the young," as Aristotle spoke of them, have conducted themselves in similar ways for a very long time, and it is to the great writers of the past that we owe this knowledge.

We have learned that adolescents loved, dreamed, quarreled, fought, even killed, 400 years ago as they do today. We have learned that, then as now, the consolidation of the value system—the superego, in our jargon—and of character organization is the work of the adolescent years as each society defines them. Though culture shapes the forms and, to some degree, the content of these consolidated structures, and dictates the range of possibilities open to the young person's choice, the fundamental task remains the same, across divides of time and space.

Does Shakespeare provide us with additional cases? Well, yes, though they are less to our purpose. The comedies offer us the transvestite roles—Viola in *Twelfth Night*, Rosalind in *As You Like It*,—both probably intended as mid-to-late adolescent girls performing in drag. Shakespeare solves the problem of Viola's androgyny by having her represented to the Duke, whom she serves and falls in love with, as a eunuch. Thus his first perception of her (in travesty): "Diana's lip / Is not more smooth and rubious; thy small pipe / Is as the maiden's organ, shrill and sound / And all is simulative a woman's part." Or, as Malvolio describes her, "Not old enough for a man, not young enough for a boy . . . 'tis with him in standing water, between a boy and a man." Once established in her role, however, she becomes a stock character, boy outside, girl within, until, unmasked, she wins the Duke's heart. The denouement depends on Shakespeare's dramatic device in which Viola and her fraternal twin Sebastian are indistinguishable from one another—are identical. It wouldn't work with a genetically hip modern audience, but in 1600 it apparently went over well.

As for Rosalind, she adds an additional spice to the transvestite recipe; at least in 1600 she was a boy performing as a girl masquerading as a boy but pretending to be a girl. In the end, however, she too is a stock comedic figure, using her high-born wit and charm to win the young hero with whom she, like the typical Shakespearean heroine, fell in love at first sight. In the end we would, as Quennell suggests, be a lot more interested in knowing about the boys who performed in these sexually ambiguous roles than about the characters themselves.

Last of all, there is Perdita, the "lost one," in the aforementioned *Winter's Tale*. A king's daughter, left to die upon a foreign rock, she is in small measure a female Oedipus, though she threatens her deluded royal father Leontes with no more than the shame of signifying his imagined cuckoldry by his dear childhood friend Polixines. But, *The Winter's Tale* being a comedy (though a rather black one), Perdita, like Oedipus found and rescued by a shepherd, survives, to be loved at 16 by the handsome prince and reunited with her chastened father and her truly chaste mother, now restored to life. Perdita, too, is a stock figure, of unearthly beauty, noble speech and rather empty character. She makes one long for the complexities of a Juliet, the wide-eyed innocence of a Miranda, or the wit of a Rosalind—but, then, she is a secondary personage in a play that is really about Leontes' pathological jealousy. And, since Freud (1922), we all know what pathological jealousy is about. Did Shakespeare?

And what about Hamlet? The Prince of Denmark is often thought of as a prototypic adolescent, obsessionally ruminating over his oedipal conflict, impulsively striking out at his elders, beset with guilty ambivalence about his love affair with Ophelia. But Hamlet's status as an undergraduate at Wittenberg is belied by the text, which tells us that Hamlet is 30 years old. In the Gravedigger scene, that worthy tells us that he has been at his job since "the day young Hamlet was born," and that he has been "sexton here, man and boy, thirty years." So Hamlet may have been one of those perpetual graduate students who qualify as one of Siegfried Bernfeld's (1938) "prolonged adolescents," perhaps, but chronologically he falls outside our special professional scope.

Above all, we learn—or are reminded of—how great art can reach to the core of our own being, resonating with our own experience, engaging us as participants in an interactive dialogue that enlarges our grasp of ourselves and of the lives we touch. Shakespeare's adolescents are, of course, imaginary creatures, not real persons, and we need to be modest in our application of our psychoanalytic formulas to their fictive lives. But great writers—Shakespeare, Dostoevsky, Proust, Joyce—are gifted with the ability to "hold the mirror up to nature," and in that glass, if we read it right, we can see ourselves.

REFERENCES

Aarons, Z. A. (1970), Normality and abnormality in adolescence: with a digression on Prince Hal—"the sowing of wild oats." *The Psychoanalytic Study of the Child*, 25:309–329. Madison, CT: International Universities Press.

Aries, P. (1962), *Centuries of Childhood*. New York: Knopf.

Bernfeld, S. (1938), Types of adolescence. *Psychoanal. Quart.*, 7:243–253.

Blos, P. (1987), Freud and the father complex. *The Psychoanalytic Study of the Child*, 42:425–442. New Haven, CT: Yale University Press.

Brustein, R. (1996), Character and personality in Shakespeare. *The New Republic*. 214:27–29.

Dalsimer, K. (1988), *Female Adolescents*. New Haven, CT: Yale University Press.

Erikson, E. (1968), Identity confusion in life history and casehistory. In: *Identity, Youth and Crisis*. New York: Norton, pp. 142–207.

Freud, S. (1905), Fragment of the analysis of a case of hysteria. *Standard Edition*, 7:7–122. London: Hogarth Press, 1953.

———— (1922), Some neurotic mechanisms in jealousy, paranoia and homosexuality. *Standard Edition* 18:223–232. London: Hogarth Press, 1955.

Kiell, N. (1959), *The Adolescent Through Fiction*. New York: International Universities Press.

Kris, E. (1952), Prince Hal's conflict. In: *Psychoanalytic Explorations in Art*. New York: International Universities Press, pp. 273–288.

Piaget, J. (1969), The intellectual development of the adolescent. In: *The Psychology of Adolescence*. ed. A. Esman. New York: International Universities Press, pp. 104–108.

Quennell, P. (1963), *Shakespeare*. London: Weidenfeld Nicholson.

3 NIETZSCHE AND THE ROMANTIC
CONSTRUCTION OF ADOLESCENCE

VIVIAN M. RAKOFF

Given the history of studies in adolescent psychiatry for approximately the past 50 years, it would be immodest to try to encompass what has become a vast territory, mapped out in terms of the disciplines of sociology, anthropology, psychoanalysis, developmental psychology, and epidemiology. Each of these gives a different picture, like the classical blind men feeling their way around the elephant. So I will fudge the task and try to summarize a personal thread of thought which borrows eclectically from all these fields, without my pretending to complete scholarship in any of them.

Inevitably I am a product of the orthodoxies of my time. I am also, sometimes, uncomfortable with these orthodoxies. Even though I am not an anthropologist, certain social/cultural facts of my early years provided a critical matrix for my later formal education.

If I may be a little more explicitly autobiographical than is customary: I was a small child in the tiny fishing village of Port Nolloth, on the northwest coast of South Africa. The entire population was no more than a few hundred people, and they were divided up in the terrible (but not unique) South African fashion. The "whites" were divided principally into English speaking Anglicans and Dutch speaking Afrikaans, who were Reformed Christians. Then there was a very small group of Catholics and a half dozen or so Jewish shop-keeping, hotel-owning families. Caught between the white and nonwhite population there were the marginalized not-quite-white, not-quite-black people of St. Helenan descent who lived in the ragged territory of the "white" village. And to complete the identifiable groups there were the intermarried Scots Cornish and Namaqua families who lived in a long "barracks" of corrugated iron and wood houses facing the sea, where their moored fishing boats remembered Europe in their names: Sporran, Clyde, Fergus, and so on.

Over the hill and behind a barricade of shifting sand dunes, the major part of the population, the Namaqua people, lived in a make shift "location". Their houses were put together out of scraps of iron, cardboard, reed matting and flattened tin cans.

There was no water borne sanitation in the entire village, (apart from the small two storied hotel my father had built); for the rest there was a system of out-houses served by a village management board, but even this was available only to the white and the marginally white populace. I never knew what people did in the location, until in later years I became aware of figures modestly squatting behind the scrubby little thorn bushes which dotted the dry veldt.

As it was with the bodily necessities, so it was with the spiritual needs of the community—dreadfully separate and dreadfully unequal. In the white village there were three churches for the small clutch of pale believers: three little corrugated iron buildings as minimal as "Monopoly" houses, each with its own little bell tower.

The Catholics were different in an important way: they slopped over the outlines of the segregated village. The nuns and the occasional errant alcoholic priest ran a school for "coloured" children. For some reason this was allowed and on the edge of the white village they taught reading, writing, embroidery, and household crafts. Now and again a daughter of one of the white families who was not sent to the big city of Capetown, was instead sent for high school education to the nuns who taught the single adolescent in a manner befitting a grand European bourgeoise; she was taught French, literature, piano, household management, and even some mathematics—in this remote foggy village where the public school system stopped at "standard six" (the class for 12-year-olds).

The fates of the growing children of these separated communities were as different as if they lived not only in separate territories, but as if they lived in different centuries. In this one, minute community, we had landless peasants; the occasional hunter-gatherer who wandered in from the surrounding veldt with some skins of small antelope and boxes of wild edible roots: *uintjies* and *kannies*; factory workers craftsmen and apprentices; school children and some absentee university students, merchants, and engineers. For some existence and expectation were, in European terms, medieval or even pre-medieval, and for others it was early capitalism. For my siblings and me, and a couple of others, there was the privileged fate of higher education, travel abroad, and the huge world of Western culture.

In terms of adolescence—modern, mid to late 20th-century adolescence—there were perhaps five of us in the village who may have made a journey of relative self discovery, struggled with an Eriksonian moratorium, created an authentic identity, and so forth. The others did what most of humankind has always done: they did what they could find to do.

Of course the inner lives of the economically and socially deprived youngsters were probably much the same as those who got to see Oxford, Cambridge, London, Paris, Rome, the Louvre, the Prado, the Metropolitan Museum, who gazed in wonder at the Parthenon, the Great Wall, the Taj Mahal, the pyramids, Katmandu, Tokyo, or who wrote poetry, struggled with essay deadlines, and so on. But the turbulence of their defenses, the qualities of their character had little to do with their fates in life. Their destiny was accurately apprehended two hundred years ago when Gray (1768), poised on the brink of the industrial revolution, in his elegy mourned for the unexpressed potentiality of the buried village Cromwells and Hampdens.[1]

But we are not here to reiterate indignation and frustration at the lives diminished by oppression and injustice. The question for the moment is: How did the formulations of Erik Erikson and Anna Freud become the almost unquestioned map of our expectations of adolescence—put forward not only as a description of a particular group at a given time in history, but also putatively as a universally valid model of normative psychosocial development, one so inevitable and democratic as physical puberty? Their descriptions became the basis for individual and group expectations and a guide to formal diagnosis and psychotherapeutic practice. They were the launching pad for many college counseling programs and they provided the framework for curricula in all sorts of educational institutions. And for a time they were almost unquestioned.

Both Anna Freud and Erik Erikson would have defined themselves as products of Freudian psychoanalysis, indeed, in spite of their own emphases, as loyal heirs and apostles of the core teachings. When it came to adolescence, however, they developed matters beyond the for-

---

[1] Gray's concern for the drab lives of unsung villagers didn't stop him from being carried in a sedan chair over the Alps, in the company of his friend Walpole (Schama, 1995, p. 448).

mulations of Sigmund Freud. They were at pains to present their theories as if they were seamless developments of Freudian thought, but they were different in their conceptions of the life stage. Their commited focus on adolescence, quite apart from its content, was a major departure from Freud's life map.

For Freud the adolescent was not a central figure in an existential drama, and the "privileging" of adolescence as a life stage is not a significant component of his elaborate developmental schema. He views the end of childhood and the beginning of adulthood as a way-station, not a project. There are only five explicit uses of the term "adolescence" in his collected works, and they are passing observations in essays on other topics. They are worth citing since they show how limited Freud's conception of adolescence was. In fact a number of the references in the *Standard Edition* of his works occur, as it were, by proxy in essays shared with Joseph Breuer (Breuer and Freud, 1893–95). Freud described a young woman whose hysterical symptoms were a foreshadowing of a later diagnosis of dementia praecox (p. 95); in the same paper he tells his Viennese contemporaries that adolescents may have more sexual knowledge than is generally assumed (p. 134). Breuer, in his contribution, recognizes that adolescence may be a time of conflict over masturbation for morally strict young men (p. 210); he warns of cases where unusual energy, indeed talents, in adolescents may presage later hysteria (about which he sounds oddly complimentary, citing one of his colleagues who conjectured that hysterics may be the "flower" of humanity) (p. 240). He is however less sanguine when he notes that previously well young people may fall into hysteria during adolescence, (p. 244) and that constitutes the total range of Freudian references to adolescence.

This is not the case with puberty. It is true that Freud may have used puberty as a term interchangeable with adolescence. In doing so he would have followed the example of centuries of European usage. As Aries (1962) has written, the labels youth, child, young person, and adolescent were frequently interchangeable. But even if this were the case, Freud's use of the term reflects a relatively constricted meaning. The emphasis is on the erotic developmental aspects of the pubertal stage, and not the complex social definition of "the youth". It is most clearly expressed in the well-known summation in the "Three Essays on Sexuality":

The final outcome of sexual development lies in what is known as the normal sexual life of the adult, in which the pursuit of pleasure comes under the sway of the reproductive function and in which the component instincts, under the primacy of a single erotogenic zone, form a firm organization directed towards a sexual aim attached to some extraneous sexual object [Freud, 1905, p. 197].

He emphasises this construct repeatedly. "Thus the establishment of that primacy in the service of reproduction is the last phase through which the organization of sexuality passes" (p. 199), and "Puberty represents the second of the diphasic stages of the selection of erotic object choice. It is a culmination, and an end of the psychosexual object choice struggle which had its first phase in infancy" (p. 200). Then the description becomes orgiastic.

Finally it must be added that during the transition period of puberty the processes of somatic and of physical development continue for a time side by side independently, until the irruption of an intense mental erotic impulse, leading to the innervation of the genitals, brings about the unity of the erotic function which is necessary for normality [p. 235].

Freud finds in the surrounding culture of his time a vivid clarifying metaphor of the process as he conceived it: all the component instincts combine. "A normal sexual life is only assured by an exact convergence of the affectionate current and the sensual aim. . . . It is like the completion of a tunnel which has been driven through a hill from both directions" (p. 207).

The fusion or meeting he announced required a metaphor different from his fundamental dialectical Hegelian model that served very well to unify the constant conflict between the thesis of the id drives, the antithesis of the controlling superego, and the synthetic resolution on the ego. The metaphor is one of a powerful, hidden subterranean process. Its source is, of course, the series of great railway tunnels driven through the Alps just before Freud wrote his essays published in 1905; the Mont Cenis, eight miles long; the St. Gotthard, nine and one-quarter miles long; and the longest of that generation of tunnels, the 12 and one third mile, 7000 feet deep Simplon, finished in 1898 after seven years of work. These were the moon flights of Freud's generation and in their yielding up of a unifying metaphor they were part of "the day residue" of his own creativity.

Freud's more customary tragic metaphor is one of unremitting conflict, whereas the tunneling metaphor makes vivid the fusion of complementary, not contradictory, opposites: animal physiological lust meets the elevated psychological (in another time the term might have been "spiritual") feelings of affection. In this image of fusion rather than contradiction Freud anticipated the ego psychologists, among whom of course are Anna Freud and Erikson, the particular foci of this discussion.

Esman (1996) has given an elegant and concise summary of the expansion of Freudian drive models into the more wide ranging models of ego psychologists as they were applied to adolescence.

In structural terms, the resurgence of the id impulses and their associated fantasies generates, initially, a disorganization of the ego and its appendage, the superego. It is the task of adolescence to achieve a new alignment of these structures, to create a mature character (Blos), a definitive identity (Erikson), predicated on the primacy of genitality over pregenital infantile sexuality (Freud).

Anna Freud (1936) returned to the fundamental Freudian metaphor for her historic descriptions of the normative struggle of puberty and adolescence. Her emphasis was not on the complementary fusion of her father's model, but rather a heightening of the dynamic conflict-laden process of psychic existence. She expanded the pubertal task of fusion and object choice into a life-phase specific period of enormous destabilisation. It is unnecessary here to give an exhaustive picture of the dynamic formulations of adolescence, but I should like to emphasise certain salient aspects of the by now classical descriptions given by Anna Freud (1936) in "The Ego and the Id at Puberty" and later (1958) in her paper "Adolescence" in which she described the characteristic ego defense structure during adolescence: it was a turbulent and ever changing ego that attempted to cope with new and powerful passions and the resurgence of Oedipal desires. She asserted that distinctions between normal and pathological adjustment during adolescence were difficult and "perhaps impossible." Indeed she took her position further by suggesting that a nonturbulent adjustment was suspect. It was as though she pictured adolescence as being normatively on the verge of near psychosis.

But for all its emphasis on major psychic destabilisation during the adolescent period, Anna Freud's focus is contained and small—one is even tempted to say, constricted, when compared with Erikson's heroic-existential vision of the life task.

Erikson's well-known formulations are also cast in the form of a struggle; but it is a struggle going much further than the arena of the individual and his or her intimates. The scope is grand and takes in history and society. The hermetically sealed Freudian drama, which has a cast of characters drawn almost entirely from the immediate family, is extended to the entire social context and its defining rituals and expectations to a far greater extent than Freud's admission of societal values into the superego.

The successful adolescent emerges from the Eriksonian struggle with that peculiarly modern achievement, an "identity"; and if not he suffers a vitiatingly chaotic state of psychic disorganisation, "identity diffusion". The difference in scope becomes dramatically apparent when one considers Freud's narrow bore, tunneling, indeed claustrophobic metaphors, with Erikson's (1950) wide landscape. He writes:

> The growing and developing youths, faced with this psychological development within them, are now primarily concerned with what they appear to be in the eyes of others as compared with what they feel they are, and with questions of how to connect the roles and skills cultivated earlier with the occupational prototypes of the day [pp. 227–228].

And consider these characteristic descriptions in Erikson's (1968) writings: "Young patients can be violent or depressed, delinquent or withdrawn, but theirs is an acute and possibly passing crisis, rather than a breakdown of the kind which tends to commit a patient to all the malignant implications of a fatalistic diagnosis" (p. 17). And, "Without an ideological simplification of the universe, the adolescent ego cannot organize experience according to the specific capacities of its expanding involvement (p. 27). . . . They are having an identity crisis, because they know they are supposed to have it" (p. 29).

Far from being inside the mountain, the struggle for an Eriksonian identity takes place in the domain of public history, as it were, on the top of the mountain. And the self in Erikson is defined in concentric layers, of which the erotic is an important layer but, significantly, not the only or even central component.

Erikson's expansion of the Freudian model may have been considered heretical in the earlier stages of psychoanalysis. He explicitly challenges a central developmental concept in his comments regarding the Oedipus complex, the central tenet of the Nicean creed of psychoanaly-

45

sis as dogma. "The Oedipal trinity is not an irreducible schema for man's conduct" (p. 47). He elaborates his notion of identity and writes "What I have called ego identity governs more than the mere fact of existence; it is, as it were, the ego quality of this existence" (p. 50). And he takes it even further when he speaks of the support for the individual in the struggle for identity: "Such identity depends on the support which the young individual receives from the collective sense of identity characterising the social groups significant to him; his class, his nation, his culture" (p. 89). From this base of the entire society and its representation within the psychic life of the individual, he casts the adolescent in an heroic role that surpasses his individual quest and invokes redemption and renewal of the entire society. "Adolescence is thus a ritual regenerator in the process of social evolution, for youth can offer its loyalties and energies both to the conservation of that which continues to feel true and to the revolutionary correction of that which has lost its regenerative significance" (pp. 134–135).

Just in case one wonders if the adolescent as heroic social regenerator is a chance reference or a slender thread in Erikson's writing, the heroic theme swells and he writes of the need to move beyond identity to "self-transcendence", invoking the towering figures of John Keats (p. 135), and William James. His particular citation of a passage from James's correspondence with his father reads like a compressed capsule of the thought of Nietzsche and Schopenhauer with its references to the "will" and to suffering and creating.

Hitherto when I have felt like taking a free initiative, like daring to act originally, without carefully waiting for contemplation of the external world to determine all for me, suicide seemed the most manly form to put my daring into; now, I will go a step further with my will, not only act with it, but believe as well; believe in my individual reality and creative power. My belief, to be sure, can't be optimistic—but I will posit life (the real, the good) in *the self-governing resistance of the ego to the world*. Life shall (be built in) doing and suffering and creating [pp. 154].

In this passage Erikson sets before us an ideal of aspiration which melds the grave battle readiness of a Schopenhauerian "grim-faced knight" with Nietzsche's hortatory injunction to "become who you are" (or were) in the service of the Eriksonian task of the creation of a secure identity—and beyond.

In due course Erikson will devote his most extended discussion of individuals, not to a discretely disguised "ordinary person", some "Anna O" or a "Rat man," but to the genius figures of Luther and Ghandi—neither of them adolescent at the point of self-discovery and self-transformation, by even the most generous expansion of the label.

As different as Sigmund Freud's, Anna Freud's, and Erikson's descriptions of the adolescent appear to be—and they are in many ways very different—they all share a common thread: a set of implicit assumptions about adolescence as a time of great intra-psychic struggle and achievement. Although Freud pauses for a consideration of the pubertal fusion as a stage on life's way, and Miss Freud places her emphasis on the the restructuring of the defences in that curiously military metaphor of the analytic construct, and Erikson marshals the youth into the grandest work of self-creation, they all make the adolescent a hero. The heroism is not only in the task itself but in the narrative of the task. Their respective narratives of the adolescent stage use metaphors of extraordinary energy and grandeur: the great tunnels under the alps, the battle strategies of the chaotic defences, the hovering tutelary examples of great geniuses. The metaphors are, I propose, all Nietzschean, and it should not be surprising.

Freud and his circle lived in a Vienna in which Nietzsche's influence was inescapable. As Carl Schorske (1980) has written, cultivated Vienna read, heard, and saw echoes of Nietzsche in the theatre, in music and painting (pp. 221–228) the plays of Hugo von Hoffmansthal (p. 230) and Schnitzler, in Rilke's poetry and Thomas Mann's novels, in Richard Strauss's tone poem *Thus spake Zarathustra*, and in Gustave Mahler's third symphony, with its choral setting of a poem taken from *Zarathustra* (p. 230). The very walls and ceilings of official Vienna were decorated by Gustav Klimt using acknowledged Nietzschean imagery. And it was not only Vienna that was soaked in Nietzsche's thought and imagery. His influence hovered over the culture of Europe at the end of the nineteenth century and the first decades of this century. He was inescapable and his followers were protean in their variety: Ibsen, Yeats, Martin Buber, Achad Ha'am, the Zionist theoretician, Rilke, Robert Graves, D'Annunzio, Gide, Shaw, and Mann, to name only a few, were explicitly Nietzschean. And one should add, more recently, A. S. Neill and R. D. Laing. His message was complex and subject to contradictory interpretations but the core of his message—if one dares define a core—was a sceptical rejection of past values and all received ideas. He articulated the late nineteenth century version of the right, indeed the moral imperative, to pursue an individual destiny; to become what one "truly" was. He praised courage, resolution, loneliness and strength. He valued myths, dreams, passion, and sensuality. He regarded rational Socratic thinking as an historical corruption of European thought. And he frequently invoked the redemptive power of youth.

Given the extraordinary range and influence of Nietzsche's thought, one asks why Freud was so inconsistent and reluctant, at times, to acknowledge Nietzsche's influence. As one reads the Ernest Jones (1954, 1955, 1957) biography of Freud one finds references to Freud's awareness of Nietzsche which coalesce into ambivalent admiration. At times Freud claimed that Nietzsche had no influence on his ideas. He said, for example, that he was uncomfortable in the domain of Nietzsche's thought. At a meeting of the Vienna Psychoanalytic Society in April 1908 when Hitschman read a section of Nietzsche's *Genealogy of Morals*, Freud admitted that he found the abstractness of philosophy "unsympathetic". He allowed that he had tried to read Nietzsche but found the work "too rich" and had abandoned the attempt.

At a later meeting of the Society to discuss Nietzsche's work, however, Freud said that Nietzsche had a "more penetrating knowledge of himself than any other man who has lived or was likely to live". (Jones, 1955, p. 385). Jones cites other instances of Freud's mixture of knowledge of Nietzsche alongside a claimed lack of understanding: in a letter to Arnold Zweig who had sent him a book on Nietzsche's illness, he wrote "You over rate my knowledge concerning N. so I cannot tell you anything of much use for your purpose. For me two things bar an approach to Nietzsche's problem. In the first place one cannot see through anyone unless one knows about his sexual constitution and with N. this is complete enigma" (Jones, 1957, p. 203). The letter continues in a way that suggests that Freud was, in fact, very much in touch with the lore surrounding Nietzsche:

There is even a suggestion that he was a passive homosexual and that he acquired syphilis in a male brothel in Italy. Whether that is true: quien sabe. In the second place he had a serious illness and after a long period of warning symptoms a General Paralysis became manifest. Everyone has conflicts. With a general Paresis the conflicts fade into the background of the aetiology [p. xx].

There was less prevarication when Freud wrote "Nietzsche is a philosopher whose guesses and intutions often agree in the most astonishing way with the findings of psychoanalyisis" (Ellenberger, 1970, p. 277). This may suggest two great minds coming independently to similar conclusions. After all Freud and Nietzsche were overlapping contemporaries; they experienced (created) the social and intellectual currents of their time. And they both shared in the late nineteenth century climate of what Ludwig Klages, the antisemitic graphologist and avowed Nietzsche disciple called "truth telling and uncovering" (Ascheim, 1992, p. 78). But the fact is that the primary author of the shared concerns of Europe—the Europe outside Freud's immdediate and still small circle—was Friedrich Nietszche.

Other psychoanalysts were less reluctant to see a direct connection between their school of thought and Nietzsche. For instance, Hans Sachs, during a visit to Nietzsche's sister, biographer, and literary executrix (distorter and traducer some might say), commented on the similarity between Nietzsche and Freud (Jones, 1955, p. 97). (This must have given great pleasure to the delusionally antisemitic Elizabeth, who in one well-known photograph is shown in *Völkisch* costume smilingly welcoming Adolf Hitler to the Nietzsche archive of which she was the dragon-guardian, Ascheim, 1992, photographic plate 16, pp. 200–201.) Alfred Adler clearly owed his idea of "masculine protest" and constant struggle for power to Nietzsche's idea of "The Will to Power". (Jones, 1955, p. 148).

Other psychoanalytic theoreticians have been more explicit in their recognition of Nietzsche. Karen Horney (1942), writing about envy, says "The envy has a quality of what Nietzsche called *Lebensneid*, an envy which does not pertain to this or that detail but to life in general" (Vol. 2, p. 59). And Phyllis Grosskurth (1986) in her biography of Melanie Klein, records that Nietzsche, together with Schopenhauer, was a strong influence on her circle of friends. Melanie Klein in her youth belonged to a group of intellectual students among whose heroes was Nietzsche; her brother Emmanuel modeled his style on Nietzsche's aphorisms and he subscribed to Nietzsche's affirmation of "the superman who must abandon conventional morality and live at a level of passion and creativity" (p. 17). And Chapman (1955) has made a careful compilation of Nietzsche's influence on Freud as represented in the writings of Ernest Jones and Henri Ellenberger.

While it may not have been clear to Freud, his debt to Nietzsche was apparent to others, and has been increasingly noted. Kauffman (1968) appears to accept without the need for discussion that Freud was in the cultural shadow cast by Nietzsche. A case in point: when Jung commented on the theoretical struggle between Adler and Freud, he wrote "Freud himself had told me that he never read Nietzsche: now I saw Freud's psychology as, so to speak, an adroit move on the part of intellectual history, compensating for Nietzsche's deification of the power principle. The problem had obviously to be rephrased not as Freud versus Adler, but Freud versus Nietzsche" (Mahony, 1982, p. 213). Jones provides further support for the position that Freud's disclaimer of lack of knowledge of Nietzsche was disingenuous. As early as 1897 he echoed a phrase of Nietzsche's when he wrote of the "collapse of all values". (Jones, 1995, p. 391).

To be fair, Nietzsche's phraseology was so soaked into the discourse of *fin-de-sìecle* Europe that Freud may have picked up specific ideas and phrases "through the air," but there are many examples of Freud's use of specifically Nietzschean phraseology that suggest more than a casual connection. In a letter to Karl Abraham in 1917 Freud quoted one of Nietzsche's more hermetic ideas, "the eternal recurrence of the same" (Jones, 1955, p. 218). For Freud it was an apt encapsulation of the idea of the repetition compulsion. In a similar appropriation, Jones draws the comparison between Nietzsche's notion of the "bad conscience" and Freud's "superego". Both are described in terms of the turning inward of unexpressed drives that become distorted and punitive (Jones, 1955, p. 306–307). Both terms "sublimation" and "id" were used by Nietzsche before Freud and with very similar meanings. (It should be noted that "id" came to Freud by an indirect source—George Groddek's "Book of the Id.")

Nietzsche himself did not claim to have had an intellectual immaculate conception. His fundamental contraposition of the intellectual Apollonian, and the instinctual Dionysian forces in the individual psyche, vividly shown in his early prodigious *Birth of Tragedy* (1872), is a borrowing from the pioneer anthropologist Bachofen—a contemporary of his at the University of Basel. But the conduit of this reformulation of ancient ideas was not the relatively obscure Bachofen (1861, cited in Pletsch, 1991), but Nietzsche.

Apart from specific terms and larger ideas Freud and Nietzsche share a sceptical attitude to the conventional truths of human existence. "It was Nietzsche's concern to unveil how man is a self-deceiving creature, who is also constantly deceiving his fellowmen. Indeed Nietzsche is inexhaustible in his attempts to show how every possible kind of feeling, opinion, attitude, conduct, and virtue is rooted in self-deception or an unconscious lie" (Jones, 1955 p. 273). And Ellenberger draws the comparison even more closely: "The work of the analyst like the Nietzschean quester after truth is to uncover and to unmask" (Ellenberger, 1970 p. 273).

So without explicitly citing or having read him—as he claimed—Freud echoed the Nietzschean zeitgeist in the value he placed on dreams, on the power of the instincts and passions, in his mining of classical mythology for metaphors (the most powerful of which was of course Oedipus). But apart from explicit borrowings or influences, Freud adopted a form of discourse which Mayer (in Mahony, 1982) suggests was Nietzsche's characteristic style; a rhetorical blend of fact and metaphor; a blending of Dionysus and Apollo which fuses art and science. "Mayer rejects the scientist-artist dichotomy even on theoretical grounds; the boundaries between fiction and nonfiction have become blurred, at least since Nietzsche, if not before" (p. 14). When Freud wrote of the innervation of the genitals in puberty he was using a chracteristically Nietzschean blend of intellectual categories, and when he wrote of the tunnels, he reflected the characteristically Nietzschean use of the mountain as an image of the place where self-discovery occurs.

That invitation to self-discovery, which now seems to be a natural right ensconced in political fact, became increasingly accepted after the Enlightenment and the French Revolution and American Revolution. By the end of the 19th century it reached the intelligentsia and specifically cultivated youth—such people as Freud and his circle, and the others of whom I have already written. But the actual numbers of adolescents or students who were influenced by Nietzsche's heroic vision of a turbulent, self-discovering life were few. As Hobsbawm (1987) writes:

The educated bourgeois youth which welcomed Nietzschean irrationalism were small minorities. Their spokesmen numbered a few dozens, but their public essentially belonged to new generations of the university trained, who were outside of the United States an exiguous educational elite. There were in 1913, 14,000 students in Belgium and the Netherlands but of a total population of 13 to 14 million, 11,400 in Scandinavia (minus Finland) out of almost 11 million, and even in studious Germany only 77,000 out of 65 million [p. 260].

But this small group became the progenitors of a vision of youth for the next century.[2]

It was a vision that would become disseminated in therapeutic circles, through Anna Freud and Erik Erikson. In the market place of politics and ideas a similar vision was encouraged by political movements, increased prosperity, a longer life span, and the increasingly democratisized belief in the pursuit of happiness.

The model of adolescence propagated by Anna Freud and Erikson is steeped in Nietzschean thought. Its positive aspects are obvious: greater freedom, a respect for personal development, a sceptical attitude to received values. The downside was a sometimes impossibly heroic aspiration, a reinforcement of the dangerous push to anomie—to isolation and rootlessness.

The difficulty in translating the grand utterances of courage, scepticism, and passion into daily life is inherent in Nietzsche's expression. He was certainly not unique in his emphasis on individual freedom; it was after all the central political struggle of the 19th century, and the free expression of feeling was a tenet of romanticism. But what sets Nietzsche apart is that he is a great dramatist of ideas. The aphorisms are passionate and poetic. In his person and in his writings he gave a human form to the intensely academic and philosophically dense arguments of his near contemporaries. The danger of his model is, however, that the passion he proclaimed seemed to have little to do with ordinary existence; it lacks dailiness. His dramas belong to dreams and operas: "Go apart and be alone with my tears, my brother. I love him who wants to create beyond himself, and thus perishes" (Kauffman, 1968, p. 90–91). The grandeur of the utterance stirs a red-necked pragmatism, and one wants to ask; how exactly does one "go apart" and "be alone" with one's tears. And in a nearly infinite regress one can see how it can generate a sense of despair and inadequacy in the good enough student, the pretty enough young woman, the more or less conventional young person who has never heard of Nietzsche. But while they haven't heard of him, much less read him, they have heard the distant echoes of his call to become "what you

---

[2] It was said that German soldiers went to fight in World War I with Nietzsche in their back packs. This was more than a metaphor. The German government printed a special 150,000 edition of *Thus Spake Zarathustra* (Nietzsche, 1883) for distribution to the troops. The war was even labeled "Nietzsche's War." As Ascheim (1992) writes, "Gavrilo Princip, the radical Bosnian student whose assasination of Archduke Franz Ferdinand of Austria in Sarajevo sparked the beginnings of the War, liked to recite from Nietzsche's *Ecce Homo*: "Insatiable as a flame, I burn and consume myself" (p. 134).

are", to "love your fate", to aspire to their being a "superman", to court the fall from life's tightrope, on which each dances his or her personal dance.

There are some sad ad hominem comments that are irresistible. Anna Freud, for all her descriptions of normative turbulence, lived in the domain of her father's thought; she was a kind of nun, or rather abbess of psychoanalysis. More egregiously Erikson, who is the theorist of identity and authenticity for our time, obscured his Jewish origins (Roazen, 1976, p. 95), changed his name and when he came to delineate the interesting—and implicitly valuable—life concentrated his attention on great geniuses. Nietzsche led him, one might say, to a disdain of the ordinary. The self to be discovered in the Eriksonian moratorium is a very grand and romantic self—so romantic that the daily lives that most of us succeed, with some difficulty, in making must always seem pale and unfulfilled.

Although it was certainly not his intention, Erikson has colluded in the decontextualization of the young, and indeed of the not-so-young. When Erikson (1968) suggests that the puberty rites and confirmation in what he calls "primitive societies" (p. 87) help to integrate and to affirm the new identity, he does not confront the paradox that the identity conferred by pubertal rites is not the identity he espouses, one of individual authenticity or self-discovery. It is closer to donning a psychic uniform, not the discovery of a true self hammered out in the smithy of an individual soul. Paradoxically, for all the panoply of ritualised suffering associated with many pubertal "rites of passage", they are not tailored to individual identity but are intensely stereotyped. Stereotypy is an essential characteristic. One may suffer during pubertal rites, but one need not be a "hero". The individual needs only to submit and conform to their ritualised cruelties, eventually to emerge from the trials of adolescent *rites de passage* to achieve self-acceptance and acceptance into the continuing historical entity of the society (Rakoff, 1995). The pubertal ceremonies with all their predictability and social context are among the major instruments preventing the loneliness of the individual which Durkheim (1950) labeled anomie.

When Durkheim wrote his great treatise on suicide in 1911 and identified anomic suicide, he emphasised that poverty and deprivation are less likely to cause self-murder than a debilitating disatisfaction with what is. A constant devaluing of the given in the present and a yearning for an ever more glowing future is a profoundly destabilizing force in individual lives. It is an implicit criticism of the Eriksonian idea of the extended moratorium and of life as a constant route of self-discovery.

The grand vision of self-realization generated by the major theorists of contemporary adolescence may be suffering from its own dialectical tensions. By neglecting the need for context and the demands of the ordinary they were part of the great movement toward freedom from which most of us have benefited. They may also have encouraged the loneliness endemic in modern urban society and thus helped to generate impossibly tormenting models of the normative.

One of the dangers of this kind of essay is that one appears to be making whole cloth out of one thread. I am not suggesting that the Nietzschean current running through the Freuds to Erikson and outward to an entire generation is the only cause of anomie, suicide, and the disorders of adolescent aspiration, of which, after suicide, the eating disorders are the most sinister. The general loss of social structures, intense mobility, loss of belief systems, are obviously powerful additional forces, particularly for Native American youth whose society is in radical transition. Their suicide rate is 5 times greater than for the general Canadian population. However, having made this reservation I read, as I was writing this last paragraph, a report on youth suicide in the *Toronto Globe and Mail* of November 16th, 1996. The report once again documents the increase in suicide among adolescents since 1950. The rise for females is about 4%, for males it is approximately 20%. Some years ago Gerald Klerman (1988) produced similar findings, and he speculated about what might be the causal factor. Perhaps the list of reasons for staying alive carefully written down by a 17-year-old patient at the Toronto Hospital for Sick Children points us in the direction of that cause. At the top of her lists written three months apart are "to become a high school graduate," "to be able to become a writer," and "might be-come famous . . . because I might discover the cure for some disease." The first is simple and modest, the others reverberate with a dangerous heroism. An ordinary life in the context of intimate relationships seems tame, an unworthy goal. Fame and great deeds are the hero's quest: they emit a seductive music most clearly sounded for our century by Nietzsche and propagated unwittingly by theoreticians of contemporary adolescence.

REFERENCES

Aries, R. (1962), *Centuries of childhood.* New York: Knopf.
Breuer, J. & Freud, S. (1893), On the psychical mechanisms of hysterical phenomena. *Standard Edition*, 3:25–39. London: Hogarth Press, 1962.

Ascheim, S. E. (1992), *The Nietzsche Legacy in Germany 1890–1990*. Berkeley: University of California Press.

Breuer, J. & Freud, S. (1893–95), Studies on hysteria. *Standard Edition*, 2. London: Hogarth Press, 1955.

Chapman, A. H. & Chapman-Santana, W. (1995), The influence of Nietzsche on Freud's ideas. *Brit. J. Psychiat.*, 166:251–253.

Durkheim, E. (1950), *Suicide*. New York: Free Press.

Ellenberger, H. (1970), *The Discovery of the Unconscious*. New York: Basic Books.

Erikson, E. H. (1950), *Childhood and Society*. New York: Norton.

———(1968), *Identity*. New York: Norton

Esman, A. (1996), The ego-psychological approach to adolescence. Presented at the Annual meeting of the American Society for Adolescent Psychiatry, Marina-del-Rey, CA.

Freud, A. (1936), *The Ego and the Mechanisms of Defense*. New York: International Universities Press, 1966.

———(1958), Adolescence. *The Psychoanalytic Study of the Child*, 13:255–278. New York: International Universities Press.

Freud, S. (1905), Three essays on the theory of sexuality. *Standard Edition*, 7:130–243. London: Hogarth Press, 1953.

Gray, T., (1768) Elegy written in a country churchyard. *The Oxford Book of English Verse*, ed. Sir Arthur Quiller-Couch. London: Oxford University Press, 1974.

Grosskurth, P. (1986), *Melanie Klein*. Toronto: McClelland & Stewart.

Kauffman, W. (1968), *Nietzsche*. New York: Vintage Books.

Klerman, G. (1988), Youthful melancholia. *Brit. J. Psychiat.*, 152:4–14

Hobsbawm, E. (1987), *The Age of Empire 1875–1914*. London: Weidenfeld & Nicholson.

Horney, K. (1942), *Collected Works of Karen Horney*. New York: Norton.

Jones, E. (1954), *The Life and Work of Sigmund Freud Vol. 1*. New York, Basic Books.

———(1955), *The Life and Work of Sigmund Freud, Vol. 2*. New York; Basic Books.

———(1957), *The Life and Work of Sigmund Freud, Vol. 3*. New York; Basic Books.

Mahony, P. (1982), *Freud as a Writer*. New York: International Universities Press.

Nietzsche, F. (1872), *The Birth of Tragedy and The Case of Wagner*, trans. W. Kaufman. New York: Vintage Press, 1967

————(1883), *Thus Spake Zarathustra*, trans. R. J. Hollingdale. Harmondsworth: Penguin Books, 1969.

Pletsch, C. (1991), *Young Nietzsche*. New York: Free Press.

Rakoff, V. (1995), Trauma and adolescent rites of initiation. *Adolescent Psychiatry*, 20:109–124. Hillsdale, NJ: The Analytic Press.

————(1989), The emergence of the adolescent patient. *Adolescent Psychiatry*, 16:379–386. Chicago: University of Chicago Press.

Roazen, P. (1976), *Erik Erikson. The Power and Limits of Wisdom.* New York: Free Press.

Schama, S. (1995), *Landscape and Memory.* New York: Knopf.

Schorske, C. E. (1980), *Fin-de-Siècle Vienna, Politics and Culture.* New York: Knopf.

PART II

CLINICAL ISSUES IN ADOLESCENCE

Clinical considerations are, of course, central to adolescent psychiatry, as they are to all mental health disciplines. In this section a number of vital clinical issues are discussed, from a number of persepctives. Drs. Jeammet and Chabert, presenting a European psychoanalytic point of view on the increasingly global problem of eating disorders, stressed what they regard as their central problem, the unresolved conflict around dependency. Drs. Hendren and Butler survey the disorders of impulse control from a biological and behavioral point of view, offering valuable suggestions about the clinical management of these difficult cases. Dr. Miller is concerned with what he sees as failures in the efforts of the judicial justice system in dealing with delinquent youths, and sets forth a program for ameliorating this situation. Dr. Glenn returns us to our clinical origins in Freud's "Dora" case, teasing out the special role of sadistic and masochistic fantasies in her psychopathology; Drs. Aronson and I engage him in a discussion of his ideas. Finally, Dr. Kernberg provides a careful and systematic protocol for the asessment of severe character pathology in adolescents.

4   A PSYCHOANALYTIC APPROACH TO EATING DISORDERS: THE ROLE OF DEPENDENCY

PHILIPPE JEAMMET AND CATHERINE CHABERT

Although they have been observed for centuries and were mentioned by Freud (Breuer and Freud, 1895) in the past 30 years eating disorders have taken on a new dimension and significance. This is quite certainly due to their extension, most clearly seen in bulimia, or in bulimiarexia, an association of anorexia nervosa and bulimic binges rather than in the purely restrictive forms of anorexia. But this is especially due to the questions these disorders confront society with as well as their specific psychopathological characteristics.

In many ways eating disorders can be seen as the symbols of psychopathology at the end of the twentieth century, in the same way hysteria was at the end of the nineteenth century. Pursuing this analogy, they can be thought of as the privileged instrument to question and reassess metapsychology, as hysteria was in its time one of the most important bases for metapsychological elaboration.

Brief Review of the Basic Psychoanalytic Models

We will restrict our review to the tenets which underlie the conceptualizations of major psychoanalytic authors who have dealt with the subject of eating disorders. Several books and articles offer a complete inventory: Schwartz (1988) in the United States and the work of Kestemberg and Decobert (1972) and Brusset (1977) in France.

It is interesting to note that although Freud was not specifically interested in eating disorders, he nevertheless indicated in a few brief notes some of the essential directions that were later to be developed.

First and foremost, it is hysteria that served in the 1890s as a reference in the initial writings where anorexia was mentioned. Freud (1894) described the case of anorexia nervosa in a young mother (see also Breuer and Freud, 1895; and Freud, 1950, letters of June 20, 1898 and December 9, 1899). Reference to hysteria is not surprising at a time when it represented the essential material for the elaboration of psychoanalytic theory. The accent was placed upon the repression of oral eroticism and upon disgust—to block the course of sexual impulses—as well as on the importance of oral-erotic fixations and the buccolabial erogenous zone. Also, in two letters to Fliess, dated December 11 and 22, 1897 (Freud, 1950), without speaking directly about bulimia, Freud, as Catherine Couvreur (1991) notes, speaks about masturbation as being the "primal addiction" for which other forms are only substitutions, and about dipsomanic attacks as a substitute compulsion for the repressed sexual drive. Freud (1895) links "eating binges" to anxiety and sees "a quantum of free-floating anxiety" in them, ready to connect with any representative contents. In 1912, he will say that actual neuroses are based on a somatic sexual manifestation that constitutes the material of excitation that will then be "psychically selected and enrobed" to form psychoneuroses. In later writings, as Catherine Couvreur remarks, Freud will make several references to drinking compulsions and drug-related addictions as protective measures that are likely to be transformed into compulsive actions against obsessive affects. He insists upon their anesthetizing function and their role as a protective shield.

It is particularly in *Civilization and its Discontents* (Freud, 1930), Catherine Couvreur recalls, that Freud tackles the study of this withdrawal into the self, and speaks about what he calls "the toxic aspects of psychic processes," which is likely to modify the conditions of our sensitivity.

But alongside the models of hysteria and actual neurosis, Freud (1895) also raised the question of depression and more specifically, of melancholia in the G manuscript where he wrote, "the food neurosis called 'anorexia' can be compared to melancholia." He mentions the possible role "of an as yet incomplete sexuality" in the case of anorexia and a loss in the field of instinctual needs in the triggering of melancholia.

Without ever specifically treating eating disorders, Freud opened all of the perspectives that have since been followed to understand the metapsychology of this pathology: 1) hysteria with its double polarity of oral fixations of the libido, factors of regression, and sexual fantasies displaced onto orality and repressed; 2) melancholia with the issue of object loss, but also of a loss in the field of instinctual needs. Freud speaks of an anesthesia that encourages melancholic thought, opening a direction in research which has a certain connection to the third perspective; 3) actual neurosis that leads us to the triple question of the weight of conjunctural actuality, of somatic and infrarepresentational factors, and finally, the failures of the ego and capacities for elaboration.

As seen through this division, the three metapsychological viewpoints are each solicited in turn: the topographical point of view in the first case, the dynamic one in the second, and the economic one in the third.

As with other fundamental points of his theory, Freud will not choose between these diverse modes, no more than he will abandon the theory of traumatism or reject the first topography after having elaborated the second. We defend this point of view, considering that more than any other behavior, perhaps because of its junctional position which was mentioned earlier, eating disorders bring us to theorize the articulation between these different viewpoints. Each one plays a role that varies from case to case and according to the particular phase of evolution, but it does not assume its full meaning or pathogenic effect except in respect to the rest, making it insufficient to consider one to the exclusion of the others.

Abraham (1922) describes several cases of feminine and masculine bulimia. He makes a connection between them and morphine addicts and drinkers, opening the way to what Fenichel (1945) will later describe as "drug-free addictions." Abraham (1925) also mentions the presence of other impulsions besides bulimia that have "escaped from all socialization" and that "spring from the same instinctual sources" (p. 248). In the "manifestations of the castration complex in women," he feels that the fact of eating usually has the unconscious meaning of becoming pregnant and can thus bring about feeding inhibitions (p. 257). His essential contribution is, however, more indirect, coming by way of the importance of oral sadism and of anal control, and also through the contribution of Melanie Klein and her students, who, by underlining the importance of archaic fantasies of sadistic devouring, destruction, and poisoning, have furnished a frequently used model by which to understand eating disorders.

In earlier times, psychoanalysts who dealt specifically with eating disorders considered them to be a symptom more than anything else, and they paid little attention to the organization of the personality.

Indeed, the drive conflict seems clear when seen through the avoidance of genital sexuality by anorexics and the erotization of eating in both disorders. The first psychoanalysts were thus led to emphasize the importance of *the role of regression in the face of genital sexuality and the role of fantasies of oral impregnation and oral incorporation of the paternal penis* (Waller et al., 1940; Masserman, 1941; Lorand, 1943). These themes will be tackled again by Fenichel. For all these authors a double tendency affects genital sexuality: one tendency displaces sexual representations onto orality then conflictualizes orality which becomes an object of disgust, inhibition and repression; the other tendency, more authentically regressive, leads to a reactivation of object relations and of an eroticism that belong to earlier stages of the anal and oral libido. We are thus in connection with anality: reaction formations, feeding rituals, obsessive thought, verification, the fecalization of food, of the body and of needs in general, in counterpoint to an idealization of the intellect and to the thin and erect body, and to the overinvestment of control, of muscular hyperactivity, of manipulating and influence-exerting relationships over objects. On the other hand, the reactivation of incorporation mechanisms and of their inhibition, the importance of envy, of all-or-nothing relationships, of greed and instability as they appear during bulimic binges, belong more to the realm of orality. Regression also leads to drive defusion and to a liberation of a free-floating aggressiveness (death instinct?) that nourishes the anorexic symptom.

However, confronted with the complexity of each case and the frequent severity of its evolution, the pathology of the personality has taken on a greater and greater importance in psychological research. It was never totally absent from earlier work and Lorand (1943), for example, made reference to a "psychogenetic disorder in the evolution of the ego," but it disappeared behind the apparent symbolic transparency of the symptom. Progressively, studies have begun to insist upon the complexity and the opacity of anorexic behavior that cannot be reduced to its symptom, no more than the symptom can be reduced to a banal symptom of hysteria. The phenomenological studies (Binswanger, 1944; Kuhn, 1953; Boss, 1954; May, 1958) already emphasized the existential dimension of anorexia and the implication that the whole personality was marked, beyond the symptom, by a profound feeling of despair and abandonment. Meyer and Weinroth (1957), for example, no longer confer upon the symptom the sense of a way out of drive conflict but instead give it the meaning of a finality that can respond to the psychotic-type defects in ego-organization, through an attempt to re-establish mother-child unity. It is the desire to separate the anorexic symptom from the more specific pathological organization that leads authors like King (1963) or Bruch (1973) to propose a distinction between primary and secondary anorexia.

However, the Göttingen symposium under the direction of Meyer and Feldman (1965) can be thought of as the definition of a turning point in the psychopathological conceptions of anorexia. Here are some of the common conclusions that emerged: 1) mental anorexia has a specific structure; 2) the essential conflict is situated at the level of the body and not at the level of sexually invested feeding functions; and 3) it expresses the incapacity to assume the genital role and the body transformations that emerge with puberty.

These conclusions have not been questioned since and have been taken up and developed in specific ways by different authors. Bruch (1973) believes that the fundamental, pathognomonic disorder is a body image problem, secondary to disturbances of interoceptive perception. These disturbances are linked to a defect in the recognition of the body's sensations and needs, which is itself secondary to troubles appearing in the first learning experiences during which the mother imposes her own sensations and her own needs onto the child instead of helping him or her perceive and recognize his own. The result is that the child is unable to recognize the limits of his or her ego, and has a defective construction of body image and a defective recognition of interoceptive perceptions (such as hunger, satiation, cold, fatigue, sexual sensations, and beyond them, emotional states). In this context, it is the child's identity that is weakened and thus remains deeply dependent on those around him. Feelings of impotence, inefficacy, and dependence are the inevitable corollaries. The extent of this triad (problems with body image, interoceptive perception, and autonomy) takes on an unreal or even delusional character and place primary anorexia, for Bruch, in the lineage of schizophrenias among which it constitutes a particular form.

The struggle to achieve autonomy and the recovery of a feeling of efficacy, exercised through body control, are the essential traits of anorexia nervosa.

Before she changed her orientation towards systemic family therapies, Mara Palazzoli-Selvini used the works of Melanie Klein to make anorexia nervosa a form of "monosymptomatic psychosis" which she qualified as "intrapersonal paranoia," halfway between the schizo-paranoid and depressive positions. It is the body, split from the rest of the ego, that is the persecuting object which must be controlled and kept at a distance. The body is the bad object filled with the attributes of the primary maternal objects that were massively incorporated during the first mother-child relationship to which it passively subjected itself.

Kestemberg et al. (1972) noticed and described the modalities specific to regression and to instinct organization. The regression is "vertiginous" in that it does not encounter any point of fixation or organization at the level of the erogenous zones. They are, in their specific organizational modes of the object relation, "erased" and "swept away" by regressive movement. This movement can not stop before reaching what the authors call the level of precursors of the relation with the object and of the ego organization, which they conceptualize in a very original version of the self.

The instinctual organization is characterized by its specific recourse to primary erogenous masochism where pleasure is directly linked to the refusal of need satisfaction. Pleasure does not accompany the feeling of having something inside oneself but rather eroticizes the nonsatisfaction of a vital need. The same is true of relationships where the constant search for pleasure of dissatisfaction dominates. "The orgasm of hunger" is the best example. The hedonization of refusal becomes a guarantee of the feeling of being or existing on one's own and bodily activity and the body are thus withdrawn from any external control.

John Sours (1980) developed a genetic perspective by referring to the developmental model of the North American psychoanalytic school. The developmental history of these patients reveals evidence of a parental insistence concerning the control of pleasure, and the importance of activities of anal control. Oral gratifications are only tolerated for a brief period and the infant is prematurely invited to adapt to the parental style of social conformity. The child is perfectly taken care of but this is performed without pleasure and the parents discourage any tendencies toward separation and autonomy: desires for independence, attitudes of opposition and negativism do not emerge. The mother anticipates the needs of the child and struggles against her own fantasies of food restriction and her incorporating and cannibalistic desires. The child cathects the mother object instead of his own self and he lives in fear of losing this object, becoming, Sours says, "a suitor and a denier." Later on, sibling rivalry, separations from the mother and oedipal competition threaten this symbiotic relationship with the mother and precipitate regression.

This brings up the problem of the nature of their object relation, and in so doing, the status of the eating disorders' premorbid personality.

Must we deduce, along with the Anglo-Saxon developmental psycho-analytic school (Sours), that it is the effect of a failure of the first sepa-ration-individuation process that the second stage at adolescence reveals by a regression to an archaic level of nondifferentiation of the self? Or rather, should we infer, along with Kestemberg et al.—and this would not be incompatible with the first view—that there is a defect in the constitution of the internal object that produces, along with psy-chosis, one of the forms of failure of the hallucinatory satisfaction of desire? This failure, even though relative, brings about a weakness in the constitution of the internal object leaving the subject to remain dependent for the most part on the external object for the regulation of her pleasures, her internal tensions, and her self-esteem. Here we can find the origin of an early failure of auto-eroticism and of the function of the protective shield.

Dependency in Eating Disorders

These different psychopathological studies, each one with its own approach and theorization, place the problems of identity at the heart of anorexia nervosa. They underline the importance of the dependency/autonomy conflict and the fundamental vulnerability of the anorexic. It is possible that this vulnerability is linked to powerful, passive desires, which result in a constant fear of intrusion and particularly of bodily invasion by the object they depend upon. The specific terms of the prob-lem show the paradox of the anorexic: she destroys herself to insure her existence. The destructive effect is not sought out for itself, and, from this point of view, anorexia is not a suicidal behavior, even if we can see it as the result of defused aggressiveness and the turning against the self of a fantasy of object incorporation that is experienced as destructive. It is the consequence of using a physiological need indispensable to sur-vival to preserve the feeling of autonomy. In so doing, which is the sec-ond paradox, the anorexic now finds herself even more dependent on the environment which she was trying to free herself from. By making refusal the instrument of her liberation, she alienates herself from the object of refusal which she can neither lose nor internalize.

Eating disorders share these characteristics with other behavioral disorders with which they are frequently associated. Indeed, a certain number of clinicians who work with adolescents and young adults, including us, have proposed arguments that prompt them to widen the spectrum of addictive behaviors beyond drugs and alcohol. No one questions the fact that tobacco addiction and the abuse of psychotropic drugs (in particular tranquilizers and sleeping pills) should be included. It is not as accepted in the case of bulimia, which as early as 1945 was included by the well-known psychoanalyst Otto Fenichel in "drug-free addictions." Yet, many authors have emphasized in recent years its comorbid connections with alcoholism and other addictions as well as its impulsive character. The same can be said of pathological gambling, what anglo-saxons call "excessive gambling," which many consider the behavior closest to chemical addictions, and pathological buying, named "compulsive spending" (Marks, 1990) by some. The question is more controversial for other behaviors such as kleptomania, so frequently associated with the above, trichotillomania, pyromania, self-mutilations, certain forms of repetitive suicide attempts of youths or anorexic individuals. Last of all, dependency behaviors have also included those involving a compulsive search for sexual partners which psychoanalysts have designated as "object addiction," certain forms of suicide attempts, particularly in young people, or even particular types of relationships to work, sports, or other forms of sensation seeking.

An entire framework for dependency is thus likely to be developed as a defense against affective dependency perceived as a threat to the subject's identity and an alienation from his objects of attachment. It is a system whereby the subject tries to substitute bonds of control and ascendancy to his affective, relational ones, which are experienced as so much more threatening in that they are more necessary. The point is to introduce substitute objects between the subject and his possible attachments which he thinks he controls: food in bulimia, drugs, and so on.

Here, we can clearly witness the controlling function of distance in a relationship through this behavior. It allows the subject to maintain apparently satisfying relationships and a relatively diversified social life. But the price is paid with the splitting of the ego. The addictive relationship repairs the most conflictual but also the most cathected aspect of relational needs, and leaves little possibility for exchanges that begin to take on a very artificial, ready-made character. Anything that calls to mind an affective bond is rejected. The behavior becomes more and more delibidinalized, purely mechanical, as all fantasy activity attached to it disappears. Autoeroticism loses its erotic, pleasurable dimension. The experience of pleasure is replaced by the need for violent sensations so that the subject can feel that he exists.

A certain number of clinicians base themselves on clinical data to justify the regrouping of such behaviors under the heading of addictive behaviors. They do not mean to say that dependency alone can account for the appearance of these disorders, nor that no other conflicts exist, but rather that these conflicts, although they are indispensable for the manifestation of these addictions, can not, on their own, enable us to understand a certain number of common characteristics. On the other hand the notion of dependency can shed a new light and provide a model which can guide our therapeutic attitudes.

If the concept of dependence does not belong, properly speaking, to classic psychoanalytic vocabulary, it is nonetheless employed by a great number of psychoanalysts. It is probably with Mahler's description of the separation-individuation process as a fundamental developmental stage of the child that this notion is most used, and adolescence, the second process of separation-individuation for Peter Blos, is considered to be the critical stage or the stumbling block of this work toward autonomy.

But even in France where psychoanalysts generally consider Mahler's approach and that of her successors as too descriptive, in the tradition of Hartmann's autonomous ego, and too separated from the conflictual, instinctual current and from sexuality, it seems difficult to completely give up this notion of dependence. Thus, without explicitly defining it, Kestemberg and Decobert (1972) imply it several times. Speaking of anorexic patients, they consider that the "foundations of their personality are experienced in terms of dependence and non-dependence" (p. 164). They also attribute "the blockage of associative possibilities and the limited contact that patients have with their own history which remains vague" (p. 37) to a very regressive position of struggle against dependence. In the same perspective, they insist several times on the role played by the lack of distinction of the imagoes and the blurred limits between the subject and the object. It is indeed "the preservation of a relative indistinction between subject and object at the fantasy level or even deeper in the Self which forces the subject into a permanent struggle against his desires for the object" (p. 164).

André Green (1982a) also refers to the pair of opposites, dependence–autonomy, as archaic. His point of view gives meaning to an entire series of behaviors which it would otherwise be hard to unite. This point of view is all the more interesting in that it brings these notions closer to the concept of the archaic, described from the angle of loss of boundaries and confusion, particularly between desire, its object and the ego. Indeed, these threats upon limits, the unsuccessful differentiation of imagoes, the factor of dedifferentiation which adolescence is specifically liable to mobilize all play a central role in the actualization of the dependence issue (Jeammet, 1989).

Thus, considered from the point of view of psychic functioning, dependence can be described as the use for defensive purposes of perceptive-motor reality as an anticathexis for a failing or threatening internal psychic reality. In this perspective, dependence is a potentiality if not a constant of mental functioning, because there always exists a dialectic game of cathexis and anticathexis between internal psychic reality and the external reality of the perceptive-motor world.

Addictive behavior can thus be described as the search for an external contribution that the subject needs for his equilibrium and that he cannot find at the level of his own internal resources.

In this perspective, we must grant a determining role to the secure relationship with the environment as well as to the link between the quality of this relationship and the quality of pleasure that the subject can experience through the use of his capacities. The experiences of separation during childhood show the quality and the reliability of these acquisitions. They enable us to differentiate between children for whom recourse to autoeroticism efficiently compensates for the absence of attachment figures from those who must replace this by a perceptive-motor cathexis of the environment or by the establishment of repetitive auto-stimulation behavior. These latter behaviors are all the more massive, mechanical, painful, and even mutilating for the subject when the bond is weak and the relation to pleasure absent.

The interest of genetic models is that they illustrate the dialectical relation between the individual's capacity for autonomy, the quality of his or her internal resources, and the quality of his or her first object relations.

What we call narcissistic foundations is what provides the continuity of the subject and the permanence of his cathexis of himself. They are based on various supports, all of which have in common their dialectical opposition to what remains available for object cathexis. However, it is a dialectical opposition based on a double paradox: the narcissistic foundations were only able to construct themselves on the basis of the object relation (but in such a way that the opposition between subject and object was not even an issue); and the "object longing" will be felt as all the less "anti narcissistic", to use Francis Pasche's expression, when the narcissistic foundations are more solidly established.

These narcissistic supports seem profoundly differentiated and are structured hierarchically from the most primitive elements to mechanisms that are already very elaborated. They can be described in terms of primary identifications, narcissistic identifications, support mechanisms (Jean Laplanche, 1987) primary homosexuality, and the establishment of the first autoeroticism of the self (Kestemberg, 1981). What they have in common is that subjects build themselves on the quality of the relationship formed with the object, but in such a way that the questions of heterogeneity between the subject and the object is never brought up. This ambiguity is preserved by the functioning of Winnicott's transitional space. It is on this conflictual basis and these internalized acquisitions that secondary identifications will later develop. The more this foundation is secured the more it will be harmonious and narcissistically pleasing for the subject. In such a case, introjections will be experienced as a blooming of the ego's potentialities and as the accomplishment of the subject's desires according to a process very clearly described by Torok (1968), in the line of Sándor Ferenczi. Using these basic acquisitions, the progressive subject/object differentiation can happen by limiting itself to conflicts between desires without identity being too strongly implicated, while an internal differentiation between agencies and the internal duplication of the subject–object difference is established according to the "double-limit" Green mentions (1982b).

On the opposite pole of this harmonious evolution, everything that makes the child prematurely feel the weight of the object and his impotence regardless of whether it is schematically, by lack of or excessive presence, liable to pave the way toward an antagonism between the subject and his or her objects of cathexis. The narcissistic foundations are no longer constituted with and by the object, filled with the quality of the relation thus established, but against the object, admittedly to quite different degrees. This work of object exclusion is also perceived in the quality of autoeroticism that is displayed, not so much because of its aggressive instinctual quality but above all because it threatens the subject's integrity. It is no longer a question of positive, libidinal, binding autoeroticism that can contain experiences of pleasure associated with objects, causing the subject to dream, to search for the hallucinatory satisfaction of pleasure and to perform the work of representation. It is its opposite: negative, destructive autoeroticism with an antiintrojection, antithought function in as far as introjection and thought are linked to objects. Instead a quest for sensations and essentially somatic stimulations which occupy the place of the object and permit the subject to feel that he or she exists, is substituted but at the price of growing self-reinforcement and progressively as the relationship becomes object free (Jeammet, 1990).

Any situation causing early conflictualization between the subject and the object and provoking the appearance of this antagonism between object cathexis and the preservation of the subject's integrity, that is, which confers an important antinarcissistic function on object cathexis, inevitably hinders introjection mechanisms and the quality of the subject's internalizations. This will bring about precocious ego-splitting and marked difficulties in the process of individuation, with the establishment of indistinct zones between the subject and the object, of reciprocal overlapping and of interfering object incorporations (Torok, 1968). In short, an entire pathology of boundaries. But most important, the corollary of this insufficiency of internal narcissistic foundations is that narcissistic equilibrium remains largely dependent on external object relations that are given the mission of countering an internal reality that threats the subject with disorganization. It is the permanence of relationships, in general more or less idealized, with one or more particularly cathected persons, that assures the subject's continuity when recourse to only internal objects is not sufficient.

The weight of external reality is, of course, more or less restrictive. It will be all the more so in cases with more failures to internalize reassuring and differentiated objects. Here again, situations vary greatly and although anticathexes always slow down the work of internalization, and thus of identification processes, the constraints can remain limited to only certain cathexes or spread like an oil stain.

A "dependent" subject is, however, not condemned to suffer from dependence any more than he or she is to have behavioral problems during adolescence.

Defenses against objectal dependence experienced as a narcissistic threat will have the common objective of protecting narcissism and of controlling the object of desire as well as possible. It will be all the more powerful in that it has the complicity of the subject's objectal desires and a desire for identification that previous failures of internalization have made sharper.

What changes might be able to break this former equilibrium in the interplay of cathexes and counter-cathexes? Those that will increase the weight of objects and accentuate the attraction they exert. Certain types of cathexes are obviously less tolerable than others. This is the case of cathexes concerning objects towards which the subject has, often unconsciously, a relationship of expectation and authority. The sexualization of this type of relationship is a powerful factor in the arousal of dependence fears: it is the case for relationships that have or acquire an incestuous dimension, and those that summon fantasies of passive receptivity. The solicitation of homosexual desires combines all of these factors, both in its narcissistic and sexual polarities. For the latter, the sexual polarity, the activation of anal penetration fantasies represents a particularly active source of intrusion anxiety. Relationships that set off identification processes have the particular potential of combining all of these factors, as is the case at adolescence.

They are also the relations which thwart the defenses mentioned above such as, for example, a brutal deidealization or the sexualization of a relationship that had been preserved up until then. In fact, any source of disequilibrium of object relations is likely to allow the emergence of phenomena of envy, handing over more power to the objects. This movement can be due to the object itself, or the internal world of the subject, such as the sudden pressure of identification desires.

Adolescence cumulates all of these factors. Its function is to reveal the internalization difficulties of early childhood and the dependence issues which have remained latent up until then. The effects of potential dependence, of the sexualization of one's body and relations, and of the reawakening of the oedipal conflict will unite to intensify the traumatic effects of each factor taken separately, mutually reinforcing each other. The deferred action effect of puberty can thus be double: a revelation of the genital sexual nature of childhood events and fantasies; a revelation of nonresolved dependence situations from childhood and the power these confer upon objects whose "influence on her" is suddenly recognized by the adolescent, as well as the narcissistic threat they represent. This double, deferred action effect could well account for the traumatic potential of puberty on some personalities. The dependence on external objects thus gives the incestuous fantasy an undeniable mark of reality. These two problem configurations, dependence and sexualization, combine their effects around identification, making it impossible to complete the identification processes which thereby lose their symbolic weight by making fantasies concrete: to identify with is not to become like the other but to take his place. Incestuous and parricidal fantasies thus take on a reality that even makes thinking about them a dangerous act (Sprince, 1988).

This threat to narcissistic autonomy represented by the awakening of object needs can easily spread to the need itself, that is, to the instinctual source. It is no longer perceived as the emergence of the subject's desire, a potential enrichment for the ego, but as a threat. The subject therefore feels dependent on the object of satisfaction, which causes it to treat desires and instincts as external objects and to apply the same defensive measures to them.

Bulimic binges as well as anorexic behavior can thus be regarded as a modality of the externalization of internal contents. They are a figuration mode and a way to express those contents that makes controlling them easier than if they were internal representations. Through this externalization, a double negation takes place: the first concerns the internal sources of desire and the second their connection to infantile objects. The act replaces recollection, following the now classical process described by Freud, and it offers a means of actively mastering passivity. The latter would mean the recognition of fantasies of desires linked to objects. Such recognition is the root of mental functioning itself, which is subverted by an effect of concealment concerning its generic mechanism: the hallucinatory satisfaction of desire and its derivatives, the pleasure of using association, the capacity to dream, the desire to cathect, all elements that presuppose the role played by difference, presence, and absence–precisely what such a behavior manages to abolish. It is all of these introjective capacities that are thus hindered by this radical attempt to displace through externalization the internal source of excitation (generating the search for the object and the reactivating of paths to the hallucinatory satisfaction of desire) upon a vector of excitation linked to a need, such as appetite, which it now becomes possible to control as an element of external reality, that is, outside of the psyche. The use of a physiological need as a neo-object (generating those "neo-objects" described by Braunschweig and Fain, 1975) replaces the objects of external reality previously used but which have now become dangerous. This procedure reminds us of what Freud said about the treatment of internal instinctual rejects as well as external perceptive elements, leading to the production of hallucinations (in the psychiatric sense of the term) by a path that is opposite to that of the hallucinatory satisfaction of desire, as Angelergues (1980) reminds us. Recourse to bulimic activity as well as to anorexia and drug addiction divert and pervert the very range of instincts and desires. Indeed, these behaviors not only offer a means of appeasement and control over instincts by the fact that they furnish a neo-object lacking the status of a desiring subject and thus meant to be under their control, but they go even further. They add a new source of excitation to the internal instinctual sources and their desires. This source, at the border between inside and outside, constantly renewable and mechanical, is a physiological function, the appetite, or a drug addiction.

This behavior, which is "at the subject's disposal," has the simultaneous effect of creating a source of internal excitation and its potential relief, of illustrating the possible internal emptiness (in its dimension of distress or depression) and its concealment.

What might be the metapsychological status of this neo-object? Because of its location at the borders of inside/outside, one might think of the transitional object. In fact, it is located at the opposite pole.

Eating disorders are not what enables the creation of a space of free exchange between the subject and the object, in which a shared pleasure can be taken without wondering about the respective roles of the subject and the object in the genesis of this pleasure. Quite to the contrary, it is there to reassure the subject as to the preservation of his limits and his power over the object, an object under control that has many of the characteristics of the fetish and that leads us to think of eating disorders in terms of a perverse adaption.

Let us recapitulate the classic ideas about perversion since Freud's time: splitting of the ego and denial of castration, authorizing the co-existence of areas of the ego with different functioning and with an opposite relationship to reality. To these we must add the failure of repression, expressed by the formula "neurosis the negative complement of perversion" whose corollary is the emergence of partial instincts. Later on, many studies emphasized the specificities of perverse relationship (Greenacre, 1960; Schmideberg, 1930; Chasseguet-Smirgel, 1984; Khan, 1979) as well as the importance of neoteny in the human being and of dependence (Barande and Barande, 1982). These works seem to us to be particularly enlightening for the understanding of bulimia. The role of economic and dynamic factors is emphasized; these are precisely the factors that confer upon bulimic behavior its most remarkable characteristics: (1) the importance of a controlling relationship; (2) the movement of delibidinization and of unbonding; (3) the role given to sensations, particularly cutaneous ones, and to the gaze, to the detriment of emotions; (4) the refusal of interiority to the benefit of exteriority, and more precisely of surface, and in correlation, a will to objectify relationships to the detriment of the empathy bond; (5) the omnipresence of death which can take the form of destruction (of the object and of the ego), or of fusion, with a total loss of limits; (6) a repetitive need to generate the regular emergence of excitation, of which the outcome, potentially threatening for the identity, must constantly be controlled; (7) an excitation that, however, is necessary for the preservation of the feeling of continuity; (8) all in all, a constant reaffirmation of limits in the face of desires (of which the "contract," as a condition of access to orgiastic pleasure, represents one of the modalities).

This neoobject relation is the response to upheavals in the relation of dependence to infantile objects introduced by puberty. In the face of threats brought on by introjective desires, the sexualization of bonds, and the loss of their narcissistic supportive function, this response offers a particularly effective compromise. The perverse adjustment safeguards the objectal bond, but reduces it to a superficial bond of contact; thus it avoids the dangers of internalization and of loss, offering by the control it authorizes an effective counterweight to destructiveness. The contact guarantees the presence of the object and its nondestruction, all the while securing its extraterritorial status and so safeguarding limits and identity. The counterpart is that the source of excitation must itself remain external and must be constantly renewed. The anchorage of this excitation upon a physiological activity authorizes its control and its apparent independence in relation to cathected objects, and this is accomplished all the more easily when the food function can be perceived as an activity of the ego more than a desire confused with its object, generating violent affects of love and hate that make it impossible to ignore the profound dependence on desired objects. The expression proposed by Khan of "ego orgasm" to qualify certain perverse adjustments, seems pertinent for the bulimic orgy. It emphasizes that the experience of plenitude achieved through orgasm is sought at the very heart of the ego, because a union with the object is too fraught with danger. The "food orgasm" proposed by Rado (1926), or the "orgasm of hunger" of Kestemberg and Decobert (1972), as concerns anorexia nervosa, is situated in the same perspective of substitution of the function for the object. It is also the role of sensations to repress the internal world of emotions with the objectal bond that they include. As for the partial instincts activated by regression, they focus on exhibitionist and sadomasochistic types of problems.

Here again, the sadomasochistic relationship tends to become delibidinalized and loses its dimension of interaction to the benefit of a frozen, stereotyped antiobjectal defense where the principal aim is opposition to the object or even its denial to the detriment of interaction. This negative dimension of bulimic behavior was underlined with pertinence by Igoin (1981) who remarked, quite rightly, that it infiltrated the entire therapeutic process by a constant disruption of the work of interpretation, a compensation for the excess of meaning of the patient's fantasy production.

Khan (1979) recalls that Anna Freud saw in the pervert's negativism the effects of his fear of emotional submission and of the threat of annihilation.

What can be said of the denial of castration? To us, castration anxiety does not seem to be central in these cases, and fades out to the benefit of separation anxiety and its oscillation between abandonment and intrusion. The extent of the regressive movement and the level of infantile fixations do not permit the difference between genders to play its organizing role, just as the relative failure of autoerotic resources prevents the erogenous zones from providing their anchoring function for the object relation. This relation will operate at a more archaic level and with a greater dispersal of erogenous zones: touch, sight, and physiological functions will be the points of subject/object connection. By contrast, castration anxiety often plays a triggering role for the regressive movement, and it can reintegrate its place during the course of the treatment. At such a moment, we realize the potential function occupied by the phallic theme in these personalities and its possible crucial role in the equilibrium between objectal and narcissistic polarities. The road to being "cured" passes through the adjustment of a narcissistic, phallic organization, which to us seems to be the most accessible defensive narcissistic adjustment, or the least inaccessible to eating disorders. There is a whole range of possibilities depending on the earlier acquisitions of the personality: this goes from the point where the adjustment of bisexuality makes an opening toward genital sexuality possible, to its opposite, dominated by very undifferentiated narcissistic functioning (Gonzales, 1988). Through the phallic organization, the patient authorizes herself a fantasy of bodily completeness that enables her to appropriate the alleged omnipotence of the object of desire and to deny her need and the dependence that results from it.

Through the control of needs, it is the body that is also targeted, probably in its capacity as the representative of the primal scene of the combined parents in the act of coitus that gave birth to the subject, and of maternal femininity as a model of identification. The instinctual feminine body is a foreign body for the ego because it has become unfamiliar. To this body is opposed the machine-body, the tube-body, reduced to its functional level and the object of total control, a fetish-body, phallic and upright, whose firmness and invariance constitute the protective

shield, the neutral, material screen that protects the anorexic from traumatic contact with the object and from invasive, uncontrollable affects
which might be provoked.

Dependency and Treatment Management

The consideration that addictive behavior is an attempt at regulating
a relationship to external objects, which have been given the function of
organizing the internal psychic equilibrium and of anticathexes of internal objects, has concrete consequences for our approach and our therapeutic attitudes toward addictive patients. The difficulty resides entirely
in the necessity of soliciting a wish for objects made tolerable without
recourse to addictive activities.

In these conditions, the treatment objective is not only to make the
unknown infantile events of the patient knowable and thus controllable
but also and especially to make them tolerable. Such work implies, in
our opinion, a reinforcement of the patient's narcissistic foundations
and of measures of "acceptability" of the object relation. This is
achieved through the quest for a minimum acceptable common language by the patient, and through the necessity of speaking his or her
language and thus knowing how to "use" defense modes in order to
progressively include an objectal dimension that may offer the possible restoration of his or her objectified autoeroticisms (as they were
previously defined). This is the condition, in our opinion, for insight
and for the capacity to step back from oneself, experienced neither as
a destruction of bonds to objects and as a mirror of the self, nor as an
obsession to understand, dominated by the sole will to control, which
anticipates any possible surprise in relationships with objects. Such an
evolution depends, on one hand, on what remains of the subject's
capacities to resort to individual autoerotic resources, more or less promoted by the quality of environmental support, on the other hand on
the quality of the transferential relationship. The therapeutic relational
style and interpretative activity will greatly depend on these parameters. The more narcissism is supported and the more efficient the transferential help (because it is well tolerated), the closer we are to
classical therapy.

We are thus obliged to adopt a very pragmatic attitude in treatment
methods and to be able to accept only what the patients can tolerate.
Because of this, psychoanalytical psychotherapy and *a fortiori* psycho-

analysis are not the systematic orientation of treatment. The establishment of a psychoanalytic process remains a constant perspective, inscribed from the beginning in the organization of the terms of treatment. Whatever the diversity of methods used, the therapy tries, at every step, to put the patient into contact with the reality of her internal world and her mental functioning, but all the while adapting to what seems possible for her to hear, constantly trying to help her rediscover pleasure in cathecting psychic functioning, and working to restore a more positive image of herself.

It is thus the entire treatment system for eating disorders that can be placed under the auspices of a psychoanalytic conception of this pathology. It is present at each step of the treatment and determines the therapeutic objective: to give back to the psychic apparatus its functions of conflict elaboration, adjustments and mediations for internal and external constraints and the protection of the subject. This objective is asymptotic. It is always "to come" but must not, itself, weigh upon the treatment like a restrictive ideal. It offers an orientation to each approach that encourages anything that might facilitate the subject's opening up to her internal world. It familiarizes her with this world by tolerating its contradictions without becoming disorganized. But this is done depending on the capacities of each individual, leading toward the increase of these capacities without pushing.

Basically, the authoritative medical prescription partially takes on the function of the symptomatic behavior in the patient's psychic economy and, in so doing, lessens its restrictive character. Just like the symptom, it hides the true desires of the patient, intervenes between her and her parents, opening up a possibility of differentiation if not autonomy. It occupies a function of ignorance, halfway between insufficient repression and a splitting of the ego with pathogenic effects because they leave entire chapters of the patients' psychic lives out of reach of the ego's elaboration capacities. The prescription also has the function of being a third party which relays and if possible reactivates an oedipal organization and a paternal function that has trouble taking on its role as differentiator and protector of the patient's identity. The "weight contract" in the case of anorexia exemplifies and supports the functions of the medical prescription we have just described.

The medical prescription must be inscribed and acquire meaning in relation to the patient's psychic economy. It has the merit of recalling the symptom's function in this economy, which we might otherwise tend to forget and consider in terms of the classic neurotic symptom that should disappear spontaneously when changes in the psychic economy brought about by treatment render its existence unnecessary. Once again, this would be forgetting precisely what is specific about these patients' mental functioning. Of course, it is not true of all patients nor of every period in their evolution. In some cases it is preferable to "ignore" the symptom, leaving its management to the patient, either because its weight in the psychic economy is sufficiently limited or in order to stop making it a stake in a controlling relationship with the therapist.

But usually ignoring the symptom would mean running an important risk and quite often, underestimating its effect upon the current mental functioning of the subject. In such cases, the symptom signals its own presence by a sudden aggravation that necessitates external intervention; it empties the psychotherapy of its meaning and of any dynamic effect by installing, de facto, a split that keeps the essential conflictual elements out of the therapy's reach. Here we can witness a true perversion of the therapy following the same perverse adaptation modalities that are used in the eating disorder itself: preservation of a controlling bond that is all at once of indefinite duration, protects from separation anxiety, lacks the potential to mobilize and to do the work of internalization, thus remaining at the ego's periphery, and protects it from the anxiety of intrusion and annihilation, all of which make the denial of castration anxiety possible.

The essential psychotherapeutic work is carried out in a way that largely depends upon the organization of the personality, which serves as a context for the eating disorder once the specific framework adjustments mentioned earlier and links to the particularities of these behavioral troubles are taken into account. These adjustments, which precede the psychoanalytic therapy, also accompany and permeate its course during a variable amount of time. They necessitate a certain caution, and the more classical psychoanalytic work, that is, the lifting of repression and the expression of fantasies, the handling of transference and actual interpretative work, needs to be soft-pedalled. Each one of these points is liable to reactivate the weakness of the narcissistic foundations and the exciting power of the object.

The therapist quickly finds himself confronted by a situation of incestuous character, or by a potentially passionate bond of homosexual nature. The weakness of the narcissistic filter makes lifting repression explosive and fantasy becomes confused with reality. Psychic reality is quickly overwhelmed, leading to an inevitable recourse to acting out as a form of defence according to two preferential modalities: the interruption of therapy or the aggravation of symptomatic behavior. The possibilities at the disposal of the psychotherapist are limited, in that interpretation only increases his power of attraction. Bifocal or plurifocal therapy can demonstrate its usefulness here, by permitting the nonpsychotherapeutic clinician to intervene, thanks to his distance, and help the patient to better test reality. He may even have an interpretative activity that can be heard but not recognized as such because of the different nature of the bond. The massiveness of the transferential bond with the psychotherapist endows him with maternal qualities, and most importantly, dedifferentiates him, making him appear like an engulfing, totalitarian narcissistic object, in the image of the patient's own voracity, fuelled by his narcissistic failings. The more neutral clinician appears like a differentiator, a third party, inscribing himself in the paternal differentiating lineage.

We can imagine that the course of these psychoanalytic therapies can often be very atypical, and especially very diverse in their modalities. Some will have several sessions per week, others are more spaced out. They can last a long time or be carried out in spurts—as in one case where regular therapeutic work was unthinkable until the patient had made several attempts to interrupt the therapy and became convinced that she was able to break off her dependence of the therapist. We can also imagine that in such a framework of plurifocal therapy we can accept, and eventually interpret, the possibility of carrying out simultaneously other individual or group therapeutic modalities of a more directive type. They reassure the patient and can help her gain back her narcissism, notably through their homosexual contribution, not experienced as such by the patient. That can be furnished by the support of a group of peers or by a same-sex therapist with whom the relationship is strongly mediated by the active character of the technique. The patient can benefit from the relationship and feed on it without feeling that she is part of a relationship.

This type of patient, by making the therapist break out of his or her usual framework, has helped psychoanalysis to better understand the importance of context, in particular the narcissistic context in which the fantasy is inscribed, and has given new impetus to the dynamic and economic metapsychological points of view that were momentarily eclipsed by the importance given to the structural point of view.

Before we finish, we should mention what seems to be an increase in the frequency of these disorders in western countries, or in the countries whose lifestyle is becoming westernized, and the interest that these same disorders inspire both in the general public and among researchers and therapists. It is likely, in fact, that there is a connection between the two phenomena. We are tempted to believe that this connection must be sought both in the challenge represented by these conditions and in their congruence with certain characteristics of the evolution of our societies. The challenge of these young people is, when faced with a society that extols and offers new and as yet unequalled possibilities of consumption and personal success, to respond by these behaviors of refusal and of self-destruction. This is all the more noteworthy that these are young people who usually have "everything they need to be happy." Their conduct seems like an insult to reason and common sense and makes us wonder about what might push a human being to destroy himself. The scandalous effect that was provoked in its time by the psychoanalytic discovery of the importance of infantile sexuality has been superseded by the realization by the general public, in any case, of this far more revolting scandal, because it confronts us with masochism, which is a desire for death or at least for suffering.

It is a challenge, then, but also a congruence and a resonance between these behaviors and the functioning ideal of a society that develops the cult of performance, factuality and sensations, which values the refusal to be in need and subordinates success to what can be seen. At the same time, the value of control is the only image conveyed by scientific development and the only objects that deserve observation are those that can be controlled and objectified by experimental repetition. The often vehement refusal of some researchers, including those in social sciences and psychiatry, of anything that pertains to fantasy life and interiority, relayed by the media, conveys an image of human mental functioning that is a perfect copy of the computer model, and that appears to be strangely in resonance with the denial displayed by many of these adolescents of their internal worlds and their true phobia of affective bonds and emotions.

At the same time, social evolution allows young people for the first time in the history of humanity—in any case, on such a large scale—to imagine a future different from a pure repetition of their parents' lives. This opening towards a partially unknown lifestyle, accompanied by a weakening of prohibitions but also by an increase in demands for performance and individual success, naturally favors the expression of narcissistic preoccupations and of needs for dependence, all the while diminishing the possibilities for oppositional conflicts.

We believe that these changes will have more repercussions on the expressive modes of adolescent conflicts than on the profound nature of the dynamics of adolescent crisis. Their influence will be felt through the evolution that affects family functioning where we witness the same weakening of prohibitions and limits that are replaced by the increase in narcissistic demands. The avoidance of conflicts and the loss of mediation concerning rules of life, which social consensus used to represent, favors the creation of a pseudo-family mutuality and the confusion between generations. The conflict theme, linked to strong taboos, specific of societies with rigid transactional rules, has given way to the theme of bonds in which the relational distance can no longer modulate itself by means of limits and clearly defined differences. The preservation of bonds is all the more necessary now that they are heavily loaded with reciprocal narcissistic expectations and because they serve to defend against aggressiveness that must be repressed because there are no situations to express it. The intolerance of bonding is equal to its necessity, one reinforcing the other, like the movement of a slip knot which ends up threatening the very identity of the subject.

Thus, the evolution of our societies, as seen particularly through the changes it has imprinted upon the functioning of the family unit, favors the expression of what can be termed a dependence problem. It favors them, but does not necessarily create them. Nothing allows us to assert that adolescents with difficulties today present structurally different psychopathological organizations from those of generations past. We lack points of objective comparison. On the other hand, it is clear that in many ways the faces of psychopathology, that is, its manifest expressions, have changed considerably. All cases that are gathered under the borderline heading, anaclitic or narcissistic pathology, as well as behavioral disorders and personality disorders, appear to be modern pathologies. Beyond their differences, these pathologies have a certain number of characteristics in common concerning their organization and mental functioning. However, nothing proves that these modalities did not exist in past generations, although they would not have expressed themselves in their present forms. These are the expressions that society's modern evolution favors.

REFERENCES

Abraham, K. (1922), Manifestations of the female castration complex. *Internat. J. Psycho-Anal.*, 3:1–29.

————— (1925), The influence of oral erotism on character-formation. *Internat. J. Psycho-Anal.*, 6:247–258.

Angelergues, R. (1980), *La psychiatrie*. Paris: Masson,

Barande, I. & Barande, R. (1982), Antinomie du concept de perversion et épigénèse de l'appétit d'excitation. XLIIè Congrès des Psychanalystes de Langue Française, Montréal. *Rev. Fr. Psychanal*, TXL VII, pp. 143–282.

Binswanger, L. (1944), The case of Ellen West. In: *Existence*, ed. R. May, E. Angel & H. Ellenberger. New York: Basic Books, 1958.

Boss, M. (1954), *Einfuhrüng in die psychosomatische Medizin*. Bern-Stutgard: H. Huber

Braunschweig, D. & Fain, M. (1975), La nuit et le jour. *Essai psychanalytique sur le fonctionnement mental*. Paris: P.U.F.

Breuer, J. & Freud, S. (1893–95), *Studies on Hysteria. Standard Edition*, 2. London: Hogarth Press, 1955.

Bruch, H. (1973), *Eating Disorders*. New York: Basic Books.

Brusset, B. (1977), *L'assiette et le miroir 1977*, Ed. Privat, 4è édit., 1991.

Chasseguet-Smirgel, J, (1984), *Ethique et esthétique de la perversion*. Paris: Champ-Vallon.

Couvreur, C. (1991), Sources historiques et perspectives contemporaines. *La Boulimie, Monographie, Rev. Franç. Psychanal*, Paris: P.U.F., pp. 13–45.

Fenichel, O. (1945), La théorie psychanalytique des névroses, Tome II. Paris: P.U.F., 1974.

Freud, S. (1894), A case of successful, treatment by hypnotism. *Standard Edition*, 1:117–128. London: Hogarth Press, 1966.

————— (1895), On the grounds for detaching a particular syndrome from neurasthenia under the description "anxiety neurosis." *Standard Edition*, 3:85–115. London: Hogarth Press, 1962.

————— (1912), Contributions to a discussion on masturbation. *Standard Edition*, 12:243–254. London: Hogarth Press, 1958.

————— (1930), Civilization and its discontents. *Standard Edition*, 21:64–145. London: Horgath Press, 1961.

————— (1950), Extracts from the Fliess papers. *Standard Edition*, 1:177–280. London: Hogarth Press., 1966.

Gonzales, R. C. (1988), Bulimia and adolescence: Individual psychoanalytic treatment. In: *Bulimia*, ed. H. J. Schwartz. New York: International Universities Press, pp 399–441.

Green, A. (1982a), Après-coup, l'archaïque. *Nouvelle Revue de Psychanalyse*, 26:195–215. Paris: Gallimard.

—————— (1982b), La double limite. *Nouvelle Revue de Psychanalyse*, 25:267–283. Paris: Gallimard.

Greenacre, P. (1960), Further notes on fetishism. *The Psychoanalytic Study of the Child*, 15:191–207. New York: International Universities Press.

Igoin, L. (1981), *La boulimie et son inforture*. Paris: P.U.F.

Jeammet, P. (1989), Psychopathologie des troubles des conduites alimentaires à l'adolescence. Valeur heuristique du concept de dépendance. *Confrontations psypchiatriques*, 31:177–202.

—————— (1990), *Les destins de l'auto-érotisme à l'adolescence. In Devenir adulte?* a collective work under the direction of A.M. Alléon, O. Morvan & S. Lebovici. Paris: P.U.F.

Kestemberg, E. (1981), Le personnage tiers. *Cahiers de Psychanalyse du 13ème*, 3.

—————— & Decobert, S. (1972), La faim et le corps [Hunger and the Body]. Paris: P.U.F.

Khan, M. (1974), *The Privacy of Self*. London: Hogarth Press.

—————— (1979), *Alienation in Perversions*. London: Hogarth Press.

King, A. (1963), Primary and secondary anorexia nervosa syndromes. *Br. J. Psychiat.*, 109:471–478.

Kuhn, R. (1953), Zür Daseinsanalyse der Anorexia Mentalis. *Nervenarzt*, 22:191–199.

Laplanche, J. (1987), *Nouveaux fondements pour la psychoanalyse*, Paris: P.U.F.

Lorand, S. (1943), Anorexia nervosa, report of a case. *Psychosom. Med.*, 5:282–290.

Marks, I. (1990), Behavioural (non-chemical) addictions. *Br. J. Addict.*, 85:1389–1394.

Masserman, J. H. (1941), Psychodynamics in anorexia nervosa and neurotic vomiting. *Psychoanal. Quart.*, 10:211–242.

May, R. (1958), *Existence*. New York: Basic Books.

Meyer, D. C. & Weinroth, L. A. (1957), Observations on psychological aspects of anorexia nervosa. *Psychosom. Med.*, 19:389–393.

Meyer, J. E. & Feldman, H. (1965), Anorexia nervosa. Proceedings of a symposium. Stuttgart: Thieme Verlag.

Palazzoli, M. S. (1978), *Self-Starvation*. New York: Aronson.

Rado, S. (1926), The psychic effects of intoxication: An attempt to resolve a psychoanalytical theory of morbid cravings. *Internat. J. Psycho-Anal.*, 7:396–413.

Schmideberg, M. (1930), The role of psychotic mechanisms in cultural development. *Internat. J. Psychoa-Anal.*, 11:387–428.

Schwartz, H. J. (1988), *Bulimia: Psychoanalytic Treatment and Theory.* New York: International Universities Press, 5491.

Sours, J. A. (1980), *Starving to Death in a Sea of Objects.* New York: Aronson.

Sprince, M. J. (1988), Experiencing and recovering transitional space in bulimia: Psychoanalytic treatment and theory, ed. H. J. Schwartz. New York: International Universities Press, pp. 73–88.

Torok, M. (1968), Maladie du deuil et fantasme du cadavre exquis. *Revue Française de psychanalyse*, XXXII:715–735.

Waller, J. M. et al. (1940), Anorexia nervosa. *Psychosom. Med.*, 2:3–16.

Wilson, C. P. (1985), *Fear of Being Fat* (rev.). New York: Aronson.

5 IMPULSE CONTROL DISORDERS IN ADOLESCENTS

ROBERT L. HENDREN AND KATY BUTLER

Concept of Impulse Control Disorder

Historically, the term impulse control disorder was used to refer to such behaviors as firesetting, gambling, paraphilia, kleptomania, trichotillomania, and violence. The concept is proving increasingly useful to explain the etiology of and plan treatment for externalizing disorders common in adolescence. This includes substance use disorders, suicide, conduct disorder (CD), eating disorders, a large subgroup of attention deficit hyperactivity disorder (ADHD), Tourette's disorder and obsessive-compulsive disorder (OCD). These disorders frequently are associated with depression, representing a possible form of "affective spectrum disorder" (McElroy et al., 1992). Utilizing this behavioral concept of impulse control in diagnosis and treatment leads us to shift from thinking nosologically to thinking functionally.

These disorders of impulse control have a number of similarities. This is particularly evident in the diagnostic classification overlap. The classification system used in the *DSM IV* (American Psychiatric Association, 1994) is based on statistically valid symptom clusters, not on etiology. While there are clear strengths to this approach, the weakness is demonstrated in comorbidity especially evident in the adolescent impulse control disorders. Commonly reported comorbidity clusters include ADHD, conduct disorder, oppositional defiant disorder (ODD), affective disorder, learning disorder (LD), Tourette's disorder, and borderline personality disorder (BPD) (Biederman, Newcorn, and Sprich, 1991). Any of these disorders may appear with suicide, substance use disorder and eating disorders (Kandel, Raveis, and Davies, 1991; Apter et al., 1995). These comorbid clusters may have differing risk factors, clinical courses, and pharmacological

85

responses (Biederman et al., 1991). Often, using the comorbid cluster to understand and treat the disorder is more useful than considering the diagnoses individually.

Impulse control disorders share many common neurobiologic markers of vulnerability as this paper will demonstrate. All of the disorders share a genetic relationship. In addition, brain structure and function are similar. Abnormalities in the prefrontal cortex, an area of the brain central to attention and behavioral inhibition, are common. Neurotransmitter alterations are similar as well. For instance, high levels of norepinephrine, which regulates stress response, central and peripheral arousal, learning and memory, and reward dependence, tends to result in overarousal and insensitivity. Serotonin, which regulates sleep, appetite, perception, sexual activity, learning and memory, and hormone secretion, is a behavior and impulse modulator. Low levels are associated with depression, suicide, impulsive non premeditated aggression and alcoholism whereas high levels are associated with shyness, fearfulness, premeditated violent crime and a lack of confidence. Low levels of dopamine are associated with behavioral activation, and novelty seeking (Anderson and Cohen, 1991).

The relationship of serotonin and impulse control disorder is especially clear (Zubieta and Alessi, 1993). Low CSF serotonin metabolites often found in certain depressions also are found among people who have made suicide attempts (Linnoila, 1988), who are violent (Linnoila, DeJong, and Virkkumen, 1989a), impulsive (Linnoila, 1988), arsonists (Virkkunen et al., 1994), alcoholics (Ballenger et al., 1979), and it has been found among their relatives (Rosenthal et al., 1989). Low 5-HIAA a serotonin metabolite, is associated with irritability and impaired impulse control. Impulsive alcoholic violent offenders have decreased 5-HIAA (Virkkunen et al., 1994). Male monkeys with low CSF 5-HIAA are at risk for violent aggressive behavior and loss of impulse control (Mehlman et al., 1994) and exhibit less social competence and sociability (Mehlman et al., 1995). There is a strong suggestion that cerebrospinal fluid 5-HIAA and homovanillic acid (HVA) and autonomic measures can be used to predict risk for future problems in children with disruptive behavior disorders (Kruesi et al., 1992).

Pharmacologic studies also demonstrate a clear relationship between serotonin and impulse control disorder. When serotonin is depleted by drugs and depression, aggression and impulsive behavior result. Alcohol and benzodiazapines reduce serotonin turnover and result in depression, disinhibition, aggression, and impulsiveness (Lancet,

1987). Antidepressants that enhance serotonin turnover (SSRI's, buspiron, and lithium) benefit drive dysregulation syndromes and depression. But serotonin as the neurotransmitter basis for impulse control is not quite so simple. Noradrenergic dysregulation is also related to impulsive behavior. Low MHPG levels, a measure of norepinephrine metabolism, are inversely related to sensation seeking and impulsivity (Gabel et al., 1994). High and low MAO levels correlate with disruptive behavior disorder (Stoff et al., 1989). In addition low blood glucose correlates with poor impulse control and depression (Linnoila, 1989b).

General markers of vulnerability or developmental instability also are commonly found among people with impulsive behavior (Gualtieri et al., 1982). This includes minor physical anomalies such as wide spaced eyes; fluctuating asymmetries of usually symmetrical sides of the body or extreme right or left handedness; EEG abnormalities including seizure disorders; and head trauma. These anomalies often reflect slow or abnormal growth of the brain in the first two trimesters of pregnancy.

An additional inborn marker of vulnerability is temperament (Bates et al., 1995). Infants characterized as having a difficult temperament are more likely to develop behavioral problems as children and adolescents than those with easy or slow-to-warm-up temperaments (Rutter et al.,1964). In a large longitudinal study exploring Cloninger's suggestion that boys who were high in impulsivity, low in anxiety, and low in reward dependence would be at greater risk for delinquency, Tremblay and coworkers (1994) demonstrated that kindergarten males with this combination of traits were more likely to develop a stable pattern of antisocial behavior. Increased reward dependence decreased delinquency.

Psychosocial Context

Individuals with an impulse control disorder have a distinct psychological style. Cognitively they often are selective in the information they process, have difficulty with abstraction, and are catastrophizing, overgeneralizing, and personalizing (Lee and Prentice, 1988). They are sensation and novelty seeking, harm avoidant, not particularly reward dependent, and frequently have a short attention span (Gabel, 1994). Depression is common (Riggs et al., 1995). Self-soothing mechanisms have not been developed to relieve uncomfortable symptoms. Their families have a high incidence of depression and impulse control disorders. These impulse control disordered young people and their families make frequent use of lower level defenses. Socially, these young people are likely to come from an environment that sanctions impulsive behavior, does not include a nuclear family, and has a high level of stress and geographic mobility (Ekblad, 1988).

It is important to note that the etiology of impulse control disorder is related to the additive effect of multiple factors such as, birth complications combined with early maternal rejection to predict violent crime at age 18 years. Neither of the risk factors were predictive alone (Raine, Brennan, and Mednick, 1994a). When early neuromotor deficits and unstable family environments occur together in an individual there is greater likelihood of criminal and violent behavior than with either factor alone or with normal controls (Raine, 1996). Another example of this additive effect is demonstrated by a study that found that self-regulation at four years could be predicted by maternal ratings of the child's impulsivity and attention span when combined with maternal negativity at 24 months of age (Silverman and Ragosa, 1993).

To demonstrate the usefulness of the functional concept of impulse control disorder, the etiology of the most common impulse control disorders follows. ADHD is discussed in the most detail because it is frequently comorbid with other impulse control disorders, and even if the full diagnostic criteria are not present, the symptoms of inattention and impulsivity frequently are common to all of these disorders. A common treatment approach to impulse control disorders is presented in the final section.

Attention Deficit Hyperactivity Disorder (ADHD)

The diagnosis of ADHD in children, adolescents, and adults includes impulsivity as a hallmark of the disorder. *DSM IV* (American Psychiatric Association, 1994) has three categories of ADHD: predominantly inattentive type, predominantly impulsive and hyperactive type, and a combination type. While overactivity decreases with age, impulsivity and inattention do not. Comorbid disorders increase with age. The predominately impulsive and hyperactive type occurs most frequently in preschool boys whereas the inattentive type is relatively more common in girls and in older children (Lahey et al., 1994).

The etiology of ADHD is biopsychosocial in origin, and shares this commonality with other impulse control disorders. Biological factors include perinatal difficulties, maternal substance abuse during pregnancy, genetic factors, and structural and functional brain abnormalities (Barkley, 1990). Twenty to thirty percent of people with ADHD have a family member with ADHD. The adult form may have stronger familial factor raising the question of whether or not it has a stronger genetic etiology (Biederman, 1995). Relatives of people with ADHD have higher morbidity risks for ADHD, antisocial disorders (Faraone and Biederman, 1994), and mood disorders (Biederman et al., 1990). They also have a significant family history of Tourette's disorder and substance abuse but not of anxiety disorders.

Brain function in ADHD is distinctive and involves several areas of the brain. The brainstem is implicated and it has been proposed that sensory neurons in the reticular formation regulating the discharge of locus coerruleus noradrenergic neurons are related to ADHD symptoms (Mefford and Potter, 1989). A prefrontal defect frequently is found as well. In a neuroimaging study utilizing Positron Emission Tomography (PET) of ADHD adults, Zametkin et al. (1990) demonstrated reduced global and regional glucose metabolism in the premotor cortex and the superior prefrontal cortex. However, this was not found in adolescent ADHD boys but was in ADHD girls with a lower Tanner stage, an inconsistency not yet fully explained (Ernst et al., 1994). Low striatal activity in the right frontal cortex is related to inattentiveness, poor impulse control, and disinhibition (O'Tuama, 1993).

Structural changes are found in the corpus callosum in individuals with ADHD. Smaller areas of the genu-rostrum (anterior) and splenium (posterior, Semrud-Clikeman et al., 1994) and the genu-rostrum only (Giedd et al., 1994) and the splenium only (Hynd et al., 1991) are found in ADHD. These regions are implicated in sustained attention and control of impulses. A smaller rostrum correlates with Connors Rating Scale scores of impulsivity-hyperactivity but not of inattention (Giedd, 1994). There is preliminary data to suggest that those with a smaller corpus callosum may be more likely to respond to methylphenidate. The caudate nucleus, which is involved with executive function and attention also is smaller in individuals with ADHD (Castellanos et al., 1994).

Hormones and neurotransmitters also are altered in ADHD; however, no single neurotransmitter system is implicated although serotonin and norepinephrine are most frequently altered. Low CSF 5-HT is found among aggressive but not among nonaggressive boys with ADHD (Halperin et al., 1994). Serotonin is thought to play a role in mood lability, anxiety, anger, impulsivity, and stress intolerance, but not solely with ADHD (Weizman et al., 1988). Noradrenergic reduction is reported in some but not all studies of youth with ADHD.

The use of neuropsychological tests in the investigation of ADHD has burgeoned over the past decade. Overall, neuropsychological test results support the presence of deficits in controlling and directing attention, organizational skills, and working memory (Barkley, Grodzinsky, and DuPaul, 1992). Among the deficits reported most frequently and consistently, are those on measures of executive function. For example, ADHD boys demonstrate deficits on a number of tests sensitive to frontal lobe function (a vigilance task, Stroop Color Word Test, a verbal fluency task, Rey-Osterrieth Complex Figure, and Porteus Mazes; Grodzinsky and Diamond, 1992).

Children with ADHD tend to leave out details when copying complex figures. However, this deficit in accuracy is not significantly different from normal controls when age and IQ are controlled for. Children with ADHD are impaired in comparison to normal controls on the developmental quality of their copy in terms of the integrity of the organization of elements in relation to each other, independent of age and IQ. This deficit may be related to impulsivity and poor planning, as their organization improves when they are asked to draw the figure again from memory following a delay (Seidman et al., 1995a). Although organization and attention deficits affect initial learning, they do not interfere with long-term memory. Thus, people with ADHD are able to remember information that they have been successful in encoding during the initial presentation of the material (Cahn and Marcotte, 1995).

Impaired neuropsychological test performance (Wisconsin Card Sorting Task, Verbal Learning subtest of the WRAML, Stroop, and auditory CPT) in individuals with ADHD is significantly worse in individuals with familial ADHD and comorbid LD. However, comorbidity of psychiatric factors had no differential effects on neuropsychological test performance, suggesting that these deficits are associated with ADHD (Seidman et al., 1995b). Unmedicated ADHD subjects demonstrate deficits on a task of visual-spatial attention suggestive of right-hemisphere dysfunction that may be related to reduced catecholamine activity in the right hemisphere frontal-striatal system (Carter et al., 1995).

Children with ADHD are at a greater risk than normal controls for the development of impairments in many facets of psychosocial function, including cognition, interpersonal, school, and family functioning. Comorbid diagnoses at baseline predicted the presence of related types of psychopathology at follow-up (Biederman et al., 1996). When compared with normal controls, subjects identified as hyperactive in childhood report poor self-esteem and are judged by clinicians to have lower levels of overall adjustment as adolescents. They also fared worse than controls with respect to academic achievement and occupational rank as adults (Slomkowski, Klein, and Mannuzza, 1995).

Many investigators have attempted to identify factors that are useful in establishing the prognosis for psychosocial problems associated with ADHD. For example, non-right motor preference in ADHD children has been associated with an increased risk for major depression and impaired psychosocial functioning (Biederman et al., 1994). Adverse family-environment variables, such as severe marital discord, low social class, large family size, paternal criminality, maternal mental disorder, and foster care placement, increase the risk for ADHD children to develop various forms of psychopathology (i.e., depression, anxiety, and conduct disorder; Biederman, 1995b). The degree of antisocial features such as defiance in ADHD boys predicts the degree of serious antisocial behavior (as indicated by felony offender rates) several years later (Satterfield et al., 1994).

Psychological factors include poor self-confidence, sadness and depression, and characterological problems. However, it is difficult to say which came first, the ADHD or the distinctive psychological pattern. It probably has a great deal to do with the goodness-of-fit with the family, the school and the social environment.

Stressful social factors include repeating grades, problems with authorities, and problems with peers, to name only a few. Peers perceive ADHD children as immature, irritating and often avoid or neglect them due to their low frustration tolerance, intrusive, bossy, socially inappropriate behavior. They often are teased by others and engage in controlling and dominating behaviors. Due to their problems with attention and impulsivity, they communicate less effectively and have difficulty with self-reflection. This cognitive and behavioral style may fit poorly with family, peers, school and others which results in poor self-confidence, saddness and depression, repeating grades, problems with authorities and characterologic problems (Hendren, 1991).

Conduct Disorder

The diagnostic category of conduct disorder represents a heterogeneous group having a large amount of overlap and comorbidity with other impulse control disorders and depression. The International Classification of Disease-Tenth Edition (ICD-10) (World Health Organization, 1992) takes this into account by having the combination categories of depressive conduct disorder and hyperkinetic conduct disorder. Major depressive disorder has been identified in 30% to 50% of conduct disordered youth and bipolar disorder in 25% (Arredondo and Butler, 1994).

The etiology of conduct disorder has a similar biopsychosocial basis as other impulse control disorders. Biologic factors include difficult temperament as an infant, genetic predisposition, abnormal levels of serotonin, and norepinephrine, neuroendocrine factors such as high testosterone, neurologic abnormalities, and low IQ (Hendren and Mullen, 1996b). Specific examples include reduced activity in the medial and lateral sections of the prefrontal cortex found in men and women murderers (Raine, Brennan, and Mednick, 1994b) or among youth predisposed to antisocial behavior, high autonomic arousal and electrodermal orienting is shown to be of positive prognostic significance for less criminal behavior in adulthood (Raine, Venables, and Williams, 1995).

Although very few studies of the neuropsychology of conduct disorder have been published, many investigators have studied children and adolescents manifesting delinquent and antisocial behavior, the hallmarks of conduct disorder. While normal IQ levels have been reported previously in studies of conduct disorder, a recent investigation reported a 17 point difference between normal controls and juveniles who displayed chronic aggressive behavior and met criteria for an externalizing disorder (Moffitt, 1993). Transient delinquent behavior was associated with only a one-point IQ difference. This finding supports the presence of biologic substrates to conduct disorder.

Specific deficits in language abilities, hypothesized to be related to left hemisphere dysfunction, are implicated in the etiology of conduct disorder. Several studies report significant discrepancies between verbal and performance IQ scores in delinquent and antisocial adolescents, in addition to deficits on numerous measures of verbal ability. This deficit in verbal abilities may predispose children to have difficulty developing adaptive strategies for verbally mediating their behavior and thinking through problems. Deficits in executive functions have also been linked with children's inability to control their impulsive behavior. Neuropsychological deficits in children with conduct disorder compound adverse family environments in terms of the degree of aggression toward victims and adversaries (Moffitt, 1993).

Other cognitive factors associated with conduct disorder are immaturity, misconceptions, short attention span, and poor academic achievement relative to IQ. High impulsivity, low anxiety, and low reward dependence in kindergarten predicts later delinquency (Tremblay et al., 1994). Increasing reward dependence is associated with decreased delinquency. Aggressive children pay greater attention to aggressive environmental cues than do nonaggressive children and they often misperceive cues. They quickly and impulsively think of nonverbal, action-oriented solutions to social situations (Kendall, 1993).

Many childhood problems are associated with brain dysfunction and the development of antisocial behavior (e.g., immaturity, overactivity, temper tantrums, poor attention, and poor school performance; Moffitt, 1993). Among adolescent psychiatric inpatients, those diagnosed with conduct disorder have earlier first contact with psychiatric services and are more likely to be diagnosed with ADHD than adolescents with comorbid conduct disorder and substance abuse or substance abuse alone (Grilo et al., 1996). Approximately one-half of adolescents with conduct disorder have comorbid substance use disorders across both young and old age groups. In fact, the probability of the comorbidity of these disorders was higher in younger children, suggesting that substance use and dependence develops rapidly in these youngsters following their first use of substances (Reebye, Moretti, and Lessard, 1995). Comorbidity of conduct disorder and ADHD is associated with an earlier age of onset and increased number of conduct disorder symptoms, as well as increased comorbidity of substance dependence, depression, and anxiety (Thompson et al., 1996) .

Family factors found to contribute to the development of conduct disorder are parental psychopathology, substance abuse, aggressivity, and other indications of general dysfunction. Family, peer, and attentional variables interact to predict delinquency (Hoge, Andrews, and Leschied, 1994). Sociocultural factors associated with conduct disorder include peer group rejection, low socioeconomic status, and cultural sanctions. While biologic vulnerability certainly influences the development of conduct disorder, the vulnerable child is embedded in a psychosocial environment involving family, peers, and socioeconomic factors that direct these vulnerabilites to the eventual outcome of conduct disorder.

Suicide

Risk factors for suicide include all of the risk factors previously mentioned for impulse control disorder. This includes major depression, bipolar disorder, substance abuse, and conduct disorder. Adolescents who re-attempt suicide are seven times more likely to have a mood disorder (Pfeffer et al., 1991). Substance abuse is a more significant risk factor when it is combined with affective disorder. In one study of adolescent suicide, 50% had affective disorder and 31% had been depressed less than three months (Brent et al., 1994). A study of adolescent suicide in Finland found 94% of those who committed suicide had a mental disorder: 51% had depression; 26% had alcohol abuse; 50% had a detectable blood alcohol level; and 51% had antisocial behavior. Comorbidity was common (Marttunen, 1994). Family psychopathology is yet another factor frequently associated with adolescent suicide (Brent 1993).

Almost all of the biopsychosocial factors associated with impulse control disorders previously mentioned are related to suicidal behavior. One of the most replicated findings is an association between low cerebrospinal fluid level of the serotonin metabolite 5-hydroxyindoleacetic acid (5-HIAA) in patients who have attempted suicide compared with those who have not (Nielsen et al., 1994).

Personality disorders and the tendency to engage in impulsive violence are critical risk factors in completed suicide (Brent et al., 1994). Girls are more likely than boys to have depression or situational problems and previous attempts are more common. Boys are more likely than girls to engage in substance abuse although this difference is decreasing. More severe psychopathology and recent psychosocial stressors are also found in boys. The younger adolescent who is suicidal is likely to be angry, impulsive, concrete, and externalizes conflict while the older adolescent is likely to be self-blaming and depressed, and concerned with the opinions of others (Borst, Noam, and Allman, 1991). Thus two foundations of suicidal behavior in adolescence have been proposed; poor impulse control (a wish not to be here) and depression (a wish to die, Apter et al., 1995).

Other Impulse Control Disorders

Substance Use Disorders (SUDs) are yet another form of disordered impulse control. In drug dependence, the youthful user experiences a powerlessness concerning the use of the substance, episodes of loss of control and an apparent inability to modify substance use in spite of adverse consequences. Individuals with SUDs have neurobiologic abnormalities similar to others with impulse control disorders. These include clustering of genetic relationships to impulse control disorders, alterations in serotonin and norepinephrine and their metabolites, attention and aggression problems, and sensation seeking (Hendren and

Mullen, 1996a). On the basis of these associations, Cloninger (1987) has proposed a classification scheme whereby a subgroup of substance abusers with a high genetic loading for alcoholism, an early onset of alcoholism, a severe course, and coexisting psychiatric problems are classified as Type 2. Type 1 substance abusers do not have the genetic loading or the early onset of substance abuse and behavioral problems and they have a better prognosis. Type 2 substance abusers have low serotonin turnover and are more likely to be depressed, to have attempted suicide, and to be incarcerated for violence (Buydens-Branchey, Branchey, and Noumair, 1989). Furthermore, aggressive behavior as early as six years predicts heavy substance abuse and aggressiveness in adolescence (Flannery et al., 1994). Crime, low self-esteem, depression and anxiety disorder (Burke, Burke, and Rae, 1994) and susceptibility to peer pressure (Flannery et al., 1994) are significantly associated with substance abuse in youth. Depressed deliquents have more substance dependence diagnoses and have increase anxiety, attentional problems and trauma effects (Riggs et al., 1995). Substance abusing youth are likely to come from families characterized as "disengaged" or "emeshed" (Friedman, Utada, and Morrisey, 1987), and family rituals are important in the intergenerational transmission (Wolin and Bennett, 1980).

Substance abuse in youth is associated with depression (DeMilio, 1989), suicide gestures and attempts (Brent et al., 1994), eating disorders (Killen et al., 1987), conduct disorder, and ADHD (Wilens and Biederman, 1993).

SUDs are often comorbid with other impulse control disorders. The association with suicidal behavior was mentioned earlier. There is a strong association between early conduct disorder and later substance use (Lynskey and Fergusson, 1995). The direct association of substance abuse with attention deficit disorder is controversial, but is often reported as insignificant when conduct disorder is taken into account (Lynskey, 1995).

Eating disorders share a similar etiology with other impulse control disorders. Co-twin comorbidity between anorexia nervosa, major depression, bulimia nervosa, generalized anxiety disorder, alcoholism, and panic disorder is reported (Kendler et al., 1995). Serotonin in the brain influences carbohydrate selection, intake, and termination (Wallin and Rissaner, 1994). Serotonin-mediated responses occur in eating disordered patients and appear to vary with the diagnostic subgroup (McBride et al., 1991). Psychological and cultural factors have a strong role in determining the eating disorder expression of impulse control disorder as well. Obsessive-compulsive disorder (OCD) also is associated with low serotonin levels and with disruptive behaviors (Hanna, Yuwiler, and Coates, 1995) and OCD responds to medications that raise serotonin levels.

Assessment of Impulse Control Disorder

During the interview with a child or adolescent with a suspected impulse control disorder, it is important to first establish rapport since they may be slow to trust authority figures as the result of poor past experiences. This rapport is valuable in keeping them engaged in a therapeutic alliance. Next, it is important to gather developmental and biopsychological signs and symptoms as described earlier in this review. It is important to evaluate the young person in the context of the family, school, community, and culture. Family history of ADHD, tics, alcoholism, personality disorder, and other comorbidity also are important to assess.

Rating scales that may prove helpful in the assessment process include the Achenbach Child Behavior Checklist (Achenbach, 1991) paying particular attention to the externalizing subscale; the Conners Rating Scale for parents and teachers (1973); the ACTERS for ADHD (Ullmann, Sleator, and Sprague, 1985); the Childhood Depression Inventory (CDI, Kovacs, 1991), which is helpful in determining the severity of depression; and the self control rating scale and the Self-Report Delinquency Scale for Conduct Disorder (Elliott et al., 1984). The Continuous Performance Task (CPT) is a computerized test for sustained attention or vigilance that has been used to confirm the diagnosis of ADHD and to determine the optimal dosage of medications (Corkum and Siegel, 1993). However, the diagnosis and treatment usually can be adequately determined clinically and with other rating scales without the addition of the CPT. The Wender Utah Rating Scale (Ward, Wender, and Reimherr, 1993) is useful for the retrospective diagnosis of ADHD and the Copeland Symptom checklist (Copeland 1991, 1992) is particularly helpful in diagnosing adult ADHD.

It is important to rule out medical causes of inattention and impulsivity such as hyperthyroidism, seizure disorder (particularly petit mal), migraine, traumatic brain injury, and hepatic disease. Side-effects resulting from drug or medication use (antihistamines, phenobarbital, steroids, lead, recreational drugs, and alcohol) should be ruled out as well.

Current Treatment of Impulse Control Disorders

The overall treatment approach that will now be described can be characterized as the "Impulsivity Model of Treatment." This treatment approach is based on a biopsychosocial approach and is directed toward delay of gratification and control of impulsivity. The approach is usually interchangeable across the impulse control disorders. Awareness of similarities among impulse control disorders can improve the watchfulness for symptom substitution. The roles of attention deficit and depression are central to this impulsivity model. The model works well in outpatient, residential, and alternative treatment settings. It is multimodal and works best when there is a multidisciplinary treatment team and a continuum of care available (Henggeler et al., 1991).

The biological component of the impulsivity model of treatment is described by a series of pharmacotherapy decision trees. Figure 1 illustrates the first clinical treatment decision to be made when it is determined that the young person has an impulse control disorder. This decision relates to the primacy of either attention deficit, depression, or developmental instability and leads to the next decision tree diagramed in Figures 2 and 3 or to the treatment of developmental instability. In general, improvement is usually greatest when biological treatments are used in conjunction with psychosocial interventions.

Stimulant medications are thought to act through primarily noradrenergic and modest adrenergic stimulation and decreased reuptake and degradation (Greenhill, 1992). Stimulants clearly decrease hyperactiv-

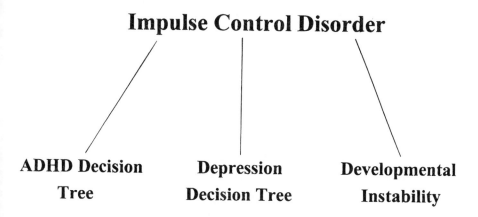

Figure 1   Impulse Control Treatment Decision Tree

ADHD Treatment Decision Tree

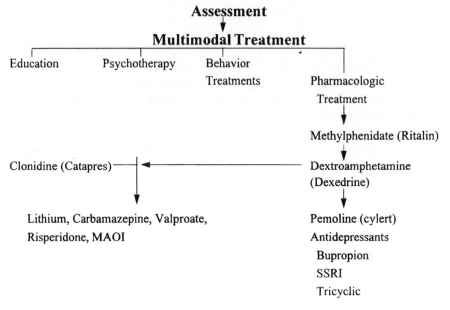

Figure 2   ADHD Treatment Decision Tree

Depression Decision Tree

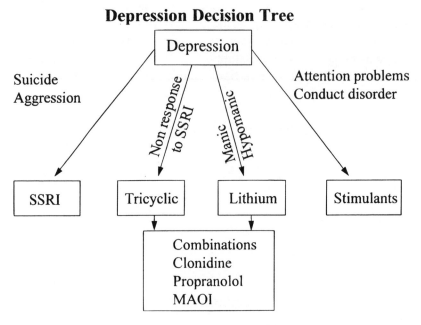

Figure 3   Depression Treatment Decision Tree

ity, inattention, and distractibility but impulsivity is not as effected nor are social relations normalized. ADHD comorbid with internalizing disorder is less likely to respond to stimulants and is more likely to have an adverse response (DuPaul and Rapport, 1993).

Tricyclic antidepressants used for attention deficit are more effective with anxious and affective symptoms and are less likely to disturb sleep than stimulants (Biederman et al., 1989). They are used when there is a failure to respond to stimulants or to avoid stimulant complications such as depression, rebound symptoms, tics, movement disorder, or relative contraindications such as substance abuse.

The SSRI's have demonstrated effectiveness in the treatment of adolescent depression (Tierney et al., 1995) and modest benefit with ADHD without depression (Barrickman et al., 1991). Depression in young people may be strongly related to serotonin deficiency while ADHD is not. Tricyclic antidepressants have been used successfully in the treatment of ADHD but are used with some reluctance due to the risk of cardiac arrythmias (March et al. 1995). Bupropion (Wellbutrin) has demonstrated notable effectiveness in the treatment of ADHD (Barrickman et al., 1995) and modest effectiveness in the treatment of ADHD comorbid and CD (Simeon, Fergurson, and Van Wyck, 1986). Trazodone (Desyrel) has demonstrated benefit in the treatment of disruptive behavior disorders in children (Zubieta and Alessi, 1993).

Pharmacology for aggression and developmental instability includes:

1. Mood stabilizers, carbamazepine (Tegretol), divalproex sodium (Depakote), and lithium (Lithane), often are useful for the treatment of intermittant explosive disorder, bipolar disorder, and for aggression especially when associated with neurologic abnormalities.
2. Alpha adrenergic blocking agents, Clonidine (Catapres) and guanfacine (Tenex), are useful in the treatment of the impulsive component of ADHD, tics and Tourette's disorder, and are most effective with overactive, uninhibited, impulsive, and aggressive youth. They increase frustration tolerance, compliance, and reduce emotional outbursts but not distractibility or inattention. They may be useful with CD and ODD when ADHD is associated (Hunt et al., 1990, 1995).
3. Beta adrenergic blocking agents, propranolol (Inderal) and pindolol (Visken), are effective with unprovoked aggressive behavior especially when there is neurologic damage, anxiety especially an-

xiety related to posttraumatic stress syndrome, and uncontrolable rage (Connor, 1993).

4. Buspirone (BuSpar) can be effective in treating impulsive and aggressive behavior in some patients especially those with anxiety and irritability.

5. Neuroleptics, especially newer agents like risperidone (Risperdal) and olanzapine (Zyprexa), may be useful in managing impulsive behavior that has not responded to other psychotropic medications.

The psychological and environmental components of the impulsivity model of treatment consist of cognitive behavioral therapy (CBT) and environmental manipulation (Spence, 1994). The early stage of therapy is behavioral, focusing on specific behaviors and situations where the impulse control disorder causes the greatest difficulty. As therapy progresses, there is more of a focus on the cognitive assumptions and distortions that have developed and the effects of these on behavior. This involves assessment of the type of distortion, problem-solving skills and coping strategies training, modeling in therapy, support groups, and keeping thought journals.

CBT has been shown to be an effective treatment for substance abuse, ADHD, conduct disorder, suicidal ideation, and eating disorders. Rotherman-Borus and colleagues (1994) describe a CBT program for suicide that consists of: 1) establish a positive family climate; 2) increase family problem-solving skills (define the problem, generate solutions, select a solution, evaluate the efficacy), 3) demonstrate therapist effectiveness; and 4) use special techniques such as tokens for positive reinforcement, a "feeling thermometer," role playing, and reframing. Wilson and Fairburn (1993) describe a three stage CBT model for the treatment of eating disorder that consists of: stage 1) evaluation and behavior monitoring; stage 2) cognitive focus, identify feelings, behavioral experiments, increased self-efficacy; and stage 3) relapse prevention.

Family counseling for family dysfunction and appropriate consistent limit setting is an essential part of therapy and parents can, at times, be trained to function as case managers for their children. Cognitive Problem-Solving Skills Training (PSST) and Parent Management Training (PMT), both family focused techniques, combine to create marked changes in antisocial behavior in children (Kazdin, Siegel, and Bass, 1992). PSST focuses on the individual child and teaches problem-solving skills to families to manage interpersonal situations. Practice, modeling, role playing, corrective feedback, and social and token reinforcement are used. Outside the sessions, tasks are assigned and parents are actively involved. PMT focuses on child-rearing practices, parent–child interactions and contingencies that can support prosocial behavior at home and school. The content of the sessions include observing and defining behavior, positive reinforcement, shaping behavior, negotiating and contracting, time out, reprimands, and special contingencies for low-scoring behavior. The child's school performance is monitored by the teacher with back-up reinforcers earned at home. The child is involved in reviewing the program and negotiating reinforcements. The combination of PSST and PMT leads to better results than with either alone.

Psychodynamic approaches to the treatment of impulse control disorders are not generally effective since they involve self-reflection which is difficult for impulsive people with a short attention span. However, one study of psychodynamic treatment for behavior disorder reports 33% of patients returned to normal function. Better results occurred when anxiety was present, treatment was longer, and comorbidity (especially developmental disability) was absent. Significant improvement was more likely to be found in children with oppositional defiant disorder than among those with attention deficit hyperactivity disorder or conduct disorder (Fonagy and Target, 1994). Individual therapy should focus on poor self-esteem and improving social competence.

A strategic structural system approach to resistance to change being the result of the usefulness of the symptom to the family in self-regulation has proven useful in engaging impulse control disorder families in treatment (Szapocznik et al., 1988). Social treatment approaches to the larger environment consist of environmental manipulation such as finding a new peer group and public education. School-based programs also have proven effective (Hendren, Weisen, and Orley, 1994). These programs can be directed to the larger school environment such as the program to prevent bullying in Norway that delivered the message that bullying behavior was unacceptable and would not be tolerated (Olweus, 1992); or they can be directed to high risk groups such as children of alcoholics, pregnant teens, or children who have been in trouble for their behavior. These programs typically involve problem-solving skills training based on cognitive behavioral techniques.

Working effectively with an impulsive patient requires regular monitoring and management of feelings aroused in the therapist by the patient. Some of these feelings are expectable reactions to undependable behaviors such as missed appointments, dangerous risk-taking behavior, impulsive thoughtless comments, and potential legal issues raised in working with these high risk patients. At times these patients can arouse countertransference feelings in the therapist as well. These feelings might range from envy and vicarious pleasure derived from exciting unrestricted behavior to anger, revulsion, indignation, and even hatred for thoughtless, destructive acts with consequences that go far beyond the patient and the therapist. Recognizing and acknowledging these feelings is the first and most important step and often keeps the feelings from becoming counterproductive or destructive. When these feelings significantly interfere with the therapy or the well-being of the patient or therapist, outside consultation should be sought.

Conclusions

Developing an understanding and effective treatment approach for impulse control disorders requires improved diagnostic specificity, outcome measurement, elucidation of neurodevelopmental influences, and investment in sociocultural programs aimed at prevention and early intervention. Comorbidity is important to recognize in understanding impulse control disorders and developing effective treatment programs. Outcome measurement is complicated by this comorbidity and should be considered in developing and evaluating follow-up studies (Offord and Bennett, 1994).

While impulse control disorders often have been attributed to a lack of will power or general "badness," we are beginning to appreciate the unique neurodevelopmental underpinnings to these disorders. Neuroimaging and neuropsychological testing are advancing our understanding of impulse control disorders as having a biological basis. Treatment and prevention efforts are benefiting from this new understanding. Psychosocial approaches such as academic skills training and school and community based interventions are proving valuable for early intervention when high-risk groups are identified.

BIBLIOGRAPHY

Achenbach, T. M. (1991), *Manual for the Child Behavior Checklist/ 4–18 and 1991 Profile*. Burlington: University of Vermont Department of Psychiatry.

American Psychiatric Association (1994), *Diagnostic and Statistical Manual of Mental Disorders (DSM-IV), ed 4.* Washington, DC: American Psychiatric Press.

Anderson, G. M. & Cohen, D. J. (1991), The neurobiology of childhood neuropsychiatric disorders. *Child and Adolescent Psychiatry* ed, M, Lewis. Baltimore, M. Wiliams & Wilkins, pp. 28–37.

Apter, A., Gothelf, D., Orbach, I., Weizman, R., Ratzoni, G., Har-Even, D. & Tyano, S. (1995), Correlation of suicidal and violent behavior in different diagnostic categories in hospitalized adolescent patients. *J. of Amer. Acad. of Child Adoles. Psychiat.*, 34: 912–918.

Arredondo, D. E. & Butler, S. F. (1994), Affective comorbidity in psychiatrically hospitalized adolescents with conduct disorder or oppositional defiant disorder: Should conduct disorder be treated with mood stabilizers? *J. Child and Adoles. Psychopharm.*, 4:151–158.

Ballenger, J. C., Goodwin, F. K., Major, L. F. & Brown G. L. (1979), Alcohol and central serotonin metabolism in man. *Arch. of Gen. Psychiat.*, 36:224–227.

Barkley, R. A., Grodzinsky, G. & DuPaul, G. J. (1992), Frontal lobe functions in attention deficit disorder with and without hyperactivity: A review and research report. *J. Abnormal Child Psychol.*, 20:163–188.

Barkley, R. A. (1990), Associated problems, subtyping, and etiologies. *Attention Deficit Hyperactivity Disorder*, ed. R. A. Barkley: New York. New York: Guilford Press, pp. 74–105.

Barrickman, L., Nayes, R., Kuperman, S., Schumacher, E. & Virda, M. (1991), Treatment of ADHD with Fluoxetine: A preliminary trial. *J. Amer. Acad. Child Adoles. Psychiat.*, 30:762–767.

———— Perry P. J., Allen, A. J., Kuperman, S., Arndt, S. V., Herrmann K. J., & Schumacher, E. (1995), Bupropion versus Methylphenidate in the treatment of attention-deficit hyperactivity disorder. *J. Amer. Acad. Child Adoles. Psychiat.*, 34:649–657.

Bates, J., Wachs, T. D. & VandenBos, G. R. (1995), Trends in Research on Temperament. *Psychiat. Services.* 46:661–663.

Biederman, J., Baldessarini R. J., Wright, V. et al. (1989), A double-blind placebo controlled study of desipramine in the treatment of ADD: I. Efficacy. *J. Amer. Acad. Child & Adoles., Psychiat.* 28:777–784.

———— Faraone, S. V., Keenan, K. et al. (1990), Family-genetic and psychosocial risk factors in DSM-III attention deficit disorder. *J. Amer. Acad. Child Adoles. Psychiat.* 29:526–533.

———— ———— Lapey K. A., Milberger, S., Reed, E. D. & Seidman, L. J. (1994), Motor preference, major depression and psychosocial dysfunction among children with attention deficit hyperactivity disorder. *J. Psychiat. Res.*, 28:171–184.

———— ———— Mick, E., Spencer, T., Wilens, T., Kiely, K., Guite, J., Ablon, J. S., Reed, E. & Warburton, R. (1995a), High risk for attention deficit hyperactivity disorder among children of parents with childhood onset of the disorder: A pilot study. *Amer. J. Psychiat.*, 152:431–435.

———— ———— ———— Guite, J., Mick, E., Chen, L., Mennin, D., Marrs, A., Ouellette, C., Moore, P., Spencer, T., Norman, D., Wilens, T., Kraus, I. & Perrin, J. (1996), A Prospective 4-year follow-up study of attention deficit hyperactivity and related disorders. *Arch. Gen. Psychiat.*, 53:437–446.

———— Milberger, S., Faraone, S. V., Kiely, K., Guite, J., Mick, E., Albon, S., Warburton, R. & Reed, E. (1995b), Family-environment risk factors for attention deficit hyperactivity disorder. *Arch. Gen. Psychiat.*, 52:464–470.

———— Newcorn, J., & Sprich, S. (1991), Comorbidity of attention deficit hyperactivity disorder with conduct, depressive, anxiety and other disorders. *Amer. J. Psychiat.*, 148:517–564.

Borst, S., Noam, G. G., & Allman, C. J. (1987), Alcohol, firearms, and suicide among youth. *J. Amer. Med. Assn.*, 257:3369–3372.

———— ———— & Bartok, J. (1991), Adolescent suicidality: A clinical-developmental approach. *J. Amer. Acad. Child Adoles. Psychiat.*, 30:796–803.

———— & Perper, J. (1993), Psychiatric risk factors for adolescent suicide: A Case-Control Study. *J. Amer. Acad. Child Adoles. Psychiat.*, 32:521–529.

Brent, D. A., Johnson, B. A., Perper, J., Connolly, J., Bridge, J., Bartle, S. & Rather, C. (1994), Personality disorder, personality traits, impulsive violence, and completed suicide in adolescents. *J. Amer. Acad. Child Adoles. Psychiat.*, 33:1080–1086.

Burke, J. D., Burke, K. C. & Rae, D. S. (1994), Increased rates of drug abuse and dependence after onset of mood or anxiety disorders in adolescence. *Hosp. Community Psychiat.*, 45:451–455.

Buydens-Branchey, L., Branchey, M. H. & Noumair, D. (1989), Age of alcoholism onset I. Relationship to psychopathology. *Arc. Gen. Psychiat.*, 46:225–230.

Cahn, D. A. & Marcotte, A. C. (1995), Rates of forgetting in attention deficit hyperactivity disorder. *Child Neuropsychol.*, 1:158–163.

Carter, C. S., Chaderjian, M., Krener, P., Northcutt C. & Wolfe, V. (1995), Asymmetrical visual spatial attentional performance in ADHD: Evidence for a right hemispheric deficit. *Society of Biolog. Psychiat.*, 37:789–797.

Castellanos, F. X., Giedd, J. N., Eckburg, P., Marsh, W. L., Vaituzis, A. C., Kaysen, D., Hamburger S. D. & Rapoport, J. L. (1994), Quantitive morphology of the caudate nucleus in attention deficit hyperactivity disorder. *Amer. J. Psychiat.*, 151:1791–1796.

Cloninger, C. R. (1987), Neurogenic adaptive mechanisms in alcoholism. *Science.* 236:410–416.

Conners, C. K. (1973), Rating scales For Use in Drug Studies with Children, *Psychopharm. Bull. (Spec. issue: Pharmacotherapy with Children)*, pp. 24–84.

Connor, D. F. (1993), Beta blockers for aggression: A review of the pediatric experience. *J. Child Adoles. Psychopharm.* 3:99–114.

Copeland, E. D. (1991), *Medications for Attention Disorders and Related Medical Problems.* Atlanta, GA: SPI Press.

Copeland E. D. & Love, V. L. (1992), *Attention Without Tension: A Teacher's Handbook on Attention Disorders.* Atlanta, GA: 3 C's of Childhood.

Corkum, P. V. & Siegel, L. S. (1993), Is the continuous performance task a valuable research tool for Use with children with attention-deficit-hyperactivity disorder? *J. Child Psycho. & Psychiat.* 34:1217–1239.

DeMilio, L. (1989), Psychiatric syndromes in adolescent substance abusers. *Amer. J. Psychiat.*, 146:1212–1214.

DuPaul, G. J. & Rapport, M. D. (1993), Does Methylphenidate normalize the classroom performance of children with attention deficit disorder? *J. Amer. Acad. Child Adoles. Psychiat.*, 32:190–198.

Ekblad, S. (1988), Influence of child-rearing on aggressive behavior in a transcultural perspective. *ACTA Psychiat. Scand., suppl.*, 344:133–139.

Elliott, D., Ageton, S., Huizinga, D., Knowleds, B. & Canter, R. (1984), The prevalence and incidence of delinquent behavior: 1976–1980. *The National Youth Survey Project Report No. 26.*

Ernst, M., Liebenauer, L. L., King, A. C., Fitzgerald, G. A., Cohen, R. M. & Zametkin, A. J. (1994), Reduced brain metabolism in hyperactive girls. *J. of Amer. Acad. Child and Adoles. Psychiat.,* 33:858–868.

Faraone, S. & Biederman, J. (1994), Is attention deficit hyperactivity disorder familial? *Harvard Rev. Psychiat.,* 1:271–287.

Flannery D. J., Vazgonyi, A. T., Torquati, J. & Fridrich, A. (1994), Ethnic and gender differences in risk for early adolescent substance abuse. *J. Youth Adolesc.* 23:195–213.

Fonagy, P. & Target, M., (1994), The efficacy of psychoanalysis for children with disruptive disorders. *J. Amer. Acad. Child Adoles. Psychiat.,* 33:45–55.

Friedman, A. S., Utada, A. & Morrissey, M. R. (1987), Families of adolescent drug abusers are "rigid": Are these families either "disengaged" or "enmeshed" or both. *Family Process,* 26:131–148.

Gabel, S., Stadler, J., Bjorn, J., Shindledecker, R. & Bowden, C. L. (1994), Sensation seeking in psychiatrically disturbed youth: Relationship to biochemical parameters and behavior problems. *J. Amer. Acad. Child Adoles. Psychiat.,* 33:123–129.

Giedd, J. N., Castellanos, F. X., Casey, B. J., Kozuch, P., King, A. C., Hamburger, S. D. & Rappaport, J. L. (1994), Quantitative morphology of the corpus callosum in attention deficit hyperactivity disorder. *Amer. J. Psychiat.,* 151:665–669.

Greenhill, L. L. (1992), Pharmacologic treatment of attention deficit hyperactivity disorder. *Psychiatric Clinics of North America,* 15:1–27.

Grilo, C. M., Becker D. F., Fehon, D. C., Edell, W. S. & McGlashan, T. H. (1996), Conduct disorder, substance use disorders, and coexisting conduct and substance use disorder in adolescent inpatients. *Amer. J. Psychiat.,* 153:914–920.

Grodzinsky, G. M. & Diamond R. (1992), Frontal lobe functioning in boys with attention-deficit hyperactivity disorder. *Develop. Neuropsychol.,* 8:427–445.

Gualtieri, C. T., Adams, A., Shen, C. E. & Loiselle, D. (1982), Minor physical anomalies in alcoholic and schizopherenic adults and hyperactive and autistic children. *Amer. J. Psychiat.,* 139:640–643.

Halperin, J. M., Matier, K., Newcorn, J. H., Schwartz, S. T., Sharma, V., Siever, L. J. & Wornell, G. (1994), Serotonergic function in aggressive and nonaggressive boys with attention deficit hyperactivity disorder. *Amer. J. Psychiat.*, 151:243–248.

Hanna, G. L., Yuwiler, A. & Coates, J. K. (1995), Whole blood serotonin and sisruptive behaviors in juvenile obsessive-compulsive disorder. *J. Amer. Acad. Child Adoles. Psychiat.*, 34:28–35.

Hendren, R. L. (1991), Adolescent hyperactivity. In: Adolescent Psychotherapy, ed. M. Slamowitz. Washington DC. American Psychiatric Press.

———— Mullen, D. (1996a), Adolescent substance abuse: Etiology, treatment, and prevention. In: *Chronic Mental Illness Through the Life Cycle* ed. Sarles R. M. & J. Talbot J.

———— ———— (1996b), Generalized conduct disorders. In: *The Comprehensive Textbook of Child and Adolescent Psychiatry*, ed. J. M. Wiener. Washington, DC: American Psychiatric Press.

———— Weisen, R. B. & Orley, J. (1994), *Mental Health Programs in Schools for the Division of Mental Health*. Geneva: World Health Organization, MNH/PSF/93.3.

Henggeler, S. W., Berduin, C. M., Melton, G. B., et al. (1991), Effects of multisystematic therapy on drug use and abuse in serious juvenile offenders: A progress report from two outcome studies. *Family Dynamics Addict.*, 1:40–51.

Hoge, R. D., Andrews, D. A. & Leschied, A. W. (1994), Tests of three hypotheses regarding the predictors of delinquency. *J. Abn. Child Psychol.* 22:547–559.

Hunt, R. D., Arnsten, A. F. T. & Asbell, M. D. (1995), An open trial of guanfiacine in the treatment of attention-deficit hyperactivity disorder. *J. Amer. Acad. Child Adoles. Psychiat.*, 34:50–54.

———— Capper, L. & O'Connell, P. (1990), Clonidine in child and adolescent psychiatry. *J. Adoles. Psychopharm.*, 1:87–102.

Hynd, G. W., Semrud-Clikeman, M., Lory, A. R., Novey, E. S., Eliopulous, D. & Lyytinen, H. (1991), Corpus callosum morphology in attention deficit hyperactivity disorder: Morphometric analysis of MRI. *J. Learn. Disabil.*, 24:141–146.

Kandel, D. B., Raveis, V. H., & Davies, M. (1991), Suicidal ideation in adolescence: Depression, substance use and other risk factors. *J. Youth Adolesc.*, 20:289–309.

Kazdin, A. E., Siegel, T. C. & Bass, D. (1992), Cognitive problem-solving skills training and parent management training in the treatment of antisocial behavior in children. *J. Consult. Clin. Psychol.*, 60:733–747.

Kendall, P. C. (1993), Cognitive-behavioral therapies with youth: Guiding theory, current status, and emerging developments. *J. Consult. Clin. Psychol.* 61:235–247.

Kendler, K. S., Walters, E. E., Neale, M. C., Kessler, R. C., Heath, A. C. & Eaves, L. J. (1995), The structure of the genetic and environmental risk factors for six major psychiatric disorders in women. Phobia, generalized anxiety disorder, panic disorder, bulimia, major depression and alcoholism. *Arch. Gen. Psychiat.*, 52:374–83.

Killen, J. D., Taylor, C. B., Telch, M. J., Robinson, T. N., Maron, D. J. & Saylor, K. E. (1987), Depressive symptoms and substance abuse among adolescent binge eaters and purgers: A defined population study. *Amer. J. Public Health.*, 77:1539–1541.

Kovacs, M. (1991), Childhood depression inventory. *Multi-Health Systems.* North Tonawanda, NY.

Kruesi, M. J. P., Hibbs, E. D., Zahn, T. P., Keysor, C. S., Hamburger, S. D., Bartko, J. J. & Rapoport, J. L. (1992), A 2-Year prospective follow-up study of children and adolescents with disruptive behavior disorders. *Arch. Gen. Psychiat.*, 49:429–435.

Lahey, B. B., Applegate, B., McBurnett, K., Biederman, J., Greenhill, L., Hynd, G., Barkley, R., Newcorn, J., Jensen, P., Richters, J., Garfinkel, B., Kerdyk, L., Frick, P., Ollendick, T., Perez, D., Hart, E., Waldman & Shaffer, D. (1994), DSM-IV field trials for attention deficit hyperactivity disorder in children and adolescents. *Amer. J. Psychiat.*, 151:1673–1685.

The Lancet (1987), 949–950.

Lee, M. & Prentice, N. M. (1988), Interrelations of empathy, cognition, and moral reasoning with dimensions of juvenile delinquency. *Abn. Child Psychol.*, 16:127–139.

Linnoila, R. A. (1988), Suicidal behavior, Impulsiveness and serotonin. *Acta Psychiat. Scand.*, 74:529–535.

Linnoila, M., DeJong, J. & Virkkunen, M. (1989a), Family history of alcoholism in violent offenders and impulsive fire setters. *Arch. Gen. Psychiat.*, 46:613–616.

——— ——— ——— (1989b), Monoamines, glucose metabolism, and impulse control. *Psychopharm. Bull.*, 25:404–406.

Lynskey, M. T. & Fergusson, D. M. (1995), Childhood conduct problems, attention deficit behaviors, and adolescent alcohol, tobacco, and illicit drug use. *J. Abn. Child Psychol.*, 23:281–302.

March, J. S., Erhardt, D., Johnston, H. & Conners, K. (1995), Pharmacotherapy for attention-deficit hyperactivity disorder. *Psychia-*

tric Clinics of North America, 2:187–213. Philadelphia, PA: Saunders.

Marttunen, M. J., Aro, H. M., Henriksson, M. M. & Lonnquist, J. R. (1994), Psychological stressors more common in adolescent suicides with alcohol abuse compared with depressive adolescent suicide. *J. Amer. Acad. Child Adoles. Psychiat.*, 33:490–497.

McBride, A., Anderson, G. M., Khait, V. C., Sunday, S. R. & Halmi, K. A. (1991), Serotonergic responsivity in eating disorders. *Psychopharm. Bull.*, 27:365–372.

McElroy, S. L., Hudson, J. I., Pope, H. G., Jr., Keck, P. E., Jr. & Aizley, H. G. (1992), The DSM-III-R impulse control disorders not Elsewhere classified: Clinical characteristics and relationship to other psychiatric disorders. *Amer. J. Psychiat.*, 149:3, 318–327.

Mefford, I. N. & Potter, W. Z. (1989), A neuroanatomical and biochemical basis for attention deficit disorder with hyperactivity in children: A defect in tonic adrenaline mediated inhibition of locus coeruleus stimulation. *Med. Hypotheses*, 29:33–42.

Mehlman, P. T., Higley, J. D., Faucher, I., Lilly, A. A., Taub, D. M., Vickers, J., Suomi, S. J. & Linnoila, M. (1994), Low CSF 5-HIAA concentrations and severe aggression and impaired impulse control in nonhuman primates. *Amer. J. Psychiat.*, 151:1485–1491.

——— ——— ——— ——— ——— ——— ——— ——— (1995), Correlation of CSF 5-HIAA concentration with sociality and the timing of emigration in free-ranging primates. *Amer. J. Psychiat.*, 152:6, 907–913.

Moffitt, T. E., (1993), The neuropsychology of conduct disorder. *Devel. & Psychopathol.*, 5:135–151.

Nielsen, D. A., Goldman, D., Virkkunen, M., Tokola, R., Rawlings, R. & Linnoila, M. (1994), Suicidality and 5-hydroxyindoleacetic acid concentration associated with a tryptophan hydroxylase polymorphism. *Arch. Gen. Psychiat.*, 51:34–38.

Offord, D. R. & Bennett, K. J. (1994), Conduct disorder: Long-term outcomes and intervention effectiveness. *J. Amer. Acad. Child Adoles. Psychiat.*, 33:1069–1078.

Olweus, D. (1992), Victimization among school children: Intervention and prevention. In: *Improving Children's Lives*, ed. Albee, G. W. L. A. Bond, T. V. C. Monsey. Newbury Park, Sage, 275–279.

O'Tuama, L. A. & Treves, T. S. (1993), Brain single-photon emission computed tomography for behavior disorders in children. *Seminars in Nuclear Medicine*, 23:255–264.

Pfeffer, C. R., Klerman, G. L., Hurt, S. W., Lesser, M., Peskin, J. R. & Siefker, C. A. (1991), Suicidal children grow up: Demographic and clinical risk factors for adolescent suicide attempts. *J. Amer. Acad. Child Adoles. Psychiat.*, 30:609–616.

Raine, A., Brennan, P. & Mednick, S. A. (1994a), Birth complications combined with early maternal rejection at age 1 year predispose to violent crime at age 18 years. *Arch. Gen. Psychiat.*, 51: 984–988.

——— ——— ——— (1994b), High rates of violence, crime, academic problems, and behavioral problems in males with both early neuromotor deficits and unstable family environments. *Arch. Gen. Psychiat.*, 53:544–549.

——— Venables, P. H. & Williams, M. (1995), High autonomic arousal and electrodermal orienting at age 15 years as protective factors against criminal behavior at age 29 years. *Amer. J. Psychiat.*, 152:1595–1600.

Reebye, P., Moretti, M. M. & Lessard, J. C. (1995), Conduct disorder and substance use disorder: Comorbidity in a clinical sample of preadolescents and adolescents. *Can. J. Psychiat.*, 40:313–319.

Riggs, P. D., Baker, S., Mikulich, S. K., Young, S. E. & Crowley, T. J. (1995), Depression in substance-dependent delinquents. *J. Amer. Acad. Child Adoles. Psychiat.*, 34:764–771.

Rosenthal, N., Davenport, Y., Cowdry, R., Webster, M. & Goodwin, F. (1989), Monoamine metabolites in cerebrospinal fluid of depressive subgroups. *Psychiat. Res.*, 2:113–119.

Rotheram-Borus, M. J., Piacentini, J., Miller, S., Graae, F. & Castro-Blanco, D. (1994), Brief cognitive-behavioral treatment for adolescent suicide attempters and their families. *J. Amer. Acad. Child Adoles. Psychiat.*, 33:508–517.

Rutter, M., Birch, H. G., Thomas, A., et. al. (1964), Temperamental Characteristics in Infancy and the Later Development of Behavior Disorders. *Brit. J. Psychiat.*, 110:651–661.

Satterfield, J., Swanson, J., Schell, A. & Lee, F. (1994), Prediction of antisocial behavior in attention-deficit hyperactivity disorder boys from aggression/defiance scores. *J. Amer. Child Adolesc. Psychiat.*, 33:85–190.

Seidman, L. J., Benedict, K. B., Biederman, J., Bernstein, J. H., Seiverd, K., Milberger, S., Norman, D., Mick, E. & Faraone, S. V. (1995a), Performance of children with ADHD on the Rey-Osterrieth complex Figure: A pilot neuropsychological study. *J. Child Psychol. Psychiat.*, 36:1459–1473.

——— Biederman, J., Faraone, S., Milberger, S., Norman, D., Seiverd, K., Benedict, K., Guite, J., Mick, E. & Kiely, K. (1995b), Effects of family history and comorbidity on the neuropsychological performance of children with ADHD: Preliminary Findings. American Academy of Child and Adolescent Psychiatry. *J. Amer. Acad. Child Adoles. Psychiat.*, 34: 1015–1024.

Semrud-Clikeman, M., Filipek, P., Biederman, J., Steingard, R., Kennedy, D., Renshaw, P. & Bekken, K. (1994), Attention-deficit hyperactivity disorder: Magnetic resonance imaging morphometric analysis of the corpus callosum. *J. Amer. Acad. Child Adoles. Psychiat.* 33:6, 875–881.

Silverman, I. W. & Ragusa, D. M. (1993), A short-term longitudinal study of the early development of self-regulation. *J. Abn. Psychol.*, 20:415-435.

Simeon, J. G., Fergurson, H. B. & Van Wyck, Fleet, J. (1986), Bupropion effects in attention deficit and conduct disorders. *Can. J. Psychiat.*, 31:581–585.

Slomkowksi C., Klein, R. & Mannuzza, S. (1995), Is self-esteem an important outcome in hyperactive children? *J. Abn. Child Psychol.*, 23:303–315.

Spence, S. H. (1994), Practitioner review: Cognitive therapy with children and adolescents: from theory to practice. *J. Child Psycho. Psychiat.*, 35:1191–1288.

Stoff, D. M., Friedman, E., Pollock, L., Vitiello, B., Kendall, P. C. & Bridger, W. H. (1989), Elevated platelet MAO is related to impulsivity in disruptive behavior disorders. *J. Amer. Acad. Child Adoles. Psychiat.*, 28:754–760.

Szapocznik, J., Perez-Vidal, A., Brickman, A. L., Foote, F. H., Santisteban, D. & Hervis, O. (1988), Engaging adolescent drug abusers and their families in treatment: A strategic structural system approach. *J. Consul. Clin. Psychol.*, 56:552–557.

Thompson, L. L., Riggs, P. D., Mikulich, S. K. & Crowley, T. J. (1996), Contribution of ADHD symptoms to substance problems and delinquency in conduct-disordered adolescents. *J. Abnormal Child Psychol.*, 24:325–347.

Tierney, E., Joshi, P. T., Llinas, J. F., Rosenberg, L. A. & Riddle, M. A. (1995), Sertraline for major depression in children and adolescents: Preliminary clinical experience. *J. Child Adoles. Psychopharm.*, 5:13–27.

Tremblay, R. E., Pihl, R. O., Vitaro, F. & Dobkin, P. L. (1994), Predicting early onset of male antisocial behavior from preschool behavior. *Arch. Gen. Psychiat.*, 51:732–739.

Ullmann, R. K., Sleator, E. K. & Sprague R (1985), Introduction to the use of ACTeRS. *Psychopharm. Bull.* 21:915–920.

Virkkunen, M., Rawlings, R., Tokola R., Poland R., Guidotti A., Nemeroff, C., Bissette, G., Kalogeras, K., Karonen, S. L. & Linnoila, M. (1994), CSF biochemistries, glucose metabolism, and diurnal activity rhythms in alcoholics, violent Offenders, fire Setters, and healthy volunteers. *Arch. Gen. Psychiat.*, 51:20–27.

Wallin, M. S. & Rissanen, A. M. (1994), Food and mood: Relationship between food, serotonin and affective disorders. *Acta Psychiat. Scand.* Suppl 377:36–40.

Ward, M. F., Wender P. H. & Reimherr, F. W. (1993), The Wender Utah Rating Scale: An aid in the retrospective diagnosis of childhood attention deficit hyperactivity disorder. *Amer. J. of Psychiat.*, 150:885–890.

Weizman, A., Bernhout, E., Weitz, R., Tyano, S. & Rehavi, M. (1988), Imipramine binding to platelets of children with attention deficit disorder with hyperactivity. *Biol. Psychiat.*, 23:491–496.

Wilens, T. & Biederman, J. (1993), Psychopathology in preadolescent children at high risk for substance abuse: A review of the literature. *Harvard Rev. Psychiat.*, 1:207–218.

Wilson, G. T. & Fairburn C. G. (1993), Cognitive treatments for eating disorders. *Amer. Psychol.*, 61:261–269.

Wolin, S. J. & Bennett, L. A. (1980), Disrupted family rituals: A factor in the intergenerational transmission of alcoholism. *J. Stud. Alcohol*, 41:199–214.

World Health Organization (1992), *The ICD-10 Classification of Mental and Behavioral Disorders. Clinical Descriptions and Diagnostic Guidelines.* Geneva, Switzerland: World Health Organization.

Zametkin, A. J., Nordahl, T. E., Gross M., King, A. C., Semple, W. E., Rumsey, J., Hamburger, S. & Cohen, R. M. (1990), Cerebral glucose metabolism in adults with hyperactivity of childhood onset. *New Eng. Med.*, 323:1361–1366.

Zubieta, J. K. & Alessi, N. E. (1992), Acute and chronic administration of trazodone in the treatment of disruptive behavior disorders in children. *J. Clin. Psychopharm.*, 12:346–351.

——— & ——— (1993), Is there a role of serotonin in disruptive behavior disorder? Literature review. *J. Child Adoles. Psychopharm.*, 3:11–35.

6 PSYCHIATRIC CONTRIBUTIONS TO IMPROVE THE EFFECTIVENESS OF JUVENILE JUSTICE

DEREK MILLER

The juvenile justice system appears to ignore what is known about child development in favor of responding to political pressures to get tough on crime. If the system were to inform itself about the efficacy of etiological diagnosis and thence the adequate treatment of young people; it could be transformed from its ineffectual state to a major contributor to public safety, as well as the betterment of individuals and families [T. Geraghty, 1997, personal communication].

The solution to the problem is not just better screening, better initial interviewing and assessment, interdisciplinary training of lawyers and judges, and more sophisticated treatment facilities. It also requires that the psychiatric profession address the needs of the juvenile justice system so that the information given is more useful than is often the case. Currently, young people who are judged as delinquent may suffer with undiagnosed handicaps. Even if they are diagnosed, not only is there a paucity of available services, but professionals often fail to be helpful in making useful recommendations.

The central issue is the diagnosis of the treatability of individual juveniles, a concept that is not adequately covered in *DSM IV*, (American Psychiatric Association, 1994) nor in most court reports submitted by experts. The capacity of individuals to make meaningful positive emotional relationships with others, both with individuals and with social systems, is a crucial issue in behavioral change. In foster care, for example, the single best predictor of a satisfactory long-term outcome is the ability of a child to form a positive relationship with an adult (Rosenfeld et al., 1977). Clinically, the same was true in psychi-

113

atric treatment programs and in a British "Approved School" for seriously disturbed adolescents (Miller, 1966a); it is true for all age groups. Those who reach adolescence are particularly able to respond as they withdraw from infantile emotional dependence on their parents, identify with significant others, and develop new ways of organizing their lives.

The inadequacies of the current situation in juvenile justice are demonstrated by the numbers of previous offenses that often appear on a charge sheet and, by implication, by the number of appearances in court. Those charged with serious crimes, such as homicide, often show striking evidence of the failure of interventions based solely on present criteria. The number of young people coming before juvenile courts appears to demonstrate the inability to rehabilitate chronic and violent offenders while, at the same time, protecting public safety. There is now a substantive and procedural convergence between the juvenile and the criminal courts that has transformed juvenile courts from nominally rehabilitative welfare agencies into scaled-down, second-class criminal courts (Feld, 1995).

Available resources for diagnostic intervention are limited and, outside of large metropolitan areas, they may not be available at all. The issue of public safety is paramount, but it does not necessarily contradict the concept of rehabilitation. The failure to rehabilitate adequately commonly leads to a repetition of an offense, which may become more dangerous as time progresses.

Adequate treatment and rehabilitation, is possible only with adequate assessment, which clarifies the biopsychosocial etiology of the antisocial behavior. Such assessments should be done for all those appearing at intake as well as for those who appear for adjudication.

The problem is compounded because becoming a juvenile court justice is usually not considered particularly prestigious. Even if judges pay more than lip service to the concept of rehabilitation, they do not have resources available, and often they do not know for which facilities they should look. They often appear not to appreciate that there are different levels of professional expertise. As rehabilitation appears to fail in any one individual, the issue of public safety appears to become the only criterion used for disposition. Furthermore, equal weight may be given to all opinions about etiology and optimum intervention, from social workers, psychologists, probation officers, teachers, and psychiatrists, each of whom has different training and experience. Sometimes it appears that the opinions of those with the least relevant clinical expertise are accepted because those people are employed by the courts or they are known to the judge or attorneys.

Juvenile Court Problems

Entry into the juvenile court system as currently constituted is thus not as valuable as it might be. Complicated as they may be, sanctions are simpler to apply than are rehabilitative techniques.

Another significant issue is that, for many reasons, juvenile courts in large cities are often overwhelmed with numbers. One reason that is modifiable, and to which psychiatry should be able to make a significant contribution, has to do with the technique of disposition prior to actual court appearance. Another possibility is assisting in more skillful disposition after the process of adjudication.

Of the referrals to juvenile court, over half are for crimes against persons or property; the rest are for offenses against public order, status offenses (21%) or drug offenses (5%) (Snyder, 1994). Status offenses are those offenses in which a minor requires authoritative intervention. These offenders include minors under 18 years of age who are absent from home without the consent of their parents/guardians/custodians, or minors who are beyond the control of their parents. Five days after the discovery of such social problems as this, the minor may be taken into limited custody and may be adjudicated as requiring authoritative intervention. Over half of the cases presented to the juvenile justice system by the police do not go to adjudication; 28% of total referrals go to formal adjudication; and 8% end with court-ordered placements. Notwithstanding these facts, the juvenile court system in the United States handled 534,000 cases of delinquency in 1985; violent crimes accounted for 18% of these; status offenses, for 88,000 cases.

A disproportionate amount of crime in the United States is committed by young people. Their arrest rates for the most serious crimes peak in mid- to late adolescence and then gradually decline (Federal Bureau of Investigation Uniform Crime Reports for the United States, 1992). As a result of the demographic "baby bust," the age group of 10- to 17-year-olds now constitutes a smaller segment of the population than it did previously. Thus, the overall contribution of these youngsters to serious crime is decreasing.

Although violent crimes constitute a much smaller component of the overall serious crime index, the rate of juvenile violence, especially homicide, has surged dramatically since the mid 1980s. Juvenile property crime arrests increased by 8% between 1988 and 1992; and by 11% between 1983 and 1992 (Snyder, 1994).

Currently, of the referrals to juvenile court, over half the crimes are against persons and property; the rest are for offenses against public order. Between 1988 and 1992, the number of violent crimes leading to the arrest of juveniles increased by 47%, more than twice the increase for persons 18 years of age or older. Most alarmingly, juvenile arrests for murder increased by 51% compared with 9% for adults (Harlanhagen, 1994). Thus, over half the referrals are for crimes against persons or property; the rest are status offenses (those against public order), or drug offenses. The portion referred to the adult courts rose from 1% to 5% from 1971 to 1987, and this population continues to grow. Since more time may be taken with transfer hearings, pressure on the juvenile courts is increased. The number of offenders who appeared before the juvenile courts increased in 1991 to 1,340,000 cases (Juvenile Court Statistics, 1991). This represents a 5% increase in the court's case load in 1990 and a 16% increase over 1987.

An additional problem is created for the courts by the apparent unavailability of psychiatric services. As psychiatric services become less available (Vaillant 1993), an ever-increasing number of emotionally disturbed youth gravitate toward the juvenile justice system. It appears that institutionalized delinquents undergo a peculiar social-sieving process in which the more disturbed and handicapped the juvenile offender, the more likely he or she is to be incarcerated.

It has been estimated that between 6% and 14% of all school-age children suffer from some type of mental or physical handicap; between 28% and 42% of confined delinquents are classified as handicapped. Mental retardation is five times as common among the delinquent population as in the population at large (Murphy, 1986).

If the nature of the offense is not to be the principal or only criterion, there is little agreement as to the qualities that should be identified in an individual which will assist in assessing what is needed for adequate intervention. Those youngsters who are seriously psychologically disturbed often present themselves to the juvenile justice system with repeated antisocial behavior. The attempted solution is often the use of objective "public safety" issues based only on the nature and frequency of the offense. For such individuals, either long-term placement in the correctional system or transfer to adult courts and prisons is usual. Often the court has no real knowledge about these facilities. Custodial and rehabilitation facilities differ widely in rehabilitative concepts, staffing, and costs. In a 1993 analysis of 14 states, 31% of juveniles housed in state training schools were considered appropriate for less secure settings (Jones and Krisberg, 1994). It has long been known that, even in societies that do not refer juveniles to adult courts, many seriously disturbed youngsters ultimately end in the adult system (Miller, 1965).

In correctional settings, services and resources are often inadequate, and diagnosis and exploration of significant biopsychosocial etiology is commonly absent. There may be little rationale for where and how effective intervention might occur. Diagnostic labeling of the syndrome from which an individual suffers is rarely effective and is often grossly inadequate (Bartholomew, et al., 1967, Jewelka, Trupin, and Chiles, 1989). In any case, diagnostic classification based on *DSM IV* (American Psychiatric Association, 1994) is of little help in assessing treatability. Even the diagnosis of some type of organic mental disorder, such as Tourettes Disorder (307.23), indicates only that biological intervention is necessary to make psychosocial intervention possible; the diagnosis of Conduct Disorder (312.8) is merely symptomatically descriptive.

The System Failure

The failure of professionals to convey the issues that ensure successful treatability and rehabilitation may lead to a repetition of antisocial behavior. Many youngsters appear before the juvenile courts because of the failure of earlier interventions. Some are then sentenced to long periods of incarceration, sometimes with the rationalization and the misunderstanding that this is a rehabilitative maneuver. Rightly, the legal system recognizes that correctional facilities are inappropriate for prepubertal children, but the confusion about the use of mental health facilities and the absence of such facilities for dangerously disturbed children often lead to tragedy.

Many teenagers are placed on probation and offered community interventions that, because of inadequate diagnosis and a shortage of resources, cannot possibly work. Perhaps because of the apparent failure of many current community-based interventions, 8% of all referrals end with a court-ordered placement (Krisberg, Litsky, and Schwartz, 1984).

Although most transfers to the adult courts are not for violent crimes, such transfers are apparently a function of the belief that the seriousness of the crime justifies a response as if the adolescent were an adult. Between 1971 and 1987 (Federal Bureau of Investigation, 225, 1988)

117

the proportion of juveniles arrested who were referred to adult courts rose from 1% to 5%. Despite a declining number of arrests, the juvenile justice system has become more formal, more restrictive, and more oriented toward punitive sanctions (Krisberg et al., 1986). Thus, not only has the current juvenile justice system contributed to historically high levels of incarcerated young people, but also the juvenile courts have become steadily more and more overwhelmed with the numbers of youngsters who come before them. Furthermore, even though the majority of cases brought to an intake unit are not petitioned, there is a lack of resources for adequate disposition, rehabilitation, and treatment.

Institute of Medicine (1989) studies of the last decade that do not include the population deemed "delinquent," estimate that in the United States 14 to 18 million children under 18 years of age, or approximately 20% of that population, suffer from a mental disorder and need psychiatric intervention. In an earlier study, three million of these children were estimated to have a serious mental illness lasting at least one year (Knitzer, 1982). While these statistics demonstrate the need for services, there is no evidence that the healthcare system ensures the adequate provision of these services even for those who are not involved with juvenile justice. For the latter, it is clear not only that there is a highly significant percentage of severely disturbed youth, but also that there is also a gross paucity of resources (Brickman et al., 1984). Not only is there limited access to care, but a further complication results from the vast numbers of those in need (Gray and McNerney, 1986). There is no evidence that there has been any improvement in these figures.

Psychiatric assistance for adolescents in the United States is now largely dominated by a preoccupation with costs. Despite efforts being made to limit the availability of care, the evidence (personal communications) seems to be that the number of psychologically disturbed adolescents needing psychiatric help has dramatically increased. For example, referrals for such care in the South Carolina State hospital system grew 50% in 1988 and an additional 30% in the first five months of 1989. These figures include adolescents who were referred by the juvenile justice system to the state psychiatric system for diagnostic assessment.

Society appears to have veered away from the concept of rehabilitation. Although many believe that punishment will act as a deterrent to juvenile crime, there is absolutely no evidence that this is so. There appears to be a belief in some quarters that long-term incarceration, initially in juvenile corrections and then with transfer to the adult system, will be rehabilitative. Nevertheless, despite the fact that a higher percentage of adolescents is incarcerated in the United States then in any large Western country, apart from demographic issues, the juvenile crime rate does not significantly decrease. Between 1977 and 1987, both in public and in private facilities, the juvenile confinement rate increased by 43%, although during that period the incidence of violent crime, other than homicide, fell. The number of juveniles sentenced to jail has remained constant, but the number of persons under 18 years of age residing in prisons increased. Because expenditures for juvenile corrections have not kept pace with inflation and because there has been minimum capital investment in the correctional system, all juvenile correctional facilities are now chronically overcrowded, physical plants are deteriorating, and many rehabilitative programs are abandoned or downgraded for lack of funds.

Although the juvenile court is guided by the concept of adolescence as a life stage in which personality development is incomplete, the United States and Iran are alone among nations in sentencing juveniles to death. The Supreme Court held in 1982 that age should be a mitigating factor in deciding whether the death penalty should apply (*Eddings vs. Oklahoma* 455 United States 104, 1982). Despite all psychological evidence about the length of time taken for personality development, particularly in those who are emotionally disturbed, the court concluded that 15 years is a minimum age for executions (*Thompson vs. Oklahoma* United States 2687, 1988).

An incorrect assumption, made by many in the juvenile justice system, is that, although the nature of the behavior indicates the danger to public safety, it also necessarily indicates the severity of the underlying personality disturbance. Sometimes, however, a relatively minor antisocial episode for which the juvenile is arraigned may be only the tip of the iceberg. Dangerously disturbed adolescents may appear with relatively mild antisocial behavior. Alternatively, a serious crime may be committed by a juvenile who is responding to extreme social pathology and who thus has responded inappropriately to acute stress. Without adequate diagnosis as to etiology it is obviously difficult to decide on an appropriate intervention based on behavior alone.

Most states, Massachusetts being a notable exception, seem to go along with the concept that punishment and incarceration are an appropriate response to the problems created by violence and antisocial behavior among youths. Punishment of one offender is believed to deter others. There is no statistical evidence that this is an accurate concept as

119

it applies to antisocial youth. The psychological evidence from interviewing many youngsters is that what happens to others is seen as irrelevant and does not serve as a deterrent.

The operation of juvenile justice often appears not to differentiate between the establishment of guilt or innocence and an appropriate disposition that will offer the maximum chance of rehabilitation. Some State's Attorneys, perhaps with an eye to reelection, appear to need to establish themselves as upholders of extreme penalties irrespective of whether such penalties produces a rehabilitated youngster—this, despite the fact that opinion polls suggest that the general public continues to be supportive of the juvenile system's traditional mission. The crisis, however, is in the teenage homicide rate. According to the National Center for Disease Control and Prevention (1994) from 1985 to 1991, the annual rates at which young males age 15 to 19 were being killed jumped 54%; 97% of this increase was due to the use of guns. Arrest rates for homicide among males aged 15 to 19 went up 127% from 1985 to 1991; it dropped to 19% for males aged 25 through 29 and 13% percent for men aged 30 to 34 in the same period. The overall homicide rate did not rise. The violence epidemic is specifically a problem of firearm deaths. Obviously, some of the pressure on the juvenile court would be relieved if society removed guns from young people and dealt adequately with drug dealing gangs.

The legal system, politicians, and the media, irrespective of the results of adequate rehabilitation, seem also to believe that to be "tough on crime" is an appropriate response to the problems created by juvenile crime. Election campaigns continue to claim toughness on juvenile offenders as an appropriate response. Those who are most vociferous in these claims often do not wish to change gun laws, which allow 60% of the adolescent population to have access to weapons.

Further, the evidence suggests that the treatment of juveniles accused in the juvenile courts of violent crimes is less lenient than it is in the adult courts. For example, in California, youths adjudicated for violent offenses confined in the California Youth Authority serve longer periods of incarceration then adults do. In other words, if a juvenile is accused of any type of violent crime and is referred to the juvenile court, he is statistically highly likely to be treated with greater severity than is an equivalent adult (Jones and Krisberg, 1996). The situation is confusing, however, because juvenile and criminal courts often work at cross purposes. Criminal courts frequently impose longer sentences on older offenders, whose rate of criminal activity is declining. They do not sentence as severely younger offenders, whose rate of criminal activity is increasing or at its peak or who pose the greater risk to public safety. Juvenile property offenders, in particular, typically receive lenient sentences when they appear in adult court as first time adult offenders (Greenwood, Abrahams, and Zimmerling, 1984).

The Classification and Placement of Juvenile Offenders

When a case is referred to the juvenile court, a decision is generally made by a court-appointed attorney or intake workers from other disciplines whether to process the case formally and file a petition or to handle the case informally. In 1991, 55% of referrals for offenses against persons resulted in formal petitions (Juvenile Court Statistics, 1991).

It is not clear which techniques, other than assessing the type of crime, are used by intake workers in deciding whether or not a youngster should be referred for adjudication. Presumably some intake workers are concerned about the social stability of the child's environment and the familial and educational status. Although not all would agree, the biopsychosocial etiology of most illness and clinical experience suggests that the more stable the family environment, the more likely the child who behaves in a criminal fashion is to be psychologically disturbed.

There is no question (Gendreau and Ross, 1987) that, if interventions are intended to be rehabilitative as a generalized approach, even without specific investigation as to etiology, the chances of the juvenile court's being swamped with repeat offenders are lessened, and the chances of successful intervention are increased (Altschuler and Armstrong 1984).

General rehabilitation approaches randomly applied produce better results than does punishment alone; nevertheless specifically applied techniques should work better to decrease both recidivism and court appearances.

Techniques for successful intervention include 1) continuous case management; 2) careful emphasis on reintegration and reentry services; 3) opportunities for youth achievement and program decision making; 4) clear and consistent consequences for misconduct; 5) enriched educational and vocational programs; and 6) a diversity of forms of individual and family counseling matching the needs of adolescents.

A number of private-sector programs, such as Vision Quest, the Associated Marine Institutes, the Ecker Foundation, and Outward Bound, are thought to be satisfactory alternatives to conventional juvenile correctional facilities. In the 1960s, the California Youth Authority randomly assigned youths to either institutions or intensive community treatment units. Those in community treatment had a much lower rate of parole failure after 12 to 24 months (Palmer, 1971) than did those sent to institutions.

There are currently two types of intervention:

1) Intervention is based on the type of crime. This approach is apparently thought to obviate the need for sophisticated diagnostic assessment about the etiology of behavior; at its best, the intervention is based on the concept of the "least restrictive environment." This constitutional concept (Hoffman and Faust, 1977) is also used in some parts of the mental health system. Under it, the justification for more intensive intervention is made on the basis of a failure to produce adequate behavioral results with a less intensive system. Although overtly less costly, when it fails, it is an expensive technique. It loads the courts with repeat offenders. It also creates the youngsters' perception that adult intervention is useless, thus ultimate rehabilitation is even more difficult than usual.

2) The alternative approach is to assign all youngsters to rehabilitative programs.

Both approaches are basically nonspecific in that they apply to all juveniles. Ignored is the possibility that there are diagnosable criteria that make for more successful intervention.

Assessment at Intake Interviews

In any setting, a youngster's capacity to respond to rehabilitation or treatment depends on his or her ability to make an emotional investment in others, to trust them, and to handle frustration in a way that others find tolerable. In the case of major crime, for example, at the preliminary interview of the offender by a member of the State's Attorney's staff, the attorney has a relatively limited role; a young person is told of his or her legal rights; and there is a preliminary investigation of the nature of the crime.

The more serious the offense, the more necessary is adequate planning for rehabilitation. All serious offenders should have a complete biopsychosocial assessment of etiology before adequate disposition can be done. Those who commit violent crimes should be routinely remanded for such an assessment before adjudication.

The initial assessment interview should decide whether the youngster is capable of forming a trusting relationship. Unless this is clear in the initial interview, at least one or two more interviews with the same professional during the subsequent week are needed. In the preliminary interview, an assessment also should be made as to whether the youngster, or his or her family, has any conflict about the antisocial behavior or merely regrets being caught.

A number of developmental issues influence the ability to make trusting relationships and tolerate frustration. Physical development and its relationship to chronological age are significant. Without physiological puberty, adolescence is not possible; but not all pubertal boys and girls become adolescents. The latter implies a capacity to become genuinely autonomous with a sense of personal security, whatever the psychological storms associated with the development of sexual maturity. Being postpubertal does not automatically enable young people to be empathic and to make trusting relationships. Without this ability, or if it is lost with minimal stress or greater, youngsters are at the mercy of their impulses and cannot move past self-involvement. They cannot internalize such concepts as honesty, empathy, productivity and care for others.

Until the middle stage of adolescence, usually age 15 or 16, most young people have not yet developed an adequate sense of time; they have little sense of the past and the future. Those who have not yet become adolescent feel both omnipotent and helpless. They do not respond to deterrence because they do not believe that there will be inevitable consequences to behavior (often there are not), and threats do not influence them.

In healthy adolescents, behavior is ultimately controlled not by fear of consequences, but by the youngster's positive feelings for people and by social systems that explicitly and implicitly exert productive behavioral control. Young people are then able to internalize controls and identify with the positive aspects of the personalities of others and the social system in which they live. If, for example, such a young person is involved with a trusted individual or group of adults who represent the positive values of society, he is highly unlikely to involve himself in antisocial behavior and will abandon behavior of this type. At the same time, even those who cannot be trusting may behave if the here-and-now controls are good enough. They may be productive if a consistent demand is made for this, but they do not internalize positive value systems and they tend to become recidivists.

An individual's developmental history should clarify the presence or absence of factors that enable the development of the capacity to be trusting. This involves the ability to make an attachment (Bowlby, 1984), which includes both bonding and dependence. The former is a biopsychosocial process involving the capacity, in an infant initially on the basis of hearing, touch, feeling, smell, and then sight, to recognize the other person as providing a safe, nurturing environment. The latter involves the visual recognition of a specific person with unique, individual qualities, and the understanding that he or she is a separate being. If a child is able to become dependent on the persons (usually mother and father) to whom he or she has bonded, the development of trust can be relatively smooth. Mothers who bond to their infants are able to recall their first interaction with the child (Miller, 1986). Usually mothers who do not have such recall have not satisfactorily bonded to their offspring.

The development of the capacity to be trusting is obviously impaired by parental brutality and rejection and by the multiple changes of caregiver that are often present in inadequate child care systems. In addition, if infants are not adequately stimulated, nurtured, and fed and the environment is not "good enough" (Winnicott, 1965), by one year of age they show significant impairment in their potential.

Child observation and clinical examinations and treatment would indicate that it is probable that, like adults, children make highly meaningful attachments to not more than two or three persons; yet in some day care centers children may be exposed to a much larger number of caregiving adults, or there may be too many children for each adult. Multiple handling is likely to produce children and adolescents who cannot make a trusting relationship with others and who find it difficult, if not impossible, to maintain an internal image of a loving other. Thus, even in the presence of an immediate supportive figure, they cannot easily control themselves. Such children commonly do not develop a capacity for self-control under stress and are likely to be highly impulsive. When they are placed in an institutional setting, often they can make only tenuous network attachments.

Adolescents may join a gang in an attempt to develop autonomy from parents, as a substitute for parents or as an outlet for violence and rage. Isolated nuclear families or single parents find it difficult to rear healthy adults. If there are no available extraparental adults or a socially acceptable network of people to whom the adolescent can relate, a gang often offers the equivalent of a tribe (Miller, 1970).

Social Etiology

The possibility of rehabilitation in the community depends to some extent on its nature, the type of neighborhood in which a youngster lives, the quality of the school attended, and the familial network to which he or she belongs.

Apart from the need for two involved parents (significantly missing in the lives of many juvenile delinquents), children need relationships with a consistent social system with relatively clear values, an emotionally involved network of adults including relatives and family friends, a relatively stable peer group, and the possibility of making firm attachments to caregivers who are not constantly changing. They also need an adequate education, and the need for vocational education is often neglected for the nonacademic. A pertinent question is whether or not the youngster allows parents to exert control of his behavior.

Differentiation is necessary between those youngsters who may present a serious danger to the community and themselves because of their severe biopsychosocial pathology and those who, while possibly requiring some assistance, are not a danger to themselves or others, and are less likely to become recidivists. Understanding the etiology of antisocial behavior and the possibility of a psychiatric disability does not influence judgments of guilt or innocence, except perhaps for those who are legally adjudged insane, but it should influence disposition.

The breakdown of the nuclear family and the disintegration of extrafamilial networks, along with changes in the preoccupations of society, have occurred in parallel with—if they are not a cause of—a situation in which many adolescents are considerably more violent than in the past (Miller, 1971). In the four years from 1987 to 1991 juvenile courts handled 54% more cases in which the most serious charge was a violent crime. The number of such young people who are able to make significant, trusting relationships with adults has apparently decreased. Young people then become more vulnerable to peer pressure. The etiology of group pressures in antisocial disturbance becomes more significant, partly because youngsters with a limited capacity to make trusting relationships with adults are likely to become highly involved with their peers and are more susceptible to the impulsive expression of antisocial behavior (Miller, 1986). These groups become highly vulnerable to contagion both in local gang structures and in the rapidly appearing and transient groups that are created with the goal of enacting a given episode of antisocial behavior.

Social agencies, including the probation services, are commonly ill equipped for adequate diagnosis and treatment, particularly for the assessment of biological etiology. Often they are unable to offer appropriate symptom control. If treatment intervention fails, young people may go through a cycle of broken relationships. These repeat the rejection often associated with the developmental trauma found in a large number of those who engage in antisocial behavior. If the relationships established with community workers are dependent on the continuance of antisocial behavior, when the value of such relationships becomes apparent and the misbehavior ceases, the care from the adult is likely to be withdrawn. For those for whom the significant etiology of the antisocial behavior is the absence of emotionally significant adult relationships, this behavior is remarkable. Not surprisingly, with the inappropriate withdrawal of adult support, the antisocial behavior is likely to recur.

Commonly, social agencies see adolescents for four or five sessions. These brief interventions are likely to be helpful only to those with no significant biological vulnerability. Also, these are people who live in a relatively stable social system, who can make an emotional investment in others, and who have temporarily been involved in antisocial behavior because of stress related to an acute focal conflict. With young people for whom previous adult interventions have not been helpful, the attitude they bring with them is likely to be that the new intervention will be useless.

Appropriate treatment recommendations require knowledge of the following issues:

1) How consistent was care given in the first five years of the person's life? Were two parents or consistent parent substitutes available in the child-rearing experience? Was a father involved in child's upbringing?
2) Was nurturing adequate? Was the child properly fed? Financial deprivation commonly means that a child suffers from lack of adequate nutrition.

3) What was the living experience of the child? What was the quality of the parenting available, either from the natural or foster parents?

4) What is the quality of the child's education? How many times has the child changed schools, and how commonly is education offered by members of both sexes? Is there any evidence of relationships with adults outside the nuclear family?

The capacity to make an emotional involvement with others can be assessed in a one-to-one interview. An intake worker able to comment on the youngster's apparent feeling on the basis of appearance or behavior, or who can offer some understanding of the youngster's emotional situation, should see a change in affect or in the content of the youth's communications in the subsequent phase of the interview. If this does not happen, the probability is that the adolescent is not invested in the interaction.

Generally speaking, an interviewer's recognition of the feeling world of the youngster should lead, for those youngsters who are able to form relationships, to a change in the way they interact. For example, to comment empathically on how nervous the youngster seems to be should make the youngster, other things being equal, feel more comfortable. The crucial issue is whether or not a trusting relationship seems possible. Those who can make trusting relationships, whatever the nature of their crimes, are almost certainly rehabilitatable. Those who cannot make such relationships almost certainly are not.

The Problem of Violence

Violence can be either emotional (affective), or it can be predatory. Affective violence appears as a stress response; predatory violence is planned, hunting behavior and does not involve rage reactions. Youngsters who are involved in predatory violence take longer to change their attitude about its acceptability than are those who are involved in emotionally charged violence; the latter often cannot be helped without a biological intervention (Miller and Looney, 1976).

For serious crimes, as defined by the FBI's crime index, the total arrests of young people for violent offenses in 1992 declined from 31% to 29%. Murder and rape combined represented less than 5% of all juvenile arrests in 1992 (Federal Bureau of Investigation, Uniform

Crime Reports, 1993) These offenses typically occur among youths who have many previous appearances in the juvenile court. Many delinquent adolescents have been so corrupted by the social world in which they live, that violence is quite acceptable to them, and they see nothing wrong in such behavior.

The assessment of potential dangerousness, with an appropriate court response, should reduce the load on the court as it will reduce the number of valueless interventions. In 1974, a district court invalidated a statute that held that if there was a serious risk that a juvenile might, before a return date to court, commit an act that, if committed by an adult would constitute a crime, freedom in the community was unacceptable. At that time, the district court concluded that no diagnostic tools had as yet been devised that could enable the most highly trained criminologist to predict reliably which juveniles would engage in a violent crime (Brooks, 1974). However, in *Schall vs Martin* (1984 S. Court 104: 2403) the Supreme Court upheld a New York statute that authorized pretrial detention. The court said that such a judgment forms an important element in many situations and "we have specifically rejected the contention that it is impossible to predict future behavior."

Tort law, represented by *Tarasoff vs. Regents* of the University of California (1976, 551 p: 2d, 334), makes it clear that there is a duty to protect individuals when a psychotherapist believes that there is a likelihood of the patient's inflicting injury on identifiable third parties. For juveniles it is reasonable to conclude that there is a duty to protect both the juvenile from committing further violent offenses and society from being his or her victim.

There are currently actuarial approaches to improve the prediction of violence as manifested by the MacArthur Risk Assessment Study (Steadman et al., 1994). In a study by Monahan (1996), risk factors fell into the following four domains:

1) Dispositional variables. These refer to the demographic factors of age, race, gender, and social class as well as to personality traits, which include impulse and anger control and such neurological factors as, for example, these due to head injury.

2) Historical variables, which are significant events experienced by subjects in the past such as family and work history, mental hospitalization, a history of violence, and a criminal and juvenile justice history.

3) Conjectural variables. These include current social supports, the balance of social stress and support, the physical aspects of the environment, such as the presence of weapons.
4) Clinical variables. These include types and symptoms of mental disorder, personality disorder, drug and alcohol abuse, and the level of social functioning.

The profile characteristics of juvenile murderers are typically those of a disruptive, behaviorally disordered youth with family and school problems; one who was reared in a violent environment and abused by one of more caretakers. There is prior evidence of difficulty controlling aggressive urges toward others and, commonly, arrests for earlier offenses (Meyers et al., 1995).

The neglect of the emotional health of delinquents, both violent and nonviolent, is very well-documented (Lewis, 1994). The problem is clear from Lewis's studies in which, for example, she demonstrated the neuropsychiatric, psychoeducational and family characteristics of juveniles who later committed murder (Lewis, Moy, and Jackson, 1985). The studies of Meyers et al. (1995) produced a similar background picture, but one that can apply to many youngsters who are not homicidal. The history includes family dysfunction, previous violent acts, disruptive behavior, failure in at least one school grade, and emotional abuse by family members. Family violence, prior arrests, learning disabilities, the availability of weapons, and psychotic symptoms are equally relevant. Except for the prevalence of weapons—and even with them—not all children and adolescents who fit these categories turn out to be repeatedly dangerous. It is also necessary to clarify other clinical and historical factors which suggest the likelihood of dangerousness.

In the assessment of dangerousness, apart from the profiles described by Lewis et al. (1985) and Monahan (1996), interviewers should have the following in mind:

(1) Can the youngster form a trusting relationship, and is honesty possible? Does the boy or girl lie by omission, commission, or both?
(2) Is the youth capable of remorse? Is guilt possible?
(3) How easily are others dehumanized?
(4) What is the extent of current social pathology, and what has been the nurturing experience of the youngster?

The assessment of dangerousness, like that of treatability, involves an assessment of the capacity under stress to make a meaningful emotional investment in others and be empathic. This capacity is based to a considerable degree on the person's developmental experiences as well as the possible presence of organic brain damage. It requires an understanding of the way that frustration is handled and the person's capacity for anti-social and violent behavior. Those who commit violent acts are said to have had a severely disturbed childhood, to have committed previous acts of violence, and often to suffer from bipolar illness (Yesavage, 1983). These are predictors for violence, but a significant issue is whether or not violence is egosyntonic and acceptable to the person.

Depending on how people learn to express anger, they may handle it by withdrawal from reality into fantasy, by projection onto others, or by actions by which they constructively or destructively try to alter the situation. The appearance of violent outbursts is influenced by a number of factors: the existential support that the child feels from the family and others, the strength of the child's own personality, the internalization of the image of loving parental figures, the stresses that the child experiences, the intensity and quality of the mood shifts, and how much these are a function of neuroendocrinological vulnerability.

Particularly significant in the potential for dangerousness is the ease, under stress, in which a victim is dehumanized. The likelihood of dangerous or antisocial behavior being repeated, as had been said, is particularly dependent on the youngster's capacity to form meaningful emotional and trusting relationships. If this capacity appears impaired and if dehumanization easily occurs, there is an indication, whatever the nature of the offense, for further investigation.

The Concept of Humanization and Dehumanization

Whether or not violence is directed toward other people depends on the ability to perceive them as warm, feeling, and alive—whether they are seen as "human." Humanization is an essential quality of life. It relieves anxiety about the unknown by offering explanations in terms of human behavior. For example, primitive people explained the violent forces of nature in human terms; today hurricanes are given the names of people. This type of anthropomorphic thinking helps explain the inexplicable—animals become human, the earth becomes a mother. This tendency to humanize depends on appropriate nurturing and stable attachments in the first three years of life. In children it indicates the beginning of an ability to be empathic; it is first seen intermittently when children are about three years old. This ability may be lost with the experience of frustration or in response to parental attitudes:

> A three-year-old child was waiting for his mother to collect him from a hospital waiting room. While the child was waiting, he picked up a cockroach from the floor and began talking to it and stroking it as if it were a person. Then his mother hurried in and grabbed the little boy by the hand; he dropped the cockroach on the floor and stomped on it. [Miller, 1986].

Dehumanization, on the other hand, relieves painful internal tension by making projection easy, as it removes the human element from people. A decrease in a person's perception of others' human qualities also reflects a decrease in a person's sense of his or her own humanity. From clinical observation of bullying in school, the ability to dehumanize first appears in children from about the age of six or seven. In adults, it has its own language: for example, Jews are "kikes"; black people are "niggers"; and whites are "honkies." In wars, this language is common; to the British in the Falklands War, the Argentinians became "Argies"; to Americans in the Vietnam War, the Vietnamese were "gooks" (Gault, 1971). In street gangs, outsiders are given special names, and, especially under conditions of economic and emotional deprivation, these groups may be exploited for material or instinctual satisfaction. So Latino street groups in Chicago hunt the "White Unknowns," or vice versa. In correctional centers, the weak and young are abused as if they were objects rather than people.

It is clear from such sexual abuse as gang rape that the dehumanization of others also involves the self, and the two aspects are mutually reinforcing. A boy who took part in a gang rape explained, "I don't know what happened; I became an animal"; a boy who was raped in prison said, "They didn't care; all they wanted was my ass. I was a thing."

Dehumanization may vary in intensity; sometimes individuals are perceived as subhuman, and sometimes they become inanimate, despicable objects (Barnard, Ottenberg, and Redl, 1965).Dehumanization includes a number of psychological defense mechanisms: denial, repression, and depersonalization. Pathological dehumanization is responsible for people's ability to tolerate mass homicide; it was clearly a factor in the Holocaust. The coldness of pathological dehumanization is apparent in severely disturbed prepubertal children and in postpubertal teenagers, especially when they engage in homicidal or sexually aggressive behavior (Szymuiska and Lesniak, 1972).

Dehumanization may be intermittent, and some types of behavior demonstrate the rapidity with which conscienceless pathological behavior can appear. Among the violent gangs of Chicago, it is not uncommon for one group member to cross another's turf and be caught. He may be murdered in an apparently inconsequential way. However, an alien gang member may take his girl friend home in absolute safety. It is only after he leaves her house that he may be "wasted."

Sometimes intermittent dehumanization is a function of stress; one boy became homicidal only when sexually stimulated:

One seventeen-year-old said, "Sometimes I see a lady in the super-market and she turns me on. Then I follow her home and try to get into her apartment if she is alone. I like to have her give me a blow job, and I like to bite her tits. If she refuses, I hit her, and if she yells, I will kill her."

Projective identification, in which an unacceptable part of the self is split off and projected onto others who, because they are the recipients of the projection, become nonhuman, requires partial dehumanization. Projective identification is also an important determinant of prejudice. For example, adolescents in normative conflict about their own sexual identity may use derogatory words to describe others, such as "fag" or "faggot" for boys whom they do not like or with whom they are angry. A late-maturing boy may, however, be constantly taunted as a "fag" because his lack of masculine qualities poses a threat to postpubertal youths, particularly in the intimacy of locker rooms. This is a transient phenomenon for these youngsters, but adults in conflict about their own sexuality may even see homosexuals more definitively as the cause of their country's decline in status and influence. That is, they dehumanize those who are homosexual and wish to have them isolated or eliminated. Such individuals are apparently defending against intolerable anxiety by projecting an unacceptable part of themselves onto dehumanized others and then demanding their elimination.

Partial dehumanization is common. It is adaptive for society at large and is part of all complex social systems. In hospital emergency rooms, medical staff often do not give prime attention to a patient's pain if analgesics make diagnosis impossible; thus the staff cannot allow themselves to be too empathic with the patient. In prison systems, guards may work in conditions that ignore both their own and the inmates' humanity; they are dehumanized by the state. In school systems, teachers and pupils may be transferred from school to school in pursuit of goals that ignore the here-and-now experience of the children and staff. The boundary between adaptive dehumanization and pathological dehumanization is thus blurred. When predatory violence toward others is present in peacetime, dehumanization is pathological. The same attitude in wartime is considered adaptive. It is often used as an excuse to deny situations that would otherwise be intolerable; that is, it allows empathy to be sidestepped. Thus poverty in the abstract can be discussed without considering what it must be like not to have adequate food and shelter. Partial and intermittent dehumanization may therefore temporarily remove the humanity from groups and individuals so that they need to be considered only in the abstract.

The more that persons are dehumanized as children, the more likely they will, as children, teenagers, and adults, dehumanize others. Compared with nonabused siblings, abused children are more likely to have been separated from their mothers in the first 48 hours after birth, and they are often products of abnormal pregnancy, labor, or delivery (Lynch, 1975). These people also may become child abusers themselves, often because they really wish their infants and children to look after them. According to Bowlby (1984), most, perhaps all, parents who expect their children to look after them, experienced very inadequate parenting themselves. When young people become the victims of dehumanized inmate violence, as they are in many correctional centers, they are likely to be more violent when they leave than when they were admitted.

The Probability of Dangerousness

The most dangerous young people are those who behave with affective violence under stress, who find the violence acceptable or enjoy it, who dehumanize others and in whom the stress is inevitable; adolescent sexual frustration, for example. Equally potentially dangerous are the nonrelating, cold people to whom others are things to be eliminated. These people have a high risk of becoming dangerously violent. Some, however, require permission from significant others or groups to behave violently. Young people who kill as part of gang activity are less dangerous than are those who do not require support from others; they are less dangerous because, if they can form relationships, they have dehumanized others as part of the gang experience. The risk of violence is thus low (Miller, 1984). There are some people who, although they behave antisocially and may be judged delinquent, are not capable of violence. These are persons who have had a good nurturing experience and who find it immensely difficult to dehumanize. They may need months of attempted reinforcement of this capacity, and even then they are unable to behave in a dehumanizing way.

The delinquent population contains a disproportionately high number of adolescents who suffer from organic brain syndromes, especially epilepsy, some mood disorders, and learning disabilities. The severity of the offense does not necessarily indicate the presence or absence of such brain pathology.

Recommendations should specify both the generalized nonspecific needs of the individual delinquent and specific, individualized services that should be offered (Knesper and Miller, 1976). A specific treatment plan should clearly state the goals of treatment, but there is as yet no adequate technique of assessing the length of time before any improvement is consolidated. The issue is not only whether a youngster becomes productive and social, but what his ability will be to handle stress in the community at large without the likelihood of the recurrence of delinquent behavior. The amount of support from the environment is a crucial issue in the maintenance of productive social behavior.

Formal diagnostic assessment, if this is indicated, can occur in the community or in a special treatment center. A model used in other countries is of a diagnostic remand center in which, prior to a formal arraignment, young people are sent for a thorough diagnostic assessment. Sophisticated recommendations about potential disposition can then be made to the court.

If psychiatrists are making recommendations that are less than optimal on the basis of what is available, this oversight should be made clear; otherwise the courts have no way of knowing what might be inadequate in the recommendation. If the modification of recommendations is made by the courts on a similar basis at the expense of an optimal recommendation, it is not only ethically questionable but is probably doomed to fail. This is possibly partly responsible for the courts being overwhelmed.

Conclusion

In addition to considering the implications of behavior, one way of reducing the load on the juvenile court system is to make an adequate clarification of the biological, psychological, and social etiology of delinquent behavior.

The issue of the success or failure of previous interventions is highly relevant. Distrust is often exacerbated when there have multiple interviewers. When interviews take place without any prospect of helpful intervention, the adult world is seen as unworthy of trust. Diagnostic assessment without helpful interventions is likely to reinforce pathology.

The assessment of dangerousness is crucial. It is almost certain that there are no absolute criteria, but a reasonably accurate prediction can be made as to the likelihood of violent, homicidal, or antisocial behavior (Miller and Looney, 1974).

The treatment needs of disturbed antisocial adolescents can initially be assessed by attorneys, social workers, and youth workers who have been trained in specific diagnostic skills. These skills should go beyond being able to make a *DSM IV* diagnosis. Intake interviews should take note of at least the following issues:

1) How dangerous is the behavior of the youngster, and how likely is it to be repeated?
2) Is the youngster able to appreciate the effects of his or her behavior on others? How gratifying is the behavior? How acceptable is violence? Is there evidence of remorse? How acceptable are weapons; how accessible are they?
3) Is the boy or girl able to form meaningful emotional relationships with others? Is he or she capable of empathy?
4) Is the person willing to attack others? If so, whom? Who is dehumanized, how easily, and under what circumstances? What is the acceptability of antisocial behavior?
5) What is the social pathology to which the youngster is exposed in school and community, in relationships with peers and adults?
6) Is there any evidence of biological pathology, that is, evidence of disorders of attention; learning difficulties including an inability for abstract thought with only concrete thinking; mood disorder, including rage attacks?

7) Is the delinquent dependent on the "high" of drugs, or on the drug itself? Does the he or she deal drugs? How does the youngster afford to buy drugs?

8) What is the significant family structure: presence or absence of father; extended family; family networks of friends? Is there a history of child abuse—physical, sexual, or verbal?

The preliminary assessment should include recommendations for further diagnostic interventions. An adequate preliminary diagnosis, such as is being described, can seldom be made in one 45-minute interview.

When placement is made, staff should, minimally, clarify the explicit philosophy of the approach to the delinquent. The most potent social system reinforcements of disturbance appear either as a result of adult conflicts or as implicit permission for a whole series of behaviors that overtly are negated (Stanton and Schwartz, 1954).

The assessment of the likelihood of dangerous behavior should imply the creation of a special, secure facility for the dangerously disturbed. In this facility staff would be taught diagnostic and vocational skills as well as group counseling techniques. The recognition of the importance of group process and network relationships among both staff and inmates, as well as one-to-one relationship needs to be recognized. Institutional expectations would meet developmental needs. For example, long periods of inactivity and isolation from others are developmentally inappropriate. It is difficult to see the developmental value of chemical and physical restraint or of punitive behavioral techniques. It is not unusual to hear of adolescents forced to stand, facing a wall, for days at a time. Prolonged isolation from others in "quiet" or seclusion rooms seems of little value (Soloff, 1985).

There is a tolerable level of staff tension that can be borne without the inmate population's becoming disturbed. If the tension becomes too great, though, then disturbance takes place. Many attempts at personality development collapse because of tension in the social system in which they take place. If staff development representing a change of approach is to occur, it should be done primarily with those members of the social system who are the most powerful (Miller, 1966b).

Adequate rehabilitation depends on the capacity of the delinquent to form a trusting relationship with authority adults in a setting which can be maximally secure as well as open. Those who are absolutely unable to form such relationships are almost certainly, in the present state of our knowledge, not able to be helped. Many whose capacity to form such relations can, however, with appropriate rehabilitation, be helped.

Interviewing an antisocial youngster requires techniques different from those usually used with others. A structured interview does not tell the interviewer very much about the boy or girl's ability to form relationships and be honest—both crucial diagnostic issues. If adequate preliminary and tentative diagnoses as to etiology and personality style are made, it should be possible to clarify alternatives to the juvenile court. The solution of using adult courts and adult prisons should be abandoned in favor of adequate rehabilitation for severely disturbed and violent adolescents.

REFERENCES

Altschuler, D. & Armstrong, T. (1984), Intervening with the serious juvenile offenders. In: *Violent Juvenile Offenders*, ed. R. Mathias, P. Demuro & R. Allison. San Francisco: National Council on Crime and Delinquency.

American Psychiatric Association (1994), *Diagnostic and Statistical Manual of Mental Disorders*, 4th ed, Washington, DC: American Psychiatric Press.

Barnard, A., Ottenberg, P. & Redl, F. (1965), *Dehumanization*. New York: Science & Behavior Books.

Bartholomew, A. A., Brian L. A. & Douglas, A. S. (1967), A medico-psychiatric diagnostic review of remanded male minor offenders, *Med. J. Australia*, 11:267–269.

Bowlby, J. (1984), *Caring for the Young*: ed. R. S. Cohen, B. J. Cohler & S. H. Weissman. New York: Guilford Press, pp. 269–284.

Brickman, A. S., McManus, M., Carpentine, L. & Alessi, N. (1984), Neuropsychological assessment of severely disturbed adolescents. *J. Amer. Acad. Child Psych.*, 23:453–458.

Brooks, A. (1974), *Law, Psychiatry and Mental Health System*. Boston: Little Brown.

Federal Bureau of Investigation (1988), *Uniform Crime Reports for the United States*.

———— (1993), *Uniform Crime Reports for the United States*.

Feld, B. (1995), Youth and public policy: A case study of juvenile justice. *Minn. Law Review*, 79 ML 965 May.

Gault, W. B. (1971), Some remarks on slaughter. *Amer. J. Psychiat.*, 128:82–86.

Gendreau, P. & Ross, R. (1987), Revivication of rehabilitation, evidence from the 1980's. *Justice Quart.* 4:349–407.

Gray, B. H. & McNerney, W. F. (1986), For profit enterprise in health care, *New Eng. J. Med.*, 314:1523–1548.

Greenwood, P., Abrahams, A. & Zimmerling, F. (1984), Factors affecting sentence severity for young adult offenders, Youth Crime and Juvenile Justice in California, 12–14.

Harlanhagen, B. (1994), Office of juvenile justice and delinquency prevention fact sheet #19, *Juveniles and Violence: Juvenile Offending and Victimization*, November.

Hoffman, A. & Faust, D. (1977), Least restrictive treatment of the mentally ill: A doctrine in search of its senses. *San Diego Law Rev.*, 14:1113–1115.

Institute of Medicine (1989), *Research on Children and Adolescents with Mental, Behavior and Developmental Disorders*. Washington, DC: National Academic Press.

Jewelka, R., Trupin, E. & Chiles, J. A. (1989), The mentally ill in prisons: A review. *Hosp. Comm. Psychiat.* 40:481–491.

Jones, M. A. & Krisberg, B. (1994), Images and reality. juvenile crime, youth violence and public policy. San Francisco: National Council on Crime and Delinquency.

Juvenile Court Statistics (1991), Washington, DC: Office of Justice and Delinquency Prevention. U.S. Dept. of Justice.

Knesper, D. & Miller, D. (1976), Treatment plans for mental health care., *Amer. J. Psychiat.*, 142:1161–1167.

Knitzer, J. (1982), *Unclaimed Children*. Washington, DC: Children's Defense Fund.

Krisberg, B., Litsky, P. & Schwartz, I. (1984), Youth in confinement: justice by geography. *J. Res. Crime & Delinq.*, 21:153–181.

——— Schwartz, I., Litsky, P. & Austin, J. (1986), The watershed of juvenile justice reform. *Crime and Delinq.*, 32:5–38.

Lewis, D. O., Moy, E. & Jackson, J. D. (1985), Biopsychosocial characteristics of children who later murder: A prospective study. *Amer. J. Psychiat.*, 142:1161–1167.

——— Yeager, C. A., Loverly, R., Stein, A. & Cobham-Portorreal, C. S. (1994), A clinical follow-up of delinquent males: Ignored vulnerabilities, unmet needs and the perpetuation of violence. *J. Amer. Acad. Child & Adoles. Psychiat.*, 33:518–528.

Lynch, M. (1975), Infant health and child abuse. Lancet, 2:317–319.

Meyers, W. C., Scott, K., Burgess, A. W. & Burgess, A. G. (1995), Biopsychosocial factors: Crime characteristics and classification of 25 homicidal youths. *J. Amer. Acad. Child & Adoles. Psychiat.,* 36.

Miller, D. (1965), *The Psychosocial Treatment of Delinquent Youth.* Bloomington: Indiana University Press.

———— (1966a), A model of an institution for treatment of delinquents, *Changing Concepts of Crime and its Treatment,* ed. H. Klare. Oxford, England: Pergamon Press.

———— (1966b), Staff training in the penal system: The use of small groups. *Human Rel.,* 14:151–164.

———— (1970), *Parental Responsibility for Adolescent Maturity.* London: Churchill.

———— (1971), *Murrosika.* Helsinki, Fin.: Weilin & Goos.

———— (1984), *The Age Between.* Northvale, NJ: Aronson.

———— (1986), *Attack on the Self.* Northvale, NJ: Aronson.

———— & Looney, J. (1974), The prediction of adolescent homicide: episodic dyscontrol and dehumanization. *Amer. J. Psychoanal.,* 4:187–198.

———— & ———— (1976), Determinants of homicide in adolescents. *Adoles. Psychiat.,* 4:231–254.

Monahan, J. (1996), Violence prediction: The past twenty and the next twenty years. *Crim. Just. Behav.,* 23:107–120.

Murphy, D. (1986), The prevalence of handicapping conditions among juvenile delinquents. *Remed. Spec. Ed.* 7:7–17.

National Center for Disease Control and Prevention (1994), quoted in *New York Times,* Oct. 14, p. A10.

Palmer, T. (1971), California's community treatment program for delinquent adolescents. *J. Res. Crime & Deling.,* 8:74–92.

Rosenfeld, A., Pilowsky, D. J., Fine, P., Thorpe, M., Fein, E., Simms, M. D., Halfon, M., Irwin, M., Alfaro, J. & Saletsky, R. (1977), Foster care, an update. *J. Amer. Acad. Child & Adol. Psychiat.,* 36:448–457.

Snyder, H. N. (1994), *Juvenile Arrests.* Office of Juvenile Justice and Delinquency Prevention, Fact Sheet #3, May.

Soloff, P. H. (1985), Seclusion and restraint in 1985: A review and update. *Hosp. Comm. Psychiat.,* 36:652–657.

Stanton, A. H. & Schwartz, J. S. (1954), *The Mental Hospital.* New York: Basic Books.

Steadman, H., Monahan, J., Appelbaum, P., Grisso, T., Mulvey, E., Rotl, L., Robbins, P. & Klassen, D. (1994), Designing a new generation of risk research. In: Violence and Mental Disorder, ed. J. Monahan, & H. Steadman. Chicago, IL: University of Chicago Press, pp. 297–318.

Szymuiska, L. & Lesniak, R. (1972), Juvenile homicide and sexual behavior. *Psychologica Polska,* 62:143–149.

Vaillant, G. (1993), *Wisdom of the Ego.* Cambridge, MA: Harvard University Press.

Winnicott, D. W. (1965), *Maturational Processes and the Facilitating Environment.* New York: International Universities Press.

Yesavage, J. A. (1983), Bipolar illness: Correlates of dangerous inpatient behavior. *Brit. J. Psychiat.,* 142:554–557.

7   DORA AS AN ADOLESCENT: SADISTIC AND SADOMASOCHISTIC FANTASIES

JULES GLENN

Although Freud did not appreciate its significance, it is now generally accepted that Dora, whom Freud (1905a) attempted to analyze from October through December, 1900, was an adolescent (Erikson, 1961; Glenn, 1980). Freud at that time (almost a hundred years ago) was constructing his revolutionary theories step by step, and could not be expected to have full knowledge of all the stages of psychological development at once. Naturally, after his death, analysts continue to amplify and correct his findings.

Freud focused on Dora's hysterical symptoms and on the role of dreams in understanding her dynamics and her pathology. Her sadism and masochism have not been sufficiently discussed in the analytic literature even though Freud (1908) and others have observed that such fantasies occur in adolescents as well as hysterics (Blos, 1962; Prall, 1990; Sarnoff, 1988).

In this essay I attempt to demonstrate the importance of sadomasochism in Dora's personality and in the understanding of aspects of adolescence as well. To do this I will 1) demonstrate that Dora was indeed an adolescent, not the adult woman Freud seemed to think she was; 2) define and establish the basis on which one can diagnose sadism and masochism; 3) use Freud's clinical data to demonstrate Dora's sadomasochism; 4) discuss the psychology of adolescence, including what has been called "adolescent rebellion," to highlight the significance of sadomasochism in its formation; and 5) discuss some of Freud's emotional interactions with Dora during the analysis.

Although I will stress Dora's sadomasochism, I recognize that this emphasis only affords limited insight into Dora's personality and the dreams we shall discuss. Freud discussed many additional aspects that

I shall omit here since I have dealt with these and other issues in previous articles (Glenn, 1980, 1986, 1989, 1993).

Dora as an Adolescent

Although Freud (1905b) wrote about puberty, he did not consider fully the complicated psychological reactions to the physiological changes of puberty that occur at adolescence. Even though, as we shall see, adolescence encompasses much more, I shall define adolescence in girls as the period from the onset of menarche to the consolidation of the personality. It includes both physiological and psychological changes at the time. The term *puberty* refers to the bodily changes. (As I am using these terms, prepuberty refers to the bodily changes that occur in the few years prior to puberty, from the time hormone production increases until menarche. Preadolescence refers to the psychological changes during prepuberty.)

The hormonal and bodily changes of puberty have far-reaching consequences. A profound increase in both sexual and aggressive drives arouses sexual feelings, thoughts and activities which teenagers find difficult to deal with. They try to find adaptive ways of satisfying their urges, but often fail to do so. The recent momentous rise in teenage pregnancy and the soaring high school crime problem reflects in part the increase in sexual and aggressive drives and the insufficient channelization that our society provides. Oedipal wishes, which have been kept under control during latency, burst forth and require increased defensive activity if they are to be used adaptively. Both heterosexual and homosexual urges are aroused.

The defenses used include displacement, regression, and intellectualization. Teenagers deal with the threat of incestuous and murderous feelings toward their parents by gratifying themselves through masturbation, using fantasied nonincestuous objects, and by finding sexual partners outside the family. They may employ sublimation to find gratification through mentors or peer friends rather than overt sexual partners. As they direct drives toward their selves in a regressive way, they become narcissistic and self preoccupied. As they discover newly formed cognitive capacities they find pleasure and protection in thinking.

Adolescence, as Piaget and Inhelder (1969) have demonstrated, brings with it cognitive advance. Teenagers achieve "formal operations," that is, they become capable of abstract thinking. They can become wonderful observers and clear but often impractical thinkers. Their lack of experience may lead them to logical but realistically incorrect conclusions, but their new ideals may be admirable and breath-taking. Defensive ego regression may compromise their intellectual capacity.

Teenagers, having minds of their own, also seek autonomy. They try to become independent of those about them while craving care and dependence. Their push toward emancipation often appears as adolescent rebellion which has other determinants as well. We shall discuss this later when we tackle the sadomasochistic element in such rebellion.

Freud's description of Dora highlighted many of the characteristics of adolescents. She was the right age, almost 18, when she started her three-month-long analysis. Teenagers in Dora's day reached menarche later than in current European society. Tanner (1962) states that in 1895 the average German teenager had her first period at 16 1/4. We may assume the same was true of Austrian girls.

Dora struggled with strong but repressed drives and a marked bisexuality. She was attached to Herr K, who courted her, and to his wife, Frau K, whom she adored, as well as to the governess with whom she discussed intimate matters. Her oedipal wishes, which bore strong pre-oedipal resonances, were characterized by her love, admiration and sympathy for her father along with antagonism for her mother who had what Freud called a housewife's psychosis; Dora's mother was extremely neat and demanded excessive cleanliness.

The family setting made it impossible to find a satisfactory resolution for her oedipal longings. Even at 13 she was encouraged to use a married man, the husband of her father's mistress, as a father surrogate. Her sharp adolescent eyes enabled her to perceive with accuracy and acuity her father's affair with Frau K. Her teenage cognitive capacity enabled her to reach correct conclusions about their involvement despite their denial. She recognized that she was caught in a family conspiracy in which she was given to Herr K as her father and Frau K engaged in their romance.

As an intelligent and perceptive teenager she was interested in art and women's studies, but Victorian society gave her insufficient opportunity to sublimate to her full capacity; her brother could acquire a superb education, but as a female adolescent she could not. She longed to be independent and go it alone, but she could not survive without her parents.

Masochism and Sadism. Definitions and Descriptions

Having established that Dora was indeed an adolescent struggling with typical problems as well as the particular difficulties she encountered, I will now demonstrate her masochism and sadism as well. But first I will have to define the terms. Moore and Fine (1990) state that masochism is a "propensity to seek physical or mental suffering in order to achieve sexual arousal and gratification" (p. 116). In sadism, an individual finds sexual pleasure from inflicting pain and humiliation on others. These conditions always appear together; hence the label "sadomasochism." Sadism and masochism need not appear as overt perversions. Often they are unconscious and embedded in symptoms or behavior. The symptoms may cause pain to the masochist and to those about him or her who are hurt. In a typical masochistic enactment the person may provoke others until they attack the instigator. The very same behavior may express sadism as it hurts the object of the provocative, aggressive behavior.

Freud (1924) delineated three types of masochism which he said overlap: sexual masochism, moral masochism and feminine masochism. Many analysts have suggested that a conscious or unconscious sexual element has to be present for a phenomenon to be considered masochism or sadism (Arlow, in Panel, 1956; Coen, 1988; Glenn, 1989; Glenn and Bernstein, 1995; Blum, 1991). Otherwise one could not differentiate masochism from guilt-derived self attack, adaptive sacrifice, or tolerating child bearing pain to achieve the gratifications of motherhood. As Blum (1991) has put it: "Without sexual pleasure in suffering, masochism can hardly be distinguished from passive aggression, self-abasement, and self-defeat" (p. 433). Nor could we tell sadism from hostile aggression or angry assertiveness.

Others disagree. Maleson (1984) insists that there are many forms of self defeating behavior designated as masochism, and that conscious or unconscious sexual pleasure may or may not be present. I reject his definition as too broad, and instead offer the following more specific definition:

Masochism involves a sexual fantasy in which the subject consciously or unconsciously imagines himself harmed or humiliated; the subject finds gratification in pain, painful affect, or suffering. Sadism involves a sexual fantasy in which the subject consciously or unconsciously harms or humiliates others.

Masochistic and sadistic fantasies result from a compromise forma-tion that contains ego and superego elements as well as aggressive and libidinal drive contributants. For any individual, masochism derives from many experiences in the preoedipal and oedipal periods that are transformed and consolidated during the oedipal stage. Different peo-ple may construct masochistic or sadistic fantasies from different expe-riences. Experiences which promote erotization as a defense may contribute to sadomasochism.

Dora's Symptoms and Behavior

In order to show that Dora harbored masochistic and sadistic fan-tasies, I will examine her symptoms and behavior as well as the two dreams that Freud analyzed.

There is nothing to indicate that Dora engaged in overt sexually per-verse behavior. However, a number of her symptoms caused Dora pain and suffering, and they also distressed her parents. Dora suffered from hysteria. Among her conversion symptoms were periodic aphonia, a chronic but intermittent cough, facial pain, and uncomfortable feelings of pressure. She placed herself in situations in which she could be hurt and, in the analysis, provoked and teased Freud, for instance, by play-ing secrets.

Freud uncovered a number of determinants for her disorder, but did not pay particular attention to the masochistic and sadistic aspects. Certainly he did not label her troubles as such. Dora's symptoms and behavior strongly suggest the importance of sadomasochism; the pres-ence of sexuality in her fantasies as revealed in her dreams will signifi-cantly support that construction.

The First Dream: Masochistic Fantasies

Freud described and analyzed two of Dora's dreams with clarity. He provided enough raw clinical data to allow the reader to evaluate, criti-cize, and amplify his understanding of the case. These two dreams were the last two dreams of the analysis. After the second dream she quit. In the analysis of the first of the two dreams Freud did not present the ses-sions in chronological order. Rather, he presented the dream, some associations she provided after she told Freud the manifest content, and the interpretations he made. He then revealed the analytic events that led up to the dream. It is necessary to rearrange the material and place the events of the session in sequence.

Some days or perhaps weeks before Dora reported the first dream she "raised the question of why it was precisely she who had fallen ill. . . . [B]efore [Freud] could answer [she] had put the blame on her father" (p. 75). She recalled information she had acquired years before, after her father had visited Freud who diagnosed his syphilis. Dora had overheard the diagnosis, and an aunt who said that her father had the condition prior to his marriage. Dora had imagined that something improper that she did not fully understand had occurred. She knew that her father "had fallen ill through leading a loose life" (p. 75), and believed he had passed his ill health to her, Dora, through heredity.

For some days thereafter, Dora "identified herself with her mother by means of slight symptoms and peculiarities of manner" (p. 75). Dora felt that her father had given her mother a venereal disease which led to her mother's abdominal pains and discharge. Similarly, Dora too had a catarrh and, Freud knew, had previously experienced abdominal pain.

Freud was delighted. He was convinced that there was an excellent chance that material was emerging that would throw light on "an obscure point in Dora's childhood" (p. 64). He stated that Dora and he were "engaged upon a line of inquiry which led straight toward an admission that she had masturbated in childhood" (p. 75). He told Dora that "leukorrhea in young girls pointed primarily to masturbation . . . [and] added that Dora was now on the way to finding an answer to her own question of why it was precisely she who had fallen ill—by confessing that she had masturbated, probably in childhood. Dora denied flatly that she could remember any such thing" (p. 76).

In a session at that point Dora described the first dream. She started the session by playing secrets with Freud. As he entered the waiting room "she hurriedly hid a letter she was reading" (p. 78). When Freud asked her whom it was from, she first refused to say and then told him it was a letter from her grandmother begging her to write more often.

"Recognizing" that Dora was "on the point of allowing her secret to be torn from her by [her] doctor" (p. 78), namely, Freud, he explained to his patient that she feared that each new doctor might guess that she masturbated but was disdainful that they did not.

During the session Dora played with a reticule she wore at her waist. As "she lay on the sofa and talked, she kept playing with it—opening it, putting a finger into it, shutting it again, and so on" (p. 76). Freud concluded that this was a symptomatic act that was easy to interpret. The reticule represented her genitals. By playing with it Dora was announcing, confessing, her masturbation.

Later in the same session Dora reported the recurrent dream which she first dreamed several years previously when she and her family stayed at the K's home at L.:

"A house was on fire. My father was standing beside my bed and woke me up. I dressed myself quickly. Mother wanted to stop and save her jewel-case; but Father said: "I refuse to let myself and my two children be burnt for the sake of your jewel-case." We hurried downstairs, and as soon as I was outside I woke up" (p. 64).

Following the revelation of the manifest dream, Dora's associations pointed to the complicated relationships she had with Freud and with Herr K. Dora had first had this dream two years previously. Dora had than feared that Herr K was trying to seduce her while they were staying at the lake at L.; Herr K had taken the key to her room and entered her room. In the original dream Dora resolved to leave the house and prevent a second entry. Whereas the dream had originally signified her decision to get away from Herr K, now it expressed her wish to leave Freud whom she considered dangerous.

The events that Freud described as occurring in the sessions before Dora told the dream provided a background as well as associations connected with the dream. We can conclude that the dream is about masturbation as well as about her relationship to Herr K. The jewel case of the dream represented the reticule and in turn her genitals. Dora had to be rescued not only from Herr K and Freud but also from her masturbatory wishes and fantasies. Further—and this is the point I am emphasizing—her masturbation fantasy involved pain. It included the following:

I was given a venereal disease by my father who had given such a disorder to my mother. The venereal disease causes pain. My father thus causes me pain. I am like my mother.

The sexual fantasy is thus a masochistic one.

As the session went on, Dora provided further associations and thus elaborated on the dream's meanings. I am not suggesting that the masochism is the only significance of the dream. Nor am I suggesting that Freud should have interpreted it at that time. He had already gone much too far in his interpretations to the point of chasing Dora away.

Dora's Second Dream: Her Sadistic
as well as Masochistic Fantasies

A few weeks later Dora reported what Freud called the second dream, the last one of the analysis. It too contains self-attacking thoughts in a sexual context. In addition, it contains thoughts attacking Freud, her father, her mother, and Herr K, also in a sexual context. Hostile aggressive, indeed sadistic, feelings and ideation are more prominent in the second dream. To a great extent attacks on the self, which dominate the first dream, are turned outward.

The Dream:

I was walking about in a town which I did not know. . . . Then I came into a house where I lived, went to my room and found a let-ter from mother lying there. She wrote saying that as I had left home without my parents' knowledge she had not wished to write me to say Father was ill. "Now he is dead and if you like you can come." I then went to the station [Banhof] and asked about a hun-dred times: "Where is the station?" I always got the same answer: "Five minutes." I then saw a thick wood before me which I went into, and there asked a man whom I met. He said to me: "Two and a half hours more." He offered to accompany me. But I refused and went alone. I saw the station in front of me and could not reach it. . . . I had the usual feeling of anxiety that one has in dreams when one cannot move forward. Then I was home. . . . I walked into a porter's lodge, and inquired for our flat. The maid-servant opened the door to me and replied that Mother and the oth-ers were already at the cemetery [Friedhof] [p. 94].

Freud learned during the analysis of this dream that Dora planned to leave the analysis after two additional sessions; the two and one-half hours of the dream referred to this plan. It also referred to specific events that happened at the lake at L. two years before, shortly before Herr K tried to enter Dora's room at L. (See discussion of the first dream above.) During an excursion to the lake that Herr K and Dora took together, Herr K started to propose to Dora. He began by saying, "I get nothing from my wife." This infuriated Dora because she knew he had used the very same words he used when he tried to seduce her governess. Irate, she slapped Herr K and left him. She then *asked a man* she met how long the walk back to Herr K's house where she and her family were staying was. He told her it took *two and a half hours*. This was much too long for Dora. She therefore took the ferry on which Herr K too was traveling home. It was after that trip that Herr K obtained the key to Dora's room.

By leaving the analysis she was leaving a dangerous situation akin to Herr K's house. As she had slapped Herr K she was figuratively slapping Freud. She was taking revenge on Freud for Herr K's misdeeds. The proposal at the lake was not Herr K's only attempt at seduction. You will recall that when she was 13 Herr K had forced himself on Dora.

Dora was firing in many directions. She was hurting her father who wanted her to go to Freud who he hoped would bring her to her senses. He wanted Freud to get Dora to cease pressing him to discontinue his affair with Frau K. Dora was planning to hurt Freud, who wanted the treatment to continue for scientific reasons, that is, for his own benefit. He also had acted aggressively toward Dora, pouncing on her with premature and sexual interpretations, and thus fortifying her transference from the sexually provocative Herr K (Glenn, 1980). She was not going to work with Freud or remain friends with Herr K. She would go it *alone* as she did in the manifest content of the dream. The woods in the dream referred to the countryside at the lake.

There was more to the second dream. Freud understood that there was a sexual significance to the dream, and we will now dwell on that to indicate the sexual component of Dora's masochistic and sadistic fantasies.

Freud wrote: "[T]here lay concealed behind the first situation in the dream a phantasy of defloration, the phantasy of a man seeking to force an entrance into the female genitals" (p. 100). He postulated that the imagery of her dream was that of the female genitals—"a symbolic geography of sex" (p. 99). Although the evidence appeared slim, Freud developed a conviction about the sexual allusion in the manifest dream. A suspicion "became a certainty," he said (p. 99); surprisingly perhaps, Dora confirmed Freud's interpretation at least in part.

Daringly applying symbolic interpretation in a way he said one should not (Freud, 1900), Freud asserted that the Bahnhof [railway court], the Friedhof [cemetery, peace court] and Vorhof [fore-court] of the manifest dream represented the entrance to the female genitals. The thick woods symbolized the pubic hair, and the presence of the labia minora was indicated by an association to nymphs Dora had seen in a picture of a landscape. He thought Dora had learned of the structure of the female genitals from books and to his delight Dora appeared to confirm this by recalling, after his interpretations, another part of the dream: She went calmly to her room, and began reading a big book that lay on her writing-table (p. 100).

In further associations, Dora remembered reading an encyclopedia not to learn about sex, but to find out about appendicitis when a boy cousin became afflicted with that illness. Neither Freud nor Dora mentioned it at this point, but Dora's father had previously told Freud that "he had heard from Frau K that Dora had read Mantegazza's *Physiology of Love* and books of that sort. . . . It is most likely, he had added, that she had been overexcited by such reading and merely 'fancied' the whole scene she had described" as having occurred at the lake (p. 26).

We are accumulating a reasonable amount of evidence that the second dream referred to a sexual fantasy. In the sexual fantasy Dora is hurt and others are hurt too. I will add to the evidence by discussing Dora's associations and Freud's remarks about her being hurt and hurting others; hurting and being hurt appear in the manifest dream as well. Freud did not report the sessions in which the dream was described and discussed fully and in sequence. He said that "[in] consequence of the particular circumstances in which the analysis was broken off—circumstances connected with the content of the dream—the whole of it was not cleared up. And for that reason, too, I am not equally certain at every point of the order in which my conclusions were reached" (p. 86). Hence we shall have difficulty distinguishing Freud's thoughts from Dora's. We may assume that Freud's difficulty in this regard stemmed from his countertransference, that he was deeply hurt by Dora's ending the analysis. Freud acknowledged his emotional reaction to Dora's behavior when he wrote, "No one who, like me, conjures up the most evil of those half-tamed demons that inhabit the human breast, and seeks to wrestle with them, can expect to come through the struggle unscathed" (p. 100).

We may also assume that Freud's sexual interpretations of the two dreams facilitated Dora's sexualization of her aggressive feelings which she directed toward herself and others. Indeed he made sexual interpretations even before these dreams. Similarly Herr K's attempts at sexual seduction when Dora was 13 and 15, as well as other times also facilitated erotization as a defense. So too did her realizing that her father and Frau K were having an affair. This is consistent with the fact that events in adolescence can contribute to the development of sadism and masochism (Blum, 1978, 1985; Glenn, 1974). Dora, Freud observed, was "deeply injured by Herr K's proposal" at the lake, and developed a "morbid craving for revenge" (p. 87); she slapped Herr K as a result. She later attempted to hurt her father through a *letter* in which she threatened suicide. The manifest dream contained a *letter about her father's death*. This letter also referred to another one about her cousin's appendicitis, which she looked up in the encyclopedia (the book of the manifest dream). The chain of thoughts proceeded to the fact that Dora herself "had an attack of what had been alleged to be appendicitis" (p. 92) after her aunt died. Freud did not think that her abdominal pain and fever at that time had been conversion symptoms. Rather she had a physical disorder and menstrual period pain. However after the supposed appendicitis, she dragged her foot, a hysterical symptom that signified punishment for guilt for reading about sex and childbirth, and also carried a sexual meaning. Dora's appendicitis occurred nine months after the scene at the lake, as if she had become pregnant at the lake. The "appendicitis," had thus enabled the patient to realize a "fantasy of childbirth" (p. 95) after a misstep at the lake. We will add that sex and childbirth were pictured as painful.

Putting all this together, we may construct a sadomasochistic fantasy of Dora. *Herr K hurt me by his proposal and by making me pregnant, thus causing me the pain of childbirth. I will hurt him for these attacks.*

Freud on Masochism in Adolescence

Although Freud did not specifically state that adolescence is a time that masochism flourishes, there is evidence in his clinical material that such fantasies occur in adolescence, and result in hysterical symptoms.

Writing that "hysterical phantasies can be seen to have important connections with the causation of neurotic symptoms," Freud (1908) observed that "the common source and normal prototype of all these creations of phantasy are to be found in . . . the daydreams of youth" (p. 159). He then gave a masochistic fantasy as an example:

> After I had drawn the attention of one of my patients to her phantasies, she told me that on one occasion she had suddenly found herself in tears in the street, and that, rapidly considering what she had actually been crying about, she got hold of a phantasy to the following effect. . . . She had formed a tender attachment to a pianist who was well known in town (though she was not personally acquainted with him); she had a child by him . . . and . . . he had deserted her and her child and left them in poverty [p. 160].

151

Such an unconscious fantasy, Freud continued, "is identical with the phantasy which served [the person] in his sexual satisfaction during the period of masturbation" (p. 161).

The reader will see that Freud's patient's fantasy, which he thought was essentially derived from a masturbation fantasy that had occurred in adolescence, was a masochistic one: the patient imagined she was mistreated by a man and left in misery.

Sadomasochism in Adolescence

The psychoanalytic literature on adolescence says little about teenagers' sadomasochism. Blos (1962) and Prall (1990) mention it, but do not describe it in detail or spell out its dynamics. Sarnoff (1988) goes into more detail in a full chapter on the subject, but his description of the mechanism of formation of masochism does not appear clear to me. Anna Freud (1952), without using the term, indicates its presence.

Spiegel (1978) describes the appearance and dynamics of adolescent masochism in a clinical context. He asserts that "[t]he increased instinctual pressures at adolescence and the relatively greater ego weakness, which tend to sexualize danger situations, account for the affinity of moral masochism in adolescence" (p. 225), a conclusion similar to mine. Defensive repression, regression and erotization facilitate the appearance of masochism when oedipal threats loom.

Despite the paucity of references to teenage sadomasochism, we as therapists and parents have sensed it and suffered from it even as we are puzzled by it. Adolescents attempt to thwart adults for many reasons, including a need to torture them. They are attempting to maintain their autonomy and lash out at anyone they feel is in their way. Indeed their assertive individualism contains an aggressive bite. Their passive-aggressive stance disguises their anger even as it expresses it. Their passive-aggressiveness also provokes others to attack them. Outright adolescent rebellion also serves to maintain autonomy, attack, and provoke. Since teenagers are endowed with a plethora of sexual drives, it is not surprising that they not only struggle against their sexuality; they also use their sexual drives for defensive purposes. I shall emphasize here the defensive nature of the teenager's sadism and masochism in their interactions with their parents.

An adolescents' struggle against their attachment to their parents includes aggressive-hostile and libidinal-affectionate drive components. They fear their sexual love for the parent of the opposite sex and the parent of the same sex. Incestuous positive and negative oedipal urges must be combatted. So too must they avoid their hatred for their parents, especially because, unlike younger children, they are capable of inflicting real harm. Repression alone does not suffice. Teenagers use a number of defenses, which may also be used as adaptive mechanisms: displacement (including turning to mentors for neutralized gratification and inspiration); intellectualization; turning of love or aggression toward themselves (including increased narcissism, and when aggression is sexualized, masochism); reversal (turning from active to passive or passive to active); finding sexual gratification from the self in masturbation; and, what I am underlining, regression.

These mechanisms are used in conjunction with one another. For instance, a male teenager may attempt to avoid incestuous feelings toward his mother by repressing his sexual urges while regressing to an earlier sadomasochistic attachment. He becomes nasty to his mother while provoking her to attack him and thus gratify himself. Her attack will also serve to appease his superego through his getting punished. He will then sexualize his desires to hurt and be hurt, producing a sadomasochistic gratification, the sexual aspect of which he represses.

A similar dynamic configuration may involve a girl's loving attachment to her father or an adolescent's homosexual attachments to his or her parent of the same sex.

Regression to a sadomasochistic stance may also involve reversal. Instead of feeling an attacked victim, the child becomes the active attacker, and makes his parents the victims; the masochist thus becomes a sadist. Or the opposite can occur and the attacker reverses things so that the guilty sadist becomes the masochist.

Parents may unwittingly cooperate with their children in these battling, gratifying, and disturbing interchanges because they too are threatened by sexual and aggressive impulses toward their teenage children. They experience their children's nastiness and striving for independence as an unjustified rebellion. They resent their children's provocations and want to attack back, all the while replacing their repressed incestuous desires toward their children with sadistic or masochistic wishes which may well be unconscious. As is often true of masochists, the children will accentuate their tendencies in that direction when the parent is primarily desirous of a sadomasochistic relationship.

When teenagers enter analysis or therapy, a similar set of dynamics may occur with the therapist. Feeling an incestuous attachment to the doctor who is experienced as a parent, adolescents may defend themselves by developing a sadomasochistic attachment to the adult who treats them. They will rebel, attack, and provoke, tempting the therapist to respond with an authoritarian, attacking stance and a display of his sadism. Or the therapist may find unconscious masochistic gratification rather than a more mature but forbidden sexual gratification.

Freud's Responses to Dora's Sadomasochism

It is not surprising that Freud had emotional reactions to Dora's provocative and aggressive behavior. That the analyst reacts to his patient has long been recognized. Freud (1910) applied the term countertransference to this phenomenon and advocated its control and analysis. Others emphasized the importance of self analysis in dealing with countertransferences and other transferences to the patient. More recently analysts have called the analyst's reactive behavior enactments and have emphasized the importance of understanding the patient through recognizing the enactments and the patient's evocation of them (Jacobs, 1991).

Freud, who was the father of self analysis, may have analyzed his own emotional reactions to Dora privately, but he did not provide evidence that he did. However others have been willing to make up for this omission. In fact I will soon try to show how he reacted to Dora's sadism and masochism.

I return to the "secrets" Dora played with Freud. She hid the letter she had received from her grandmother. Freud did not play it cool and temporize until the game came into the analysis. He jumped in and asked her whom the letter was from; she refused to tell him. A teasing sadomasochistic enactment was in effect. In response to Dora's teasing, Freud thought that Dora "was on the point of allowing her secret to be torn from her by the doctor" (p. 78). If he was right, then Dora was inviting a sadistic response (having someone tear something from her). In any case Freud was responding to her with a sadistic thought.

Another enactment occurred when Dora, who had provoked and hurt Freud by quitting the treatment, returned 15 months later. Freud turned down her request to resume the analysis. From the point of view of defense, Freud was identifying with the aggressor and doing to Dora what she had done to him. From the drive perspective, he was responding to her sadistic quitting, which contained a provocative element, by behaving sadistically. I should add that many readers think Freud acted adaptively and sensibly, recognizing that Dora could not be analyzed.

Freud stirred Dora's masochism in other ways as well. He acted the superior authoritative adult when he didactically asked whether she saw the match-stand on his table and why children were prohibited from playing with matches. This quiz was a put-down that played into Dora's need to be hurt and humiliated. So too was his answer, that Dora was a bed-wetter.

Freud may have been correct, but his interpretation was one of many premature drive-oriented explanations. In 1900 Freud had not yet formulated the principles of psychoanalytic technique. Only later did he recognize that the analyst has to proceed more slowly, that one should generally start from the surface and interpret defenses before drive derivatives. And he did not realize that with Dora, an adolescent, one has to be particularly careful and avoid a seductive stance.

Freud aroused Dora's masochism in five ways: (1) he made interpretations that teenagers even more than adults experience as aggressive and attacking; (2) his interpretations facilitated Dora's use of sexualization as a defense; (3) he sometimes behaved in a demeaning authoritative manner; (4) he stirred sexual feelings to an older father-like man (Freud), which led to a defensive regression from more mature oedipal wishes to sadomasochistic desires; and (5) he acted like a parent of a teenager who, fearing sexual feelings toward his children, engages in fights with them. Parent and teenager can avoid direct mature sexual feelings through sadomasochistic interchanges that simultaneously express their attraction in a disguised way. The fights can become exciting and even fun.

Summary

I have demonstrated that not only was Dora an adolescent; although she was not overtly perverse in her sexual behavior, she was a sadistic and masochistic teenager. Her symptoms contain unconscious sadomasochistic wishes. Her behavior and fantasies confirm her sadomasochism. Freud responded emotionally to her provocative and attacking behavior as would many if not most therapists. Their interaction was similar to many teenager's relation to their parents, with whom sadomasochistic interchange can serve defensive purposes. Adolescents' experiences can contribute to their sadism and masochism.

REFERENCES

Bernstein, I. (1983), Masochistic pathology and feminine development. *J. of the Amer. Psychoanal. Assn.*, 31:467–486.

Blos, P. (1962), *On Adolescence*. New York: Free Press of Glencoe.

Blum, H. P. (1978), Psychoanalytic study of an unusual perversion. *J. of the Amer. Psychoanal. Assn.* 26:785–792.

——— (1985), Superego formation, adolescent transformation, and adult neurosis. *J. of the Amer. Psychoanal. Assn.* 33:887–909.

——— (1991), Sadomasochism in the psychoanalytic process, within and beyond the pleasure principle. *J. of the Amer. Psychoanal. Assn.* 39:431–450.

Coen, S. J. (1988), Sadomasochistic excitement: In: *Masochism*, ed. R. A. Glick & D. I. Meyers. Hillsdale, NJ: The Analytic Press. pp. 43–59.

Erikson, E. H. (1961), Psychological reality and historical actuality. In: *Insight and Responsibility*. New York: Norton, 1964, pp. 159–215.

Freud, A. (1952), Adolescence. *The Psychoanalytic Study of the Child*, 13:155–178. New York: International Universities Press.

Freud, S. (1900), The interpretation of dreams. *Standard Edition*, 4–5. London: Hogarth Press, 1953.

——— (1905a), Fragment of an analysis of a case of hysteria. *Standard Edition*, 7:3–122, London: Hogarth Press, 1953.

——— (1905b), Three contributions to the theory of sexuality. *Standard Edition*, 7:133–243, London: Hogarth Press, 1953.

——— (1908), Hysterical phantasies and their relation to bisexuality. *Standard Edition*, 9:159–166, London: Hogarth Press, 1959.

——— (1910), The future prospects of psychoanalytic therapy. *Standard Edition*, 11:139–152. London: Hogarth Press, 1957.

——— (1919), "A child is being beaten." *Standard Edition*, 17:175–204. London: Hogarth Press, 1955.

——— (1924), The economic problem of masochism. *Standard Edition*, 19:159–170. London: Hogarth Press, 1961.

Glenn, J. (1974), The analysis of masturbatory conflicts in an adolescent boy. In: *The Analyst and Adolescent at Work*, ed. M. Harley. New York: Quadrangle, pp. 164–189.

————(1980), Freud's adolescent patients: Dora, Katharina and the "homosexual woman." In: *Freud and His Patients*. ed. M. Kanzer & J. Glenn. New York: Aronson, 23–47.

———— (1986), Freud, Dora and the maid. *J. of the Amer. Psychoanalyt. Assn.*, 34:591–606.

———— (1989), From protomasochism to masochism. *The Psychoanalytic Study of the Child*. 44:73–86. New Haven, CT: Yale University Press.

———— (1993), Dora's dynamics, diagnosis and treatment. *The Annual of Psychoanalysis*, 21:125–138. Hillsdale NJ: The Analytic Press.

———— & Bernstein, I. (1995), Sadomasochism. In: *Psychoanalytic Concepts*, ed. B. Moore & B. Fine. New Haven, CT: Yale University Press, pp. 252–265.

Jacobs, T. J. (1991), *The Use of the Self*. Madison, CT: International Universities Press.

Maleson, F. G. (1984), The multiple meanings of masochism in psychoanalytic discourse. *J. Amer. Psychoanal. Assn.*, 32:325–356.

Moore, B. E. & Fine, B. D., ed. (1990), *Psychoanalytic Terms and Concepts*. New Haven, CT: Yale University Press.

Panel (1956), The problem of masochism in the theory and technique of psychoanalysis, M. H. Stein, reporter. *J. Amer. Psychoanal. Asson.* 4:526–538.

Piaget, J. & Inhelder, B. (1969), *The Psychology of the Child*. New York: Basic Books.

Prall, R.C. (1990), The neurotic adolescent. In: *The Neurotic Child and Adolescent*, ed. M. H. Etezady. Northvale, NJ: Aronson, pp. 241–302.

Sarnoff, C. (1988), Adolescent masochism. In: *Masochism*, ed. R. A. Glick & D. I. Meyers. Hillsdale, NJ: The Analytic Press, pp. 205–224.

Spiegel, L. A. (1978), Moral masochism. *Psychoanal. Quart.*, 47:209–236.

Tanner, J. M. (1962), *Growth at Adolescence*. Oxford: Blackwell.

Discussion

MORTON J. ARONSON

The magnificently written Dora case (Freud, 1905) is one of Freud's major clinical contributions to psychoanalysis and has been taught to generations of candidates. It has served to demonstrate impressively the unconscious meanings and causes of hysterical symptoms, the remarkable value of dream interpretation, and the central role of transference and countertransference in the analytic situation as well as the disastrous consequences to the treatment of the failure to recognize and deal with them. This case report contributes to our idealization of Freud by demonstrating the genius of his mind at work and, at the same time, serves to humanize him by allowing us to perceive his countertransference problems.

We are in debt to Jules Glenn for his contribution to further understanding of the Dora case. Chapters by him, Scharfman, Bernstein, and Kanzer in the book *Freud and His Patients* (1980) have become classics. "Dora As an Adolescent" is the third of Glenn's (1986, 1993) additional essays on Dora since the foregoing book. In it he makes a persuasive case for the presence of sadomasochistic features in Dora and as part of the psychology of adolescence. What is open for discussion, in my opinion, is the psychopathological significance of these conflicts. Glenn's point of view depends on what has been called the narrow definition of sadomasochism illustrated, for example, in the Moore and Fine definition that ties the search for pain and suffering to genital sexual arousal and gratification. Those who subscribe to this point of view recognize the importance of protomasochism and, I assume, protosadism in the preoedipal stages of development but believe these are consolidated into sadomasochistic conflicts in the oedipal phase, augmented by regressive defense against oedipal castration fears to the anal-sadistic level of drive organization. For those analysts who subscribe to this view, no behavior, character trait, or fantasy (conscious or unconscious) that embodies the search for pain and suffering can be considered sadomasochism unless it is for purposes of genital sexual gratification.

Freud (1924) extended the concept of masochism beyond perversion, identified masochistic elements in numerous types of sexual behavior, and saw rudiments of masochism in infantile sexuality. In addition, he described derivative forms, notably moral masochism, where the subject, as a result of an unconscious sense of guilt, seeks out the position of a victim without any sexual pleasure being directly involved.

For the many analysts who subscribe to a broad view of sadomasochism, these phenomena are ubiquitous in mental life, exist at all stages of development, serve a variety of intrapsychic functions, vary in significance from normal to psychotic, and may or may not be linked to genital sexual fantasies, conscious or unconscious. The Novicks (1987), for example, defined masochism as the active pursuit of psychic or physical pain, suffering or humiliation in the service of adaptation, defense, and instinctual gratification at oral, anal, and phallic levels. Glick and Myers (1988) connect repetitive seeking of pain, failure, subjugation, and humiliation to the maintenance of self boundaries, self-cohesion, self-esteem, object attachment, instinctual gratification and neurotic resolution of id, ego, and superego conflicts, as well as direct genital sexual discharge, but not necessarily related to sexual excitement.

Most authors agree that sadomasochistic fantasies and sado-masochistically tinged behavior are not necessarily pathologic. Kernberg (1988) describes their presence in normal sexual love making. Many aspects of normal behavior contain sadomasochistic elements as sublimated derivatives; for example, enduring psychoanalytic candidacy for so many years, a game of golf or tennis, or even discussing a psychoanalytic paper. Some analysts consider beating fantasies and rape fantasies to be a normal and transient phase in female development. The reverse may also be true. Maleson (1984) argues for a broad concept of sadomasochism with no tie to a specifically sexual dynamic since many patients with clear consensually agreed masochistic personality structures do not reveal sexual masochistic fantasies, even with analysis.

Some analysts believe that for sexual fantasies to be considered sado-masochistic their content should resemble the acts committed in sado-masochistic perversions. The three fantasies which Freud and Glenn attribute to Dora with supporting evidence ranging from some to virtually none at all bear no similarity to the acts performed by sado-masochistic perverts. Furthermore, in none of them can one demonstrate a search for pain in order to achieve sexual excitement and discharge. The venereal disease fantasy was one of many fantasies underlying Dora's multiple hysterical symptoms. Since this was one of the topics under discussion in the analysis before the recurrent burning house dream, and since there is evidence that masturbatory wishes were part of the latent dream thoughts, Glenn concluded that the venereal disease fantasy was involved in the unconscious masturbation fantasy. It may have been, but it seems very likely that, if there was a masturbation fantasy, then it involved fearful sexual wishes for Herr K, Dora's father, and Freud. It should be noted that Freud's speculation that Dora masturbated as a child became, for Freud, an established fact despite Dora's steadfast insistence that she could not remember it. The second fantasy, the fantasy of defloration, was a product of Freud's analysis of the sec-

159

ond dream. He arrived at this conclusion, that this unconscious fantasy was present in the latent content of the dream, by his interpretation of the symbols in the dream without any such associations from Dora. As Glenn says, "the evidence is slim." The third fantasy, which embodied revenge against her father and Freud, was also derived from the second dream but was here supported by elements of the manifest content and Dora's associations. Dora had ample justification for resentment of her father and Freud. To characterize the resentment as sadism, particularly in the narrow definition of the term, seems doubtful. The suffering component of Dora's purported unconscious fantasies as well as the suffering involved in her hysterical symptoms can be more easily understood as the superego demanded punishment for her incestuous wishes than by the thesis that she sought pain in order to achieve genital sexual excitement and gratification. I would agree that there is a masochistic component, but only in the broad definition of the term.

Glenn argues that Dora's adolescent sadomasochistic behavior affected her treatment, specifically that she provoked Freud's sadistic behavior towards her by playing "secrets" with her grandmother's letter and by thwarting Freud's scientific aspirations by stopping treatment. As I reread the case history I was struck by how compliant and productive a patient Dora was; she was neither hostile nor provocative, nor did she display any evidence of a negative therapeutic reaction as one would expect with a sadomasochistic patient. Her momentary teasing about her grandmother's letter was hardly very provocative, in fact, Freud was delighted because he saw it as confirmation of her sexual secrets. Similarly, to review her quitting treatment as a sadistic act, arouses doubt. She gave Freud ample warning in her first dream that she had to escape from the analysis because of her frightening erotic transference wishes, displaced from Herr K onto Freud, "But I was deaf to this first note of warning" (p. 119). Later, in his postscript, Freud believed that Dora felt deceived and rejected by Herr K and transferred this to Freud. But Dora had ample reason to believe that she was deceived and rejected by Freud as she had been by Herr K. Freud stimulated her with excessive and premature sex talk and by telling her that she wanted him to kiss her, and then displayed no interest in her intention to terminate. That she should retaliate by turning passive into active and become the rejecter sounds more like healthy self assertion than pathological sadism. The same is the case in her slapping Herr K when he used the same words to seduce her that he used with the governess: "You know I get nothing from my wife." This is not to say that these acts of rejection did not reverberate unconsciously with some measure of sadomasochism, but it seems unlikely that the sado-masochistic elements played a prominent role. It could be argued that it would have been quite masochistic for Dora to continue in a treatment that resembled what Freud later called "wild analysis" (1910).

Glenn attributes Freud's emotional reaction to Dora's provocative-ness and aggressiveness. Elsewhere, Glenn (1980), has pointed out that Freud had similar problems with his other female patients (The Homosexual Woman and Irma), but was patient with the extreme hos-tility of the Rat-Man and the apathy of the Wolf-Man. Although Freud was hurt by Dora's leaving, he was amply compensated by using her case to make major contributions to psychoanalytic theory and tech-nique. Dora did not fare so well. Despite Freud's efforts to disguise her identity, the disguise was easily penetrated and the world learned that she was Ida Bauer, the sister of a prominent Austrian figure. Her "secrets" became public knowledge. According to Deutsch (1957), who saw her for several visits 20 years after her analysis, she was a chroni-cally unhappy woman, sexually frigid, and plagued by multiple neurotic symptoms.

Beyond Dora, Glenn gives us an excellent discussion of the psychol-ogy of adolescence and makes a valuable contribution by focusing on the role sadomasochistic conflicts play in adolescent rebellion. I agree that for many adolescents sadomasochism functions as a regressive defense against castration anxiety. I do not agree, however, that this sin-gle dynamic accounts for the wide range of masochistic problems that we encounter clinically. The core mechanism of masochism is pleasure in pain or pain as a condition for pleasure. But all pleasure is not sexual. To name but a few examples: the ego experiences pleasure in moral masochism by appeasing the sadistic superego; victims of child abuse and trauma typically become sadomasochistic adults for whom pain is equated with love and pleasure is found in maintaining the tie to the object; suffering for a valued goal or at the hands of an admired or feared person may be a source of great narcissistic pleasure. Many more examples could be cited, but the conclusion is that sadomasochism is too complex a phenomenon to be accounted for by a single dynamic.

REFERENCES

Deutsch, F. (1957), A footnote to Freud's "Fragment of an Analysis of a Case of Hysteria." *Psychoanal. Quart.*, 26:159–16.

Freud, S. (1905), Fragment of an analysis of a case of hysteria. *Standard Edition*, 7:3–122. London; Hogarth Press, 1953.

——(1910), 'Wild psychoanalysis' *Standard Edition*, 11:221–227. London: Hogarth Press, 1957.

——(1924), The economic problem of masochism. *Standard Edition*, 19: 159–170 London: Hogarth Press, 1961.

Glenn, J. (1980), Freud's adolescent patients: Katherina, Dora and the homosexual woman. In: *Freud and His Patients*, ed. M. Kanzer & J. Glenn. New York: Aronson.

——(1986), Freud, Dora and the maid. *J. Amer. Psychoanal. Assn.*, 34:591–606.

——(1993), Dora's dynamics, diagnosis and treatment. *Annual of Psychoanalysis*, 21:125–138. Hillsdale, NJ: The Analytic Press.

Glick, R. & Myers, H. (1988), *Masochism, current psychoanalytic perspectives* ed. R. Glick & H. Myers. Hillsdale N.J: Analytic Press.

Kernberg, O. (1988), Clinical dimensions of masochism. *J. Amer. Psychoanal. Assn*, 36:1005–1029.

Maleson, F. (1984), The multiple meanings of masochism in psychoanalytic discourse. *J. Amer. Psychoanal. Assn.*, 32:325–356.

Novick, K. & Novick, J. (1987), The essence of masochism. *The Psychoanalytic Study of the Child.*, 42:353–384. New Haven, CT: Yale University Press.

Discussion

AARON H. ESMAN

Dr. Glenn's essay is a rich addition to his series of reappraisals of Freud's clinical cases and, specifically, of the seminal case of Dora, surely by now the most celebrated adolescent girl of fin-de-siècle Vienna. He has enhanced our understanding not only of the complexities of this famous case, but also of the role that sadomasochistic wishes and fantasies play in the lives of adolescents in general and in their psychoanalytic treatment in particular.

My discussion will address what I consider to be some alternative ways of reading aspects of the case and of the interactions between Freud and his patient, Ida Bauer, known to the world as "Dora". This review is all the more timely in that it was just 50 years ago that Ida Bauer, a lonely refugee from Nazi persecution, died in the very institution—Mt. Sinai Hospital—in which we are meeting. Glenn emphasizes Dora's provocativeness, for instance, her "playing secrets" with Freud about the letter in the waiting room. What stands out for me in this interaction, however, was Freud's own distinctly unanalytic (by our current standards, anyway) approach—his assuming, that is, the inquisitorial stance of an angry *pater familias* in demanding her "confession." Indeed, his own sadistic fantasy is, as Glenn points out, revealed in his "recognition" that Dora was "on the point of allowing her secret to be torn from her." Dora's response can, therefore, certainly be seen as a defensive reaction to Freud's sadistic provocation rather than her own masochistic impulse.

The plot thickens further with respect to the question of the "reticule." Freud did not address Dora's action any more analytically than he had the matter of the letter; he had no idea what the reticule represented for Dora, where it had come from (also grandmother?) or why she was wearing it on that day. Rather, he made a symbolic interpretation that, given both his and the generally current views on the subject of masturbation, Dora could only have experienced as an accusation and a reproach. Again, Freud was playing the role of a "penetrating" authority figure, and this may well have shaped Dora's activity in the session.

What is remarkable, actually, is Freud's massive failure of empathy with his young patient. So great was his eagerness to prove the validity of his sexual theories of pathogenesis that he could not understand Dora's negative response at 15 to Herr K's attempted seduction as anything other than a neurotic one. Knowing as he did the intricate dramatics of the Schnitzler-like round of sexual intrigue between Dora's family and the K's, he could not see that Dora was desperately trying to preserve some sense of autonomy, to maintain some view of herself as other than the passive sexual plaything that the conspiring adults in her world sought to make of her—to, as Herr Bauer had asked of Freud, "bring her to her senses." Despite himself, it seems, Freud's notion of what would qualify as "being in her senses" was not altogether different from her father's.

We cannot, of course, know all of the factors that determined Freud's massive countertransferential behavior toward Dora. I shall be so bold, however, as to suggest one possibility. In 1900, at the time of Dora's truncated analysis, Freud's eldest daughter Mathilda had turned 14 and was, therefore, likely to have been in the throes of her pubescence. Is it possible that Freud, who by his own admission was by this time sexually inactive in his own marriage (compare Herr K's "I get nothing from my wife"), was struggling with his own counter-oedipal feelings toward a nubile daughter? Might he have been displacing such feelings toward his attractive adolescent patient and reacting against them? And might an unconscious identification with his peer Herr K have interfered with his ability to understand Dora's rejection of Herr K's seduction?

In any case, the outcome seems to me to have been determined less by Dora's sadomasochism than by Freud's insistent sexualization of the analytic exchange and of his authoritarian stance. At the least, the provocations were mutual and, as Glenn has pointed out, Freud enacted his sadism in the epilogue, when, like a spurned suitor, he rejected Dora's effort to resume the treatment. Dora—Ida Bauer—had a difficult, often painful post-Freud life, described sensitively by Hannah Decker (1991) in *Freud, Dora and Vienna 1900*. Felix Deutsch, who saw her when she was 40, described her as "one of the most repulsive hysterics" he had ever met. She was, apparently, an angry, unstable woman, and no doubt sadomasochism was a significant element in her character. But for what went on in Freud's consulting room, Freud himself must be held largely to account. By focusing our attention on the details of that interaction in the very first analytic treatment of an adolescent, Glenn has done us a valuable service, and I am pleased to have had the opportunity to discuss his fascinating essay.

REFERENCE

Decker, H. (1991) *Freud, Dora and Vienna 1900*. New York: Free Press.

Reply to Discussions

JULES GLENN

Aaron Esman and Morton J. Aronson, in their challenging discussions of "Dora as an Adolescent," appreciate many of my statements and disagree with others. Much of the controversy involves definitions while some of it stems from the fact that I have highlighted a particular aspect of Dora's psychodynamics and have omitted many others. I will therefore address the question of definition and then put Dora's sadistic and masochistic fantasies in context by discussing other contributions to our understanding of sadomasochism and to Dora's psychology.

Aronson starts by agreeing with me that students of the subject have been unable to reach a consensus as to what sadism and masochism consist of; several definitions have been proposed and even insisted on, but a single agreed upon definition has eluded us.

Linguistic confusion is not unusual in our science. It is therefore important that an author, when using complex concepts, like sadism or masochism, define his terms so that the reader or discussant will know what he is writing about. Aronson recognizes that I have used the terms sadism and masochism in a narrow sense. I state that "masochism involves a sexual fantasy in which the subject consciously or unconsciously imagines himself harmed or humiliated; the subject finds gratification in pain, painful affect or suffering. Sadism involves a sexual fantasy in which the subject consciously or unconsciously harms or humiliates others." I think a narrow definition serves us best because the broad definition includes too much; it does not differentiate masochism from psychic states in which one endures pain in order find other satisfaction, for example, childbirth or sacrifice for an ideal, or from suffering due to guilt, shame, or humiliation. Maleson (1984), who documents the numerous ways analysts conceive of masochism, does not offer a definitive definition. Aronson's definition is a fine one, but it is not the one I use here.

In other papers I have attempted to delineate the numerous factors that serve as building blocks for masochism or sadism. Freud (1919, 1924) described defensive turning of aggression inward, guilt and regression. Eidelberg (1954) described the need to avoid narcissistic mortification by controlling the degree with which one provokes people. Novick and Novick (1991) emphasize the importance of achieving narcissistic gratification, even delusionary omnipotence. Loewenstein (1957) described the importance of preoedipal patterning. I have written about psychic trauma, mechanisms of control, oedipal conflicts, and defensive sexualization and regression as determinants of masochistic and sadistic fantasies (Glenn, 1984b, 1989). Valenstein (1973) has drawn attention to a child's early attachment to pain when the mother is associated with pain. Some or all of these determinants (and others) act in conjunction with one another and can appear in different combinations. The numerous determinants can produce a masochistic or sadistic state as a final common denominator (Glenn, 1984a, 1984b, 1989; Glenn and Bernstein, 1995).

Noticing that the psychodynamics and significance of masochism and sadism in adolescence have been ignored or slighted by Freud and other students of teenagers, I decided to present a paper about Dora, and to try to correct the omissions. I did not think that sadomasochism was the only key to understanding Dora or all other teenagers. I had already written about Dora's adolescent status, her reactions to her family situation (Erikson, 1961), and to her analyst and aspects of Freud's countertransference (Glenn, 1980, 1986, 1993). I noted that Dora was an alert perceptive adolescent who, as Esman also observed in his discussion, craved independence and autonomy in a setting that sought to stifle her.

In the current essay I focus on a relatively small but, I think, significant aspect of the case. My method was to reorganize the facts that Freud presented about Dora's two dreams in order to reinterpret them and to include her sadistic and masochistic fantasies. I presented the events that preceded the dreams, the manifest dreams and her associations. I also included Freud's thoughts, his symbolic interpretation, and his other interpretations of the dreams. Using all of these data I reached conclusions that I thought would be convincing to the reader. I thought that Dora's dreams referred to her sexual fantasies and that this was in part due to Freud's influence. He helped eroticize the analytic situation. I thought that Dora's dreams referred to sexual fantasies and feelings she experienced and were intimately linked to desires to be hurt (in the first dream) or to hurt others (in the second dream). This approach requires an examination of each association and its relation to the totality of associations.

Hence, recognition of Freud's seductive and authoritarian technique, which he had used earlier in the analysis prior to the appearance of the two dreams, helps us understand Dora's reactions in the context of the analysis. Noticing that Dora's reaction was defensive or adaptive becomes part of our understanding of her masochism, not a contradiction of it. My essay demonstrates that Dora was masochistic and sadistic in the sense I use the terms. Whether the masochism and sadism started before the treatment or not is not to the point. I do believe, however, that Dora was indeed sadistic and masochistic before she saw Freud.

The reader will agree that Dora's father brought her to Freud because she had serious symptoms (in addition to the fact that he wanted Freud to make her a compliant girl who would not interfere with his affair). She suffered from depression, chronic intermittent cough and aphonia, and uncomfortable feelings of pressure and pain. She also threatened suicide and, encouraged by the adults in her life, put herself in situations that invited danger. Freud intended to treat Dora through helping her understand herself. The analytic situation is intended to facilitate revelation of unconscious thoughts and feelings, and make interpretation and insight possible. Although Freud did not conclude that Dora harbored sadomasochistic fantasies, he provided sufficient evidence for us, almost 100 years later, to do so.

Aronson and Esman agree that the paper casts light on the psychology of adolescence. Reviewing the literature, I was astonished to find that so little had been written about the role of sadomasochism in what has been called adolescent rebellion. I believe that Freud's beautifully described clinical data can be used to clarify certain neglected aspects of adolescent psychology. Aronson adds that he does not agree "that a single dynamic accounts for the wide range of masochistic problems that we encounter clinically". I totally agree. As I noted above, there are many determinants of sadomasochism which work together to produce individual clinical pictures in different persons.

Finally, Esman writes of Freud's "massive failure of empathy" with Dora. I think that that statement is extreme and requires modification. Freud was desperately trying to understand Dora, to put himself in her place as a means of achieving insight. He succeeded only partially. To the degree that he succeeded he was able to make significant theoretical advances. He also recognized that Dora was in the throes of a stifling family conspiracy and that she emphasized the role of others in part to hide her own complicity. Unfortunately, he did not realize that rushing the defensive aspect of her reactions interfered with her fully understanding the implications of the family interaction. Nor did he realize that his rapid, forceful and sexually tinged interpretations reinforced her feelings that he was like her father and Herr K. Despite that error Dora appeared to appreciate that, like her, he was searching for the truth. Decker (1991) believes that his accepting that Dora's description of her family was correct had a major therapeutic effect.

REFERENCES

Decker, H. S. (1991), *Freud, Dora and Vienna 1900*. New York: Free Press.

Eidelberg, L. (1954), *An Outline of Comparative Pathology of the Neuroses*. New York: International Universities Press.

Erikson, E. H. (1961), Psychological reality and historical actuality. In: *Insight and Responsibility*. New York: Norton. 1964, pp. 159–215.

Freud, S. (1919), "A child is being beaten." *Standard Edition*, 17:179–204. London: Hogarth Press, 1955.

———— (1924), The economic problem of masochism. *Standard Edition*, 19:159–170. London: Hogarth Press, 1961.

Glenn, J. (1980), Freud's adolescent patients: Dora, Katharina and the "homosexual woman." In: *Freud and His Patients*, ed. M. Kanzer and J. Glenn. New York: Aronson, pp. 23–47.

———— (1984a), A note on loss, pain, and masochism in children. *J. Amer. Psychoanal. Assn.*, 32:63–75.

———— (1984b), Psychic trauma and masochism. *J. Amer. Psychoanal. Assn.*, 32:357–386.

———— (1986), Freud, Dora and the maid. *J. Amer. Psychoanal. Assn.*, 34:591–606.

———— (1989), From protomasochism to masochism. *The Psychoanalytic Study of the Child*, 44:73–86, New Haven, CT: Yale University Press.

———— (1993), Dora's dynamics, diagnosis and treatment. *Annual of Psychoanalysis*, 21:125–138. Hillsdale, NJ: The Analytic Press.

———— & Bernstein, I. (1995), Sadomasochism. In: *Psychoanalysis. The Major Concepts*, ed. B. E. Moore and B. D. Fine. New Haven, CT: Yale University Press, pp. 252–265.

Loewenstein, R. M. (1957), A contribution to the psychoanalytic theory of masochism. *J. Amer. Psychoanal. Assn.*, 5:197–234.

Maleson, F. G. (1984), The multiple meanings of masochism in psychoanalytic discourse. *J. Amer. Psychoanal. Assn.*, 32:325–356.

Novick, J. & Novick, K. K. (1991), Some comments on masochism and the delusion of omnipotence. *J. Amer. Psychoanal. Assn.*, 39:307–332.

Valenstein, A. F. (1973), On attachment to painful feelings and the negative therapeutic reaction. *The Psychoanalytic Study of the Child*, 28:365–394. New Haven, CT: Yale University Press.

8 THE DIAGNOSIS OF NARCISSISTIC AND ANTISOCIAL PATHOLOGY IN ADOLESCENCE

OTTO F. KERNBERG

The most important task for the psychiatrist examining a troubled adolescent is to assess accurately the severity of the psychopathology, differentiating in the process emotional turmoil as part of a neurosis or an adjustment reaction, from early manifestations of psychosis or severe character pathology. Varying degrees of anxiety and depression, emotional outbursts and temper tantrums, excessive rebelliousness or dependency, sexual inhibition, and polymorphous perverse sexual impulses and behaviors may present in adolescents without severe character pathology as well as in psychotic youngsters and in those with very severe characterological disturbances.

Identity integration is the key anchoring point of the differential diagnosis of milder types of character pathology and neurotic personality organization, on one hand, and severe character pathology and borderline personality organization, on the other. This differential diagnosis should not present many difficulties to the experienced clinician. It is important to differentiate identity crises (a normal vicissitude of adolescence) from the syndrome of identity diffusion. Identity crises reflect the impact of the relatively rapid physical and psychological growth in these years, the changes that emerge with puberty, the adolescent's internal sense of confusion regarding the emergence of strong sexual impulses and the contradictory pressures regarding how to deal with them, the widening gap between the perception of the adolescent on the part of his or her traditional family environment and his or her self perception. Adolescent identity crisis thus refers to a significant discrepancy between a rapidly shifting self-concept and the persistence of the adolescent's experience of how others perceive him (Erikson, 1956).

169

Identity diffusion, in contrast, refers to a lack of integration both of the concept of the self and of the concept of significant others. Its roots are usually in early childhood, related to a lack of normal resolution of the stage of separation-individuation (Mahler et al., 1975). The syndrome of identity diffusion may be present throughout childhood, but, in all but the most severe cases, the protective functions of the structured environment of an ordinary childhood experience prevent the symptoms of identity diffusion from becoming evident until that protective structure loosens in the course of adolescent development.

The Diagnosis of Identity Diffusion and Reality Testing

The diagnosis of identity diffusion is the first step in the evaluation of the severity of any character pathology in an adolescent.

In response to the diagnostician's request to the adolescent to provide a brief self description, to provide a picture of himself or herself that would permit the diagnostician to differentiate him or her from all other persons, what emerges in most cases of identity diffusion is a contradictory and chaotic account. These patients lack the self-reflective capacity that would enable them to be aware of the chaotic nature of the description of the self that they convey. Occasionally, the syndrome may also be expressed in a rigid adherence to social norms, either traditional ones of family demands, or the cultural clichés of the adolescent group. This rigid style of coping with the inner experience of identity diffusion is reflected in what has been called the "quiet borderline patient" who impresses the therapist as a relatively affectless, indecisive, undefined, pseudo-submissive youngster (Sherwood and Cohen, 1994). Both rigid and chaotic self-descriptions are in sharp contrast to the rich and highly personalized image an adolescent with normal identity integration might provide. In addition, adolescents with an integrated self-concept describe themselves in ways that are harmonious with their interactions with the diagnostician, in contrast to sharp discrepancies between the description of the self-concept and the interactions in the diagnostic interviews in the case of identity diffusion.

When evaluating ego identity, the assessment of the self-concept is complemented by that of the integration of the representations of significant others. This latter aspect of ego identity deserves particular diagnostic attention because, in the special case of the narcissistic personality, a pathological grandiose self contributes to an integration of sorts of the self-concept, while the integration of the concept of significant others

170

remains glaringly absent. Lack of integration of the concept of significant others shows in the incapacity to convey to the diagnostician a live and integrated picture of the most important persons in the adolescent patient's life.

In this regard, as I pointed out in earlier work (1984), adolescents with a neurotic personality organization, severe conflicts at home, school, or both, and a rebellious and affectively unstable style of interpersonal interactions may be highly critical of the adults that surround them, particularly their parents and teachers, involved in intense conflicts of loyalties and group formation, and yet able to describe with remarkable depth the personalities of all those with whom they have intense personal conflicts. In contrast, adolescents with identity diffusion are remarkably incapable of conveying a live picture of those who are closest to them and with whom conflicts over dependency, submission, and rebellion are most intense. Therefore, the request to the adolescent to convey a live picture of the persons who are most important in his or her life—regardless of whether he or she likes or dislikes them—provides crucial information regarding the capacity for integration of the concept of significant others. Naturally, in cases where the personalities of significant others are objectively chaotic and contradictory, the adolescent with normal identity formation should be able to describe such chaos, but to do it critically, with an internal need and an active attempt to sort out these chaotic contradictions.

While lack of integration of the self-concept combined with lack of integration of the concept of significant others defines identity diffusion and, by itself, determines the diagnosis of borderline personality organization, the certainty of this diagnosis can be reinforced by the evaluation of superego functioning. One central consequence of normal ego identity integration is the maturation of the superego, that is, the completion of the process by which the earliest layer of persecutory superego precursors, the later layer of idealized superego precursors, the still later layer of realistic superego precursors of the oedipal period, and the final processes of depersonification, abstraction, and individualization of the superego are integrated. The absence of normal identity integration in the ego interferes with this process and brings about various degrees of immaturity of the superego.

In fact, the degree of superego integration is one of the two most crucial prognostic factors for all types of psychotherapeutic intervention, the other factor being the quality of the adolescent's object relations. Here the issues to be evaluated are an adolescent's capacity to invest in values beyond narrow self interests and direct narcissistic gratification: interest in work, art, and culture, commitments to ideology, and the maturity of value judgments related to such investments. Obviously, the cultural background of the adolescent will crucially codetermine his orientation toward value systems; but within any particular socio-economic and cultural background, adolescents with normal identity integration have the capacity to invest in values such as commitment to friends, loyalty, honesty, interest in sports or music, politics, the success of a group to which they belong, or the history of their particular social group. Under conditions of identity diffusion, there is a remarkable poverty of such investment in value systems. Naturally, the more severe the immaturity of the superego, the more prevalent may be the antisocial behavior that, in turn, has to be evaluated in terms of the adaptation to a particular social subgroup as opposed to individualized antisocial behavior.

An additional indicator of a normally integrated superego is the capacity for romantic idealization and falling in love. While not having fallen in love in early or middle adolescence may not yet be diagnosable as an indication of superego pathology, the presence of intense love experiences, of having fallen in love, are positive indicators of good superego integration; this capacity emerges normally, and very fully, during the latency years, and there has been a conventional underestimation of the importance of such love experiences in early childhood development (P. Kernberg and Richards, 1994).

Certain characteristics that usually indicate severe character pathology in adults are less meaningful in adolescence than the key indicators of ego identity and superego maturation. To begin with, the presence or even dominance of primitive defensive operations, typical for borderline personality organization in adults, has much less diagnostic meaning in adolescence. Given the significant regression in the youngster's early adaptation to the upsurge of sexual impulses, his or her efforts to reduce a dependency upon his or her parents and to transfer early conflicts within the home into the school, social group formation, and relations to authorities outside the home; and given, particularly, the normal reactivation of intense oedipal conflicts and preoedipal defenses against them, a broad spectrum of defensive operations—from the mature ones centering around repression to the primitive ones centering around splitting—may be activated in the adolescent's interpersonal interactions. Splitting, primitive idealization, devaluation, projection and projective identification, denial, omnipotence, and omnipotent control may coexist with an increased tendency towards repression, reaction formations, displacement, intellectualization, and various inhibitions, all of which manifest themselves in the early diagnostic interviews.

Typically, in the case of neurotic personality organization, however, once the initial anxiety of the adolescent decreases in the course of the diagnostic interviews, primitive defensive operations tend to decrease as well, although they may continue unabated in areas of conflict outside the treatment situation. By the same token, the severity of neurotic symptoms, affective crises, polymorphous perverse activities, or sexual inhibition does not, by itself, indicate severity of pathology, except in cases of a consolidated perversion with significant and dangerous sadistic and masochistic components. In these latter cases, the extent to which the superego controls protect against excessive activation of aggression becomes an important aspect of the diagnostic assessment.

All the criteria examined so far serve the purpose of differentiating neurotic personality organization from borderline personality organization. The criterion of reality testing, in contrast, permits the differentiation of borderline personality organization from psychotic personality organization, that is, to distinguish the most severe character pathologies from incipient or atypical psychotic developments. The establishment of the presence or absence of reality testing is crucial to this distinction. Reality testing, as I pointed out in earlier works (1975, 1984), consists in the capacity to differentiate self from non-self, intrapsychic from external origin of stimuli, and in the capacity to maintain empathy with ordinary social criteria of reality.

In practice, reality testing may be assessed first, by exploring whether the adolescent presents hallucinations or delusions, that is, "productive ,symptoms" of psychosis; obviously, the presence of psychotic symptoms indicates loss of reality testing. Second, in cases where there is no overt evidence of hallucinations or delusions, but where abnormal sensory perceptions or ideation are present—such as pseudo-hallucinations, hallucinosis, illusions, or overvalued ideas—it is helpful to assess the adolescent patient's evaluation of his symptoms, and his capacity to empathize with the therapist's evaluation of them.

A very helpful method for clarifying reality testing is to note aspects of the patient's behavior, affect, thought content, and formal organization of thought processes that impress the diagnostician as strange, bizarre, peculiar, or inappropriate. When tactfully confronted with the diagnostician's puzzlement over whatever seemed to him most inappropriate in the patient's behavior, affect, or thought, the adolescent may be able to empathize with the diagnostician's observation and provide an explanation that reduces the discrepancy between the observed behavior and the diagnostician's subjective experience of it as strange. When the patient's explanation in effect reduces the discrepancy, and indicates that the patient is perfectly able to resonate with the reality testing of the therapist, reality testing is considered to be maintained. When, in contrast, the adolescent patient would seem to disorganize further under the impact of this confrontation, reality testing is probably lost. This is a relatively simple procedure in the hands of an experienced clinician, and one that is of enormous value, as mentioned before, in the differential diagnosis of atypical psychosis.

For example, one adolescent became depressed because, after having been the best student in mathematics throughout elementary school and high school, he came out second in a mathematics test in his senior year of high school. On exploration of why this had produced such a depressive reaction, the adolescent insisted that he was convinced that he was "the best mathematician in the world," and this was an unforgivable failure. When the interviewer tactfully inquired how he could be sure that he was the best mathematician in the world if, for example, another young man of his age in a country totally unbeknownst to this patient might be even better in mathematics—the patient became very angry. He told the examining psychiatrist that he was "completely idiotic" and then exploded in a rage attack! Subsequent exploration of this breakdown in communication confirmed the impression that this young man's grandiose idea had, indeed, delusional qualities and was not an overvalued idea as part of a pathological grandiose self, that is, a narcissistic personality structure. The diagnosis of a schizophrenic illness was confirmed by subsequent developments.

The diagnosis of reality testing by the method described above usually solves the problem of the differential diagnosis between borderline personality organization and psychotic personality organization in one or several interviews. There are, however, some conditions that make this diagnosis particularly difficult. First there are cases with severe, chronic withdrawal from reality without any pathological sensory perception or delusion formation in which the breakdown in studies and family life and the incapacity for intimate relations represent a dramatic development to outsiders, while the adolescent patient himself appears strangely indifferent to his plight. In these cases, carefully confronting the patient with this discrepancy between his indifference and others' concern usually permits the differential diagnosis between a severe schizoid or schizotypal personality disorder and a chronic schizophrenic illness.

Second, in cases of paranoid psychosis, often the adolescent patient still knows well enough what might be considered psychotic by the diagnostician, and withholds the corresponding information. The differential diagnosis may take a much longer time than in most other cases, although it may be strengthened by independent information from projective psychological testing, observations derived from the patient's life outside the diagnostic situation, family interviews, and psychiatric social work.

A third and frequent difficult diagnostic situation is presented by patients who react in such an intensely defiant, negativistic manner in the diagnostic interviews that reality testing regarding this striking behavior cannot be successfully attempted. Here again, a careful assessment of the patient's functioning at home, in school, and in his social environment, psychological testing, psychiatric social work evaluation, together with a series of diagnostic interviews may gradually facilitate the diagnosis. Non psychotic negativism usually tends to decrease over a series of diagnostic interviews, while a truly psychotic negativism does not.

A final, relatively rare type of case where the assessment of reality testing proves to be very difficult is that of patients who describe hallucinatory or delusional experiences as having persisted for many years prior to the present symptomatology that has brought them to the attention of a psychiatrist: for example, patients who harbor the delusion, sometimes from childhood on, that they will die at a certain, early age, or who have had chronic hallucinatory experiences over many years without other indications of emotional illness. Once again, repeated evaluation of reality testing, projective diagnostic testing, and the effort to assess reality testing in all areas other than this one long-lasting symptom will eventually provide an adequate diagnostic judgment. Some of these cases with chronic hallucinatory and/or delusional symptoms, particularly if they have a depressive tone, reflect an atypical major affective illness; the search for other symptoms confirming chronic depression embedded in the personality structure may facilitate the establishment of this diagnosis.

The Diagnosis of Narcissistic Pathology

The narcissistic personality disorder is one of the most prevalent severe personality disorders. The more severe the narcissistic character pathology, the earlier its presence becomes noticeable. During the school years, children with narcissistic personality disorder may have deeply problematic relationships at home and at school. Ordinary friendships are replaced by exclusive relationships of dominance and submission and the enactment of grandiose fantasies. Within the family they attempt to exercise omnipotent control, and are unable to tolerate not being dominant or the center of attention. The lack of the capacity for mutuality, for gratitude, for nonnarcissistically gratifying object investments differentiate pathological narcissism in childhood from normal infantile narcissistic attitudes.

The cases that make their appearance first during adolescence are less severe than those diagnosed in childhood, yet usually more severe than those whose pathology first emerges in early adulthood, that is, when they prove to be unable to establish intimate love relations and begin to experience breakdown in studies and work. This relationship between severity and age of emergence of narcissistic psychopathology parallels that for borderline personality organization in general; but the narcissistic personality disorder has some particular features that permits its differentiation within the broader range of patients with borderline personality organization.

First, the syndrome of identity diffusion in the narcissistic personality shows the particularity of an apparent good integration of the self-concept; it is, however, a pathological grandiose self-concept associated with a marked lack of integration of the representations of significant others. It is characteristic of narcissistic personality disorders that they have very little capacity for empathy with others, or for commitment and loyalty in friendships. Their relationships are dominated by conscious and unconscious envy; they evince a combination of devaluation of others, of symbolic spoiling of what they receive from them, of exploitativeness, greediness, entitlement, and inability to truly depend upon anyone. The pathological, grandiose self is manifested in these adolescents by exaggerated self-reference and self-centeredness; their grandiose fantasies are very often expressed in exhibitionistic traits, an attitude of superiority, recklessness, and a discrepancy between high ambitions and limited capacities. Their excessive need for the admiration of others could be misinterpreted as their being dependent; but unlike dependent personalities they are unable to experience gratitude toward those who fulfill their needs. The shallowness of their emotional life and self-experience is often reflected in a sense of emptiness, boredom, and stimulus hunger.

Frequently a dominant symptom is a significant failure at school. As I have described in an earlier work (1984) they show great difficulties in learning, as to do so interferes with their fantasy that they know everything already, or that they can absorb knowledge automatically by mere contact with information. If the narcissistic adolescent is very bright, he may be an excellent student as long as he does not have to work at it. Often these youngsters show a combination of excellent functioning in subjects that are easy for them with total breakdown in those in which they could not excel without making an effort. Such an effort—and the unconscious envy stirred up by it—is experienced as an insult to their self-esteem. Secondary devaluation of the subjects in which they do not succeed then leads to a vicious cycle of school failure. An example was a patient who had easily learned to swim well as a small child, but was never able to learn to ski: the experience of the first lesson when he saw that his older siblings were much better skiers than he demolished his willingness to learn.

The internal experience of grandiosity and entitlement, the inordinate envy and devaluation, the limitations in empathy and commitment, cardinal symptoms of the narcissistic personality, are not always easily observable in narcissistic adolescent patients. Their surface behavior can be quite variable. In the typical case, an attitude of superiority and self-assurance, a charming, engaging, seductive friendliness characterizes the patient's early contacts, reflecting the underlying pathological grandiose self. In atypical cases, however, the surface behavior may be one of anxiety, tension, insecurity, and timidity, under the influence of pervasive fear of their superiority being challenged or of their needs for admiration going unfulfilled. In fact most narcissistic patients suffer from bouts of insecurity, and the distress of such episodes may activate the secondary defense of timid surface behavior that protects them from disappointment of their narcissistic aspirations. Sometimes, in better functioning patients, what is most apparent is a certain conventional rigidity that serves as a substitute for a normal depth of relationships, ideas, and values.

The lack of superego integration of borderline personality organization is accentuated in the case of narcissistic pathology because of the absorption of the idealizing layer of superego precursors (the ego ideal) into the pathological grandiose self. This condensation of the pathological grandiose self with the ego ideal brings about a kind of false identity integration, and facilitates nonspecific manifestations of ego strength (anxiety tolerance, impulse control, some capacity for sublimatory functioning) that makes these patients appear as functioning much better than the ordinary borderline patient.

The absorption of the ego ideal into the self results in the deterioration of the world of internalized object relations and of the capacity for nonnarcissistic object investment. The main price, however, of this condensation is significant impairment of the maturation of the normal superego. In relatively mild cases this immaturity is manifest in the persistence of childish values, including preoccupation with physical attractiveness, clothing, possessions, and various conventionally determined personal adornments. The surface manifestations depend on the cultural background of the narcissistic adolescent patient. The lack of superego integration is further reflected in inability to experience normal, mournful grief reactions, and a tendency toward reacting to lapses of behavior or judgment with severe mood swings rather than by differentiated self-criticism; self-regulation of behavior comes via avoidance of shame rather than of guilt.

In more severe cases, lack of superego integration is reflected directly in antisocial behavior. The pathological grandiose self tolerates aggression, which is manifested in forms of ego-syntonic sadistic or self-aggressive, self-mutilating, suicidal behavior. Because of the absorption of the ego ideal into the pathological grandiose self, the persecutory superego precursors can not easily be absorbed into an overall integrated superego, and are reprojected as paranoid traits. The combination, in these severe cases, of narcissistic personality disorder, antisocial behavior, ego syntonic aggression, and a paranoid orientation constitutes the syndrome of malignant narcissism, the most severe—although still psychotherapeutically treatable—form of narcissistic personality disorder. Cases where superego pathology extends further to the extent of a total absence of superego functions constitute the antisocial personality disorder in a strict sense (as opposed to the less precise definition of this personality structure in the *DSM* classification system).

The Antisocial Personality Disorder in Adolescence

The antisocial personality disorder is the most severe form of narcissistic character pathology; it may be defined as a narcissistic personality disorder with extreme absence of superego functions. Clinically, the antisocial personality proper may be divided into an aggressive type and a passive-parasitic type (Henderson, 1939; Henderson and Gillespie, 1969).

Careful exploration of nearly all antisocial personality disorders shows that symptoms of this disorder were already present in early childhood. The tendency in the *DSM-III* and *DSM-IV* nomenclature to separate "conduct disorders" in childhood from the antisocial personality disorder in adulthood, with an artificial limit set at age 18 before the diagnosis of an antisocial personality may be established, ignores this continuity (Hare, 1970; Hare and Shalling, 1978; Kernberg, 1989). The distinction between conduct disorder and antisocial personality disorder seems absurd from a psychopathological and clinical viewpoint. Given the grave implications of an antisocial personality disorder at any age, it is important that the clinician examining an adolescent with significant antisocial behavior be prepared to diagnose this disorder. I have explored the differential diagnosis between the antisocial personality disorder, the syndrome of malignant narcissism, and the narcissistic personality disorder in earlier work (1989), and shall summarize briefly the main characteristics of the antisocial personality disorder proper that enable the clinician to distinguish it from the syndrome of malignant narcissism and the less severe narcissistic personality disorder, both of which may present antisocial behaviors.

It is important to keep in mind that the passive-parasitic type of antisocial personality usually goes unnoticed during early childhood, particularly if antisocial features of the patient's family and social background absorb the patient's antisocial behavior into culturally tolerated patterns. Thus, for example, early cheating in school, stealing, habitual lying, may not be taken seriously in an ambiance of social disorganization and severe family pathology while such behavior would stand out in a relatively stable and healthy social and family environment. Antisocial tendencies or severe narcissistic pathology of the parents may provide convenient "cover-ups" for a child's passive-parasitic antisocial behavior, characterized by manipulativeness, exploitiveness, lying, stealing, and cheating at school.

The predominantly aggressive type of the antisocial personality disorder is usually more readily recognized because of the impact of this pathology upon the immediate social environment of the child. As Paulina Kernberg (1989) has pointed out, the aggressive type of antisocial personality disorder in children is characterized by extreme aggression from early childhood on, to the extent that violent and destructive behavior may be expressed toward siblings, animals, and property; the parents are usually afraid of these children. They show an "affectless" expression of aggression, chronic manipulativeness and paranoid tendencies, a marked inability to keep friends, and sometimes a true reign of terror at home or in their immediate social circle at school. Often the parents are unable to convince mental health professionals of the gravity of the situation. In early adolescence, this aggression extends beyond the family circle and may include criminal behavior.

From a diagnostic viewpoint, the essential characteristics of the antisocial personality proper are, first, the presence of a narcissistic personality disorder as described above and, second, in the case of the antisocial personality of a predominantly aggressive type, the symptoms of malignant narcissism. In the case of the predominantly passive-parasitic type, there is no violence, only passive-exploitative behavior, such as lying, cheating, stealing, and exploitation of others. Third, careful evaluation of the past history reveals the presence of antisocial behavior beginning in early childhood.

Fourth, and fundamentally, these patients prove incapable of experiencing feelings of guilt and remorse for their harmful actions. They may express remorse when these are discovered, but not so long as they believe their prohibited behavior is unknown to anybody else. It is also striking that they are unable to identify with the moral dimension in the mind of the diagnostician, to the extent that, while they may be very skilled in assessing other people's motivations and behavior, the possibility of an ethical motivation is so foreign to them that the exploration of this issue—for example, in wondering how they believe the therapist may be reacting to their antisocial behavior—often reveals their striking incapacity to imagine the sense of sadness, concern, or moral shock evoked by acts of cruelty or exploitation.

Fifth, these youngsters are incapable of nonexploitative investment in others; they display an indifference and callousness that extends also to pets, which they may mistreat or abandon without any feelings. Sixth, their lack of concern for others is matched by lack of concern for themselves; they lack a sense of time, of future, of planning. While they may carry out concrete antisocial acts with excellent short-term planning, the long-term effects of cumulative antisocial behavior are emotionally insignificant to these patients and hence totally ignored. A sense of future is a superego function, in addition to an ego function, and glaringly absent in these cases. Seventh, the lack of an affective investment in significant others is matched by a lack of normal love for the self, expressed in defiant, fearless, potentially self-destructive behavior, a proneness to impulsive acts of suicide when they experience themselves driven into a corner; and of course, under the impact of intense rage, they present the risk of severely aggressive and homicidal behavior toward others.

Eighth, these patients show remarkable stunting of the capacity for depressive mourning and grief, and marked limitation of anxiety tolerance. The latter shows up in the prompt development of new symptoms or antisocial behavior when they feel threatened or controlled by external structure. Ninth, these patients show a remarkable inability to learn from experience, or to absorb the information or moral support provided by the therapist: behind this imperviousness is a radical devaluation of all value systems, a sense that life is an ongoing struggle either among wolves, or between wolves and sheep, with many wolves disguised as sheep.

Finally, these patients are incapable of falling in love. They cannot experience the integration of tenderness and sexuality, and their sexual involvements have a mechanical quality that renders them eternally unsatisfactory. When antisocial personalities develop a sadistic perversion, they can become extremely dangerous to others. The combination of severe aggression, the absence of any capacity for compassion, and the lack of superego development is the basis for the psychopathology of mass murder as well as murder in the context of sexual involvements.

In the diagnostic interviews with these patients, their manipulativeness, pathological lying and shifting rationalizations create what Paulina Kernberg (personal communication) has called "holographic man": they are able to evoke flimsy, rapidly changing, completely contradictory images of themselves, their lives and interactions. The diagnostic evaluation of these cases requires taking a complete history from them so as to identify shifts in the versions of their past presented on different occasions, to observe their interactions with the therapist as well as with significant others, and to obtain a very full social history in order to compare external observations and information with the patient's communication.

The exploration of these patients' history should include tactful questions of why they did *not* engage in what would seem, under some specific circumstances, expectable antisocial behaviors in their case; this often reveals the lack of the capacity to identify with ethical systems even while the patient is trying to portray a picture of himself as an honest and reliable individual. Naturally, the patient who lies to the diagnostician should be confronted with that in nonpunitive ways, mostly to assess the extent to which the capacity for guilt, remorse, or shame is still available. The narcissistic personality disorder with passive-parasitic tendencies will show the same general characteristics mentioned for the aggressive type, except for direct aggressive attacks on others, on property, on animals, and on the self. Patients with the syndrome of malignant narcissism but without an antisocial personality proper, will present the capacity for guilt, concern for self, some non-exploitive relations, some remnants of authentic superego functions, and some capacity for dependency; their prognosis is significantly better.

Antisocial behavior is not in itself a diagnosis. It may appear in patients with borderline personality organization and other personality disorders, as well as some patients with neurotic personality organization and good ego identity integration. Antisocial behavior may, at times, reflect a neurosis with strong rebellious features in an adolescent, and even a normal adaptation to a pathological social subgroup (the "dyssocial" reaction). In all these cases, the antisocial behavior has an excellent prognosis with the psychotherapeutic treatment of the underlying character pathology or neurotic syndrome. Therefore, in all adolescent patients with antisocial behavior, it is essential to rule out the syndrome of identity diffusion, the presence of a narcissistic personality disorder, the syndrome of malignant narcissism, and the presence of an antisocial personality proper.

Some General Considerations About the Diagnostic Evaluation of Character Pathology in Adolescence

In general, it is very important to obtain, first of all, a full picture of all current symptoms and their respective severity: for example, severe suicidal or self-mutilating tendencies, alcohol or drug abuse or dependence, depression, or eating disturbances all may require immediate interventions that take precedence over a careful evaluation of the patient's character structure: emergencies have to be taken care of first, and the evaluation of the personality structure must wait until the adolescent is in a stable, safe, protected environment.

In all cases, the study of the personality functioning in all areas of the patient's present life takes precedence over taking a past history; and the past history must be evaluated in the light of the present functioning of the patient's personality. The comparative analysis of the information provided by the patient, the family, other sources of information—from the school or the psychiatric social worker—also needs to be matched with a careful analysis of the interaction between the diagnostician and the patient. This requires the therapist to convey honestly to the patient what will be done with the information that he is obtaining, and a careful discussion of the issue of confidentiality in their interactions.

If an adolescent shows up first with his family, there may be an advantage in seeing all of them jointly before seeing the patient alone, and not to see family members without the patient first, even if they insist on it. By the same token, should the therapist have received information about the patient before he sees him, it is important that he share this information with the patient. In families where there exists a culture of keeping secrets from each other, an important part of the diagnostic evaluation is opening all channels of communication tactfully but decisively.

The experience in the long-term treatment of patients with severe personality disorders as part of our psychotherapy research project (Kernberg et al., 1989) has taught us that there are some early priorities that require immediate attention: the existence of danger to the physical survival of the patient or of others, the danger of acute disruption of the diagnostic or therapeutic process by the patient, the danger of severe interference with the diagnostic process by the patient's or other family member's lack of honesty, and the danger of premature disruption of the diagnostic process by the breakdown of the system that supports it.

If severely regressive developments occur during the diagnostic process, such as a strong negative reaction toward the diagnostician, it is important to abandon, temporarily, the pursuit of other information and focus on the adolescent's experience of the immediate situation. Here, psychoanalytic principles of evaluating the acting out of severe negative transferences enter into play, and the experienced clinician may have to spend quite some time in ventilating such negative transference developments without losing sight of the fact that he is still in the middle of a diagnostic process. It should be clearly understood that the definite treatment will have to await the availability of complete information regarding what the difficulties are. Primitive mechanisms of projective identification, omnipotent control, and severe denial color such early difficulties and may be used to evaluate the existence of identity diffusion, narcissistic pathology, and antisocial behavior.

If the adolescent patient refuses to come to the sessions, work with the family may facilitate the creation of an immediate social structure that will bring the patient back into the diagnostic sessions. For example, the diagnostician may discuss with the family what measures they can take to bring the patient back to consultations, and help them to deal with the patient under these circumstances. Should the patient come back to the diagnostic sessions, all these preliminary discussions will have to be shared with him as well. If an acute danger exists to the patient or to the family's physical survival, or if a differential diagnosis with a psychotic process proves to be impossible to achieve in outpatient diagnostic evaluation, a brief period of hospitalization may be indicated to carry out such evaluation in a controlled, supportive environment.

It is always helpful to study the family situation of adolescents who are being evaluated for character pathology. The pathology in the social structure of the family interacts with the patient's character pathology; thus family assessment should be part of a routine evaluation of severe psychopathology. The assessment of the extent to which the patient's difficulties represent a relatively nonspecific reaction to disturbance within the family as opposed to the presence of severe character pathology in the patient himself—regardless of how intensely family pathology interacts with it—is an important aspect of this diagnostic process. Treatment strategies will vary according to the extent to which pathological character structure in the adolescent patient and pathological structure of the family at large are present.

The careful evaluation of the adolescent patient's social life outside the family structure will provide invaluable data to relate family pathology and character pathology to each other. For example, an adolescent may show severe behavior disturbances at home, while revealing in the diagnostic interviews a very active, intense, involved, in-depth life of relationships with significant friends or admired adults outside the family. Such a patients may initially treat the diagnostician as they treat their parents, but will gradually "normalize" their interaction in the diagnostic setting as they begin to differentiate the diagnostician from the family authorities. By contrast, a family's denial of severe character pathology in their child may be exposed by the adolescent patient's information about the restriction and poverty of his or her emotional investment in significant others, and his or her severe conflicts and failure in school. In all cases of significant school failure, intelligence testing, and, when indicated, testing for learning disabilities will clarify further the extent to which character pathology, particularly a narcissistic personality disorder, contributes to the school failure.

The evaluation of the adolescent patient's sexual life provides very important data regarding the capacity for developing object relations in depth, the existence of severe disturbances in sexual functions, and the existence of potentially destructive and self-destructive behaviors in the sexual area that put the adolescent at immediate risk. Sexual promiscuity in the age of AIDS may signify active, urgent danger situations that require rapid therapeutic intervention. At the same time, as mentioned before, the capacity for romantic idealization and falling in love, and, particularly, the capacity to integrate sexual and tender feelings and involvement indicate significant maturation in the area of object relations.

The adolescent's adaptation to group processes also provides important information regarding character structure. A complete absorption in the group process, the uncritical acceptance of group mores without personal reflection and differentiation of self within the group may protect an adolescent from behavioral manifestations of severe identity diffusion, such as potentially severe conflicts in intimacy, by a conventional adaptation to group mores (Kernberg, 1988). An adolescent's capacity for subtle and critical evaluation of the individual members of his group (to which he may be making a superficial adaptation) will reveal identity integration versus identity diffusion.

An adolescent's orientation to a predominant ideology of his particular group, be it a general political ideology or an ad hoc ideology of a particular gang also will provide important information regarding superego development: primitive identification with an idealized group, with a splitting off of severely hostile evaluations of outgroups, contrasts significantly with awareness that the world is not simply divided between "all good" and "all bad" people. Most political ideologies fluctuate along a spectrum from an extremely paranoid extreme, on one hand, to a trivialized and flat conventionalism on the other, with a "humanistic" differentiated middle zone that respects individual differences, sexual intimacy and privacy, and the autonomy of the individual. Where the adolescent patient fits within such an ideological continuum will reveal important information about his superego maturation.

REFERENCES

Erikson, E. (1956), The problem of ego identity, *Identity and the Life Cycle*, pp. 104–164. New York: International Universities Press, 1959.
Hare, R. D. (1970), *Psychopathy*. New York: Wiley.
———— & Shalling. E. (1978), *Psychopathic Behavior*. New York: Wiley.
Henderson, D. K. (1939), *Psychopathic States*. London: Chapman & Hall.

————— & Gillespie, R. (1969), *Textbook of Psychiatry*. I. R. C. Batchelor. London: Oxford University Press.

Kernberg, O. F. (1975), *Borderline Conditions and Pathological Narcissism*. New York: Aronson.

————— (1984), *Severe Personality Disorders*. New Haven, CT: Yale University Press.

————— (1988), Identity, alienation, and ideology in adolescent group processes. In: *Fantasy, Myth, and Reality*. Madison, CT: International Universities Press, pp. 381–399.

————— (1989), The narcissistic personality disorder and the differential diagnosis of antisocial behavior. *Psychiatric Clinics of North America*, 12:553–570. New York: Saunders.

————— et al. (1989), *Psychodynamic Psychotherapy of Borderline Patients*. New York: Basic Books.

Kernberg, P. F. (1989), Narcissistic personality disorder in childhood. *Psychiatric Clinics of North America*, 12:671–694 New York: Saunders.

Kernberg, P. F. & Richards, A. K. (1994), Love in preadolescence as seen through children's letters. In: *The Spectrum of Psychoanalysis*, ed. A. K. Richards & A. D. Richards. Madison, CT: International Universities Press, pp. 199–218.

Mahler, M. S., Pine, F., & Bergman, A. (1975), *The Psychological Birth of the Human Infant*. New York: Basic Books.

Sherwood, V. R. & Cohen, C.P. (1994), *Psychotherapy of the Quiet Borderline Patient*. Northvale, NJ: Aronson.

PART III

ADOLESCENCE AND SOCIAL CRISIS

Adolescents are, as I have noted elsewhere, on the leading edge of social crisis almost everwhere in the world. In our time, at least, this implies involvement with violent action of one kind or another. Each of the papers in this section addresses precisely this problem. Dr. Erlich studies, from the standpoint of a concerned clinician, the reactions of Israeli adolescents to the assassination of their country's revered leader, Yitzhak Rabin. The vexing, complex and intractable problem of "ethnic cleansing" (i.e., genocide) in Bosnia evokes associations with the Holocaust, and Drs. Sugar, Shaw, and Stein consider various aspects of this tragic aspect of our dying century, with Stein reporting some glimmers of hope in this otherwise bleak vista. Finally, Dr. Kalogerakis gives us a scholarly overview of theories of causation of juvenile violence, providing a broad biopsychosocial framework for the continuing study of this difficult and often contentious field.

9 ADOLESCENTS' REACTIONS TO RABIN'S ASSASSINATION: A CASE OF PATRICIDE?

H. SHMUEL ERLICH

The assassination of Yitzhak Rabin, the Prime Minister of Israel, is undoubtedly one of the more traumatic events of our times. The tremendous waves of response to this murder, coming from a wide sociopolitical spectrum, bear testimony to this. One of the most notable aspects in the spontaneous public response was the conspicuous share of youth and adolescents in it, which received wide coverage in the media as well as in the academic world. This youthful response was described as a "classical" mourning reaction following patricide, in direct reference to Freud's (1913) well-known description. In what follows, I examine and explore these two intertwined aspects: the reaction of the adolescents on one hand, and on the other, the hypothesis that this constitutes a mourning response over patricide.

As with most traumas, it can be safely estimated that we have neither yet witnessed the end of the chain of reactions and effects of this murderous act, nor of what may be termed "the successful working through" of this group trauma. Unlike the response to a personal trauma, however, it is infinitely more difficult to estimate all the ramifications of this trauma, and to relate to it through the familiar framework of reactions to stress and traumata at the individual, clinical, and therapeutic level. It is well known that the tools at our disposal, when we are called upon to comment on reactions at the level of group, social, or mass processes, are much less accurate, sensitive, and exact, especially when based upon deductions and derivations from the individual level. We must, therefore, exercise double caution when commenting on such processes, particularly since we are ourselves part of the social processes in question, which may well bias and influence our professional judgment.

For all these reasons, I did not undertake the task of dealing with the reactions of youths to the assassination lightly. Certainly because of the gravity of the subject; but also for the reason that I am not in possession of sufficient findings or clinical material on which I can base what I am about to say. The adolescents in treatment with me, perhaps to a degree that is surprising, and perhaps not, did not comment at great length on the event, even when they did not ignore it totally. I also did not administer questionnaires and do not have research findings that might throw new light on these matters. Nevertheless, I undertook this task for two reasons: (1) I have engaged in research and exploration of adolescence for many years, and I do have certain impressions of and reflections about their professed responses to Rabin's assassination as these were available for public observation; (2) I have something to say about the responses to these responses. As I said, certain explanations were put forward in the media and in the academic and professional community which I believe deserve careful examination.

Instead of clinical material, I shall offer some pictures or scenes. These scenes represent my own selections—subjective and highly personal impressions—out of the numerous and various events we all watched endlessly in the immediate postassassination period at home, on the street, and in the continuous coverage of radio and television, which, as always in times of crisis, followed us without interruption, documenting every moment, sometimes even staging and creating the event itself. There is, of course, no escape from the central, creative, and coproductive role taken up by the media in the modern age. I will offer a couple of such images, which I find myself coming back to over and over, and which still surface in my mind even now as the shocking event itself is gaining distance in time.

First scene: This scene was broadcast repeatedly in the hours and days following the event: Aviv Gefen[1] and Yitzhak Rabin embracing, and Aviv Gefen, with heavy makeup, immediately after his appearance in the town square, that had already become history. Aviv Gefen peers into the camera, smiling with pleasure and perhaps also with a bit of embarrassment or shyness, but it is the shyness of a star. It is evident that he very much enjoys the closeness and the embrace. Rabin is also

---

[1]Aviv Gefen, a very popular singer and musician, is a youth idol and represents an anti-establishment, anti-militartistic figure. In one of earlier songs he described Rabin as a "drunkard". He appeared in the public assembly just before the assassination, with a "prophetic" song (Farewell my Brother / Be strong for me up there) which became a vehicle for public and adolescent mourning immediately following the assassination.

smiling, a warm and credible smile, a smile of closeness and affection, and even appears to be placing a kiss on Aviv's off camera cheek. Rabin in this picture looks elderly, even old, bespectacled, with balding white hair, dressed rather formally in dark suit and tie, even if, in his customary way, with a bit of negligence. He is definitely initiating the approach, the closeness, the physical touch, the hug, and the kiss. Aviv, compared to him, looks like something from another world, certainly from another generation. He is dressed in highly personal fashion, decidedly "different," his face painted and made up with a heavy layer of makeup, his lips dark and glistening with lipstick. His long flowing hair and the heavy makeup on his face seem to emphasize very well the bisexual message, perhaps the asexual one, which he puts across and symbolizes. The two men embracing in this picture are two living symbols who are at the same time well aware of their being symbols, and that they allow others to use them for their own projections and identifications, which they seem to do and accept willingly. But even as they offer themselves to being used as symbols and to the symbolic nature of their drawing close, they are also themselves.

I find myself preoccupied with the question: What do they see in each other? What moves Rabin, the representative of the generation of the Palmach,[2] a man in his seventies, who has had his fill of wars and battles, of sacrifice and political intrigue, a relatively withdrawn and closed person, not given to public emotional displays (a quality that had perhaps changed recently), seasoned and mature, square and conservative in his demeanor, to embrace Aviv Gefen and to kiss him? Is it only for the sake of the cameras, as something that could be useful for future propaganda films? Does he feel he is in need of the legitimacy that Aviv Gefen can provide for him? I have to tell myself, however, that this is not really what I feel. There is something vital and believable in this gesture, something that I experience as heartfelt and genuine, so much so that the gesture even arouses in me a measure of envy: Why is he embracing *him*? Why not *me*? And how does he manage not to be repelled by him, by his vulgarly painted, almost transvestite appearance? After all, they are as different from each other as can be imagined! Here I am reminded of something Erik Erikson once said at a case conference in which, as usual, three generations of a family were described,

---

[2]The Palmach were elite units of the Haganah, the armed forces of the Jewish population in the pre-State period, in which Rabin was outstanding young commander. This generation is credited with the establishment of the State of Israel, through armed struggle and settling the land.

down to the patient himself. He told the story in which the father turns to his own father, the patients grandfather, and asks him: "Tell me, Dad, how is it that you and my son get along so well with one another? After all, he is unbearable, and we have nothing but trouble and arguments all the time!" To which the grandfather replies: "It is simple, my son. The two of us have a common enemy—you!"

The *second scene* consists of several pictures, and is connected directly with the mourning process for Rabin. The night his coffin was on public display at the Knesset, my wife and I also went there, to join the overwhelming human wave that came out to pay its last respects to our murdered prime minister. The hour was very late, much after midnight, but people streamed from all directions in indescribable masses, but also in exemplary quietness and discipline. As we reached the place itself, on our way to the open square in front of the Knesset, the same picture repeated itself over and over again: commemorative as well as ordinary candles lit on the sidewalk or the roadside, large and small handmade signs, covered with sayings and letters addressed to Rabin, some of them accompanied by a flower, a drawing, or a poem. It was evident in all of these that their creators were young children and adolescents. And further along the way, a circle of youth, and yet another, and still more were seated on the sidewalk or in the unused road, softly singing patriotic songs, beautiful, sad Israeli songs—the kind that immediately signify times of bereavement and catastrophe. Sometimes there was in the middle of the circle a national flag, sometimes a picture of Rabin. Almost everywhere were lit candles. These boys and girls did not cry, did not wail mournfully, did not in any way act hysterically. On the contrary, they seemed quiet, inwardly directed, but also well aware of the human wave, constantly flooding past them, even as they appeared totally out of touch with it. There was sadness there, but it was extremely tender; perhaps despondency is a better word to describe the feeling. But in this despondency I also felt, strange as it may sound, a certain elevation of spirit, a kind of an ascent to higher, better, more noble spheres, like in the Chassidic transformation of the soul, when it attaches itself to the spiritual otherworldliness of the Tzadik (the "Righteous One"). There was no anger, hostility, or hatred in this. Another striking aspect was that in these circles boys with knit *kipot*[3] joined alongside other youth, in blue shirts, or other signs of their

[3]The hand knit Kippa, or skullcap, is the hallmark of the national-religious, as distinct from the ultraorthodox, who wear black ones.

belonging to "secular" Israeli society. Their sitting together, intermingled with each other, seemed like the most natural event. Not for a moment did the "secular" youth, who were decidedly the majority, indicate that they were ill-disposed towards these "other" youths who joined them, who came from a patently different political and ideological camp, and such a problematic one under these circumstances. My thought was that if this is not the Party of Peace[4], it certainly is that of conciliation and wholesomeness.

I have described these scenes because for me personally they have become an inseparable part of the entire upsetting event. There were, of course, many other pictures, all of them certainly witnessed by others as well: the scenes in the town square of Tel Aviv, at the site of the assassination where we were again with the masses for the assembly that marked the end of the week's mourning period; the funeral itself, and then the visit to the fresh grave; the writings on walls, the letters—many of them actually written by much younger, latency, and preadolescent children—and the interviews with them; the pilgrimages of adolescents from all over the country to these focal points of group and public happenings, as if to become a part of something that is transpiring, something present and actual; and much more.

Reactions to these forms of massive national mourning were numerous and variable. In response to questions posed by the media, like: "Who was Yitzhak Rabin for you?" and, "Describe your feelings about . . ." many different responses and statements could be heard. As usual, there were responses that were more eloquent, more expressive, and emotionally arousing, and such that were less representative. In conversations with colleagues, a variety of very different adolescent responses came up, of which I will mention two. In the first, the adolescent says he feels guilty, as if he has killed Rabin. In the second, an adolescent in therapy says he had a powerful emotional reaction to the assassination; but even more strongly, he is astounded by the potency of his response, which raised a slew of questions about himself, his sanity, his capacities, and so on. Many more examples can be cited. What is most striking about these responses is precisely their lack of uniformity. We can see in this, of course, a general characteristic of adolescence, namely: the tremendous variability in the shading and range of available expression at the overt level of responsiveness and observable behavior. But the question still remains: is it at all possible, and what may be the ways, to understand and

---

[4]The name given to the combined political forces committed to the peace process.

characterize this wave of spontaneous adolescent reactions? How can such a variety of shades and colors of response be characterized and understood? I believe that without a theoretical approach, capable of shedding light on these phenomena from a different angle, and departing from what is observable at the level of overt behavior, we will not find a satisfactory explanation.

As I have already mentioned, several theoretical explanations were advanced. One of the ideas immediately made use of was that of patricide, including the guilt over it. Yitzhak Rabin was indeed a father figure for all of us, as prime minister, as a military and political leader with vast, almost unquestionable personal authority. His famous words, "I shall navigate!"[5] seemed to emanate directly out of an inner authoritative posture. Even if these words were unpleasant to our democratic ears, they fulfilled a deep need and wish for a strong leader who can radiate authority, safety, and confidence, who will make order for us, enforce peace and security, and look after our well-being. What are these wishes, if not the wish for a powerful and protective father? It is indeed this same emotional stance, which regarded him as a father committed to and responsible for our survival, that had formed the ground from which sprang forth the personal allegations and accusations against him following every murderous attack, as if he personally was responsible, and as if he was the one who had created the difficult and complex situation in which we live. The outcries and signs that claimed "Rabin is a traitor!" and "Rabin is a murderer!" certainly expressed the preconception that he was an all-powerful, but also disappointing father, personally and ultimately responsible for everything, perhaps as he too saw himself or wished to be at certain moments. There is thus no doubt at all about Rabin being a father figure—admired, respected, arousing expectations and projections, as well as ambivalence, discontent, disappointment, and hostility.

If this is the case, if Rabin was indeed a father figure for us Israelis, why do I doubt the explanation that adolescent reactions to his assassination are a classic response to patricide? My doubts rest on a number of reasons. In order to discuss them, I wish to explore a few aspects of the issue: (1) the myth of patricide, (2) the adolescents' actual reactions, and (3) the psychological forces at work during adolescence.

The murder of the primordial father by his sons is described by Freud (1913) as a perhaps phantasmatic, perhaps real event, that takes place

---

[5] Spoken very forcefully in his victory speech following his election.

during the primal horde, pretribal stage that marks the dawn of human civilization. The murder of the father is the response of his sons to his total domination of everything, especially of all the women, and to their being extruded by him from the horde. The exiled sons, every one of whom aspires to take the father's place and to have the same powers and privileges, build up forces within their peer relationships. Moved by this joining of forces and their common goal, to put an end to the father's absolute control over the women of the horde, they put an end to the father's life, and then eat and incorporate him in an act of cannibalistic incorporation. But the ambivalence they felt towards the father, whom they also loved and admired, arouses in them feelings of regret and guilt that lead to his being transformed into a revered and sanctified totem animal, an object of religious adoration and idolization, in the form of the totemistic animal into which he was transformed and which now symbolizes him. The ambivalent feelings find expression in the totemistic meal, which is a ritual recreating the murder of the father and his being eaten, through killing the sanctified animal and through the meal at which it is eaten by all members of the tribe. The ritual is usually accompanied by orgiastic festivities, which depict and express paradoxically the abandonment of the social and religious strictures accepted by the sons in order to prevent the recurrence of such murder and incest. The primordial father is thus an ambivalently regarded figure, whose power inhibits the growth and development of the younger generation by blocking their approach to women, through and by which alone continuity of existence and generativity can be achieved.

This is the myth that Freud created in order to supply historic, anthropological, and literary background for two basic psychoanalytic concepts: ambivalence towards the father—competition and identification with him in relation to the mother—and acceptance of the incest taboo. These two basic assumptions are the generative root of the Oedipus complex, which Freud regarded as the cornerstone of all human development, both general and personal. Both of these, the ambivalence towards the father and the incest taboo, are transmitted from one generation to the next, and constitute the rock bottom foundation without which no human civilization can develop. In the presentation of the myth of the murder of the primal father as an actual primordial event, Freud saw support and consolidation for his teachings. The historical "fact," even if only an approximate reconstruction, was perceived by Freud as an additional element of confirmation for his hypothesized oedipal dilemma. The Oedipus complex makes its appearance at the level of the individual, but is also a basic human cultural phenomenon, and thus a connecting link between individual development and social culture in general. This is actually a line of thought often met with in Freud's writings, as in many of his contemporaries, based on the well-known principle that "ontogeny repeats phylogeny," that is, that the course of individual development recapitulates the biological development of the species. Based on the logic of this premise, Freud considered that if the murder of the father actually took place in the beginning of historical time, and its recapitulation can be observed and traced in myths, religions, rituals, or in the development of individual neurosis, then this serves as further support and evidence for the existence and operation of the Oedipus complex at both the individual and the universal levels.

I have no doubt that the myth of the patricide of the primordial father contributed significantly to understanding processes observable at the group and social level, especially the unconscious and irrational ones, which received great impetus from the developments of Bion (1961) and many who followed him (e.g., Turquet, 1975; Colman and Bexton, 1975; Colman and Geller, 1985). Indeed, *it is possible to understand the general public reaction to Rabin's assassination as expressing the ambivalent wish towards him as a father figure.* Such an understanding, which confirms the existence of an unconscious, murderous group wish toward him, can serve at least as partial explanation for the widespread public reaction of remorse and guilt after his death. Such a reaction found expression in the various emotions expressed after the murder, for example in the question, "Where have you been?"[6] or in feelings like, "We did not do enough," or "We are all guilty." Indeed, this ambivalence was expressed in a number of typical forms: depression and guilt, followed by the aggression, which is an inherent component of this ambivalence and was projected on political rivals and ideological antagonists while coming out of the depression. Totemism was also expressed in this connection, for example in the public rush toward naming sites and institutions after Rabin, even if they had no clear or direct connection with him, so as to idealize and eternalize his memory.

Even though, however, this dynamic of patricide exists and explains certain phenomena at the general public level, it does not necessarily relate to, nor does it explain, the reactions manifested in the adolescent

---

[6]This question was directed by Leah Rabin (Rabin's wife) to those who came to demonstrate support after the murder, accusing them in effect of not doing enough beforehand.

population. In the first place, patricide, as was pointed out, is a phenomenon marked by ambivalence. We did see in many adolescents the adoration and worship of Rabin, their identification with him as a hero and peace maker. But did we really also observe hostility, covert or overt aggression, followed by guilt feelings, whether direct or displaced? I do not claim there were no adolescents who felt guilt, and I have brought an example before of one such youth who felt guilty as if he had personally killed Rabin. Undoubtedly such or similar isolated responses could easily be found. As a rule, however, it seems to me that the reaction of the adolescents expresses something altogether different.[7]

The second finding which we should have encountered in the wake of a phenomenon of patricide is the internalization and identification with the murdered father. Perhaps it is still too early to look for such signs, but I do not think that anyone believes that the adolescents in question are about to reestablish the Palmach, or that they will cease from giving a central place in their life to all those things to which Rabin was a complete stranger, or for which he at times expressed outright contempt. I do not see any real signs that these adolescents are truly identifying with Rabin and his memory, although some such signs may be discerned in the general population.

What then can be discerned in the reactions of the youth? In the course of a few weeks it was possible to observe how and with what speed a ceremonial culture, or subculture, was fashioned and established. It has already been observed that we witnessed a kind of Woodstock ritual, well in the spirit of that happening: the candles and songs, the tendency and purpose that were decidedly anti-war and anti-violence; a kind of reincarnation of the culture of the flower children of the sixties, down to the motto of that era: "Make love, not war." The predominant motive in all of this was one of acceptance, tolerance and a search for perfectibility. In this respect, Rabin's assassination brought up to the surface in one fell swoop an existing and rather ordinary contemporary adolescent culture, complete with all its usual components and characteristic signs—candles, flowers, pictures, songs, poetry, and reconciliation. I have described the spirit that I absorbed in those circles of singing youths, a spirit that may be described as the incarnation of

[7]There is no doubt that any statement that lumps together various adolescent reactions as if they are one misses the real variety encountered in actuality. My comments relate to the main and dominant motives discernible in the responses of youths, even if these constitute a "hegemonious voice" (Rapoport, 1996).

beauty and goodness, of spiritual transcendence the likes of which is difficult to find in ordinary times. But adolescents have first hand knowledge of this spirit; they enter this role like a well-trained and highly skilled troupe of actors, capable of mounting a familiar play with little or no forewarning. Indeed they have performed this mourning ritual on numerous occasions, mostly sad ones, such as the tragedy in Arad, and following their friends' deaths in road accidents or acts of terrorism. These ceremonials are expressive of the readiness of adolescents for immediate idealization and creation of heroes.

Where do these winds blow from? Is this pattern distinct to Israeli youth, or does it draw on universal sources? In order to answer this, we must once again turn towards theory; but rather than turn to widely accepted theory, we should make a theoretical detour and see where it takes us. Such a detour leads through looking at psychological life not by posing the question that asks what is actually happening, but how is this happening processed and experienced in our psyche. In other words, we must look at the place that experiential modalities take up in psychic life in general, and how these influence adolescence in particular. What are these modalities, what are their implications, and what is their impact?

I have suggested (Erlich and Blatt, 1985; Erlich, 1990, in press) the possibility of regarding relatedness between persons—mother and infant, lovers, man and woman, patient and psychoanalyst-therapist—as taking place at two experiential levels simultaneously. One level consists of the experience of self and other as separate from one another, possessing a different and separate internal focus, each with his own internal center of gravity. This experience incorporates the experience of self and other as having clear cut boundaries, which structure, organize, and distinguish them from one another. Their relatedness and relationship with each other is experienced and perceived accordingly and out of the experience of the differences, distinctiveness, and separateness of the one from the other. Out of this experience stems the relationship between self and other, which is therefore mainly one of a functional and instrumental nature, in which the self does, or wishes to do, to the other, or have the other do to it, in one way or another. I therefore termed this experiential modality the experiential mode or relatedness of *Doing*.[8]

---

[8]The terms *Being* and *Doing* have clear origins and parallels in the writings of Winnicott (1971). There are nonetheless, several significant differences between his usage of them and what is presented here.

The experiential mode of *Doing* is characterized by power relation-ships and thought processes of a logical, causal, realistic, and scientific nature. It is also, however, the mode at which instinctual wishes and desires operate, as these always tend toward doing to (or being done to by) an object that is to some degree experienced as separate from the self. The overall aim in the mode of *Doing* is one of achieving aims and goals, of intentionality, and often of efficiency of performance, expressed in defining the task and carrying it out to completion. Clear-cut boundaries are therefore vitally important in this mode: the sepa-rateness and individuation of self and object find expression in the clarity of definition and strength of the boundaries that separate them from one another. The experience and perception of time here is chronological and linear, as in the time dimension pertinent to heavenly bodies and other physical events. It is time that can be measured and divided, time with a beginning and an end. Reality itself is experienced as having an independent, separate and autonomous existence from the ego/self, and it is governed by the lawfulness that derives from matter itself. Man too is perceived as existing autonomically, ruled by and answerable to conditions of lawfulness and causality.

The other experiential mode, which exists simultaneously and paral-lely with the first, is not built on separateness, but on the experience of merger and fusion. Self and object here are experienced as a unit, with no boundaries and separation marking them off from each other. To the extent that boundaries exist in this mode, they are the boundaries of the container, encompassing the united self and object and protecting them, so as to enable the continuity of the experience of oneness; other-wise, boundaries become a source of frustration and can be experi-enced as a severe limitation. Reality in this mode is experienced as part of, or a direct continuation of the ego/self. The perception of reality is thus subjective, and so are thought processes. The emphasis is on processes and contents of unity, fusion and merger with the other, as well as with the universe, nature, and so on. Thought processes in this mode are not causal, but metaphoric, synthetic, and egocentric, with a marked tendency toward identity and identification of self and external world. The experience of time is not linear or physical, chronological, or measurable; it is rather time that moves in strange circles or spirals. The central wish and experience in this mode is existential, related to the experience of "being" and "being one with" (or conversely, of its absence, i.e., of "not being" or "not being one with"). I therefore termed this experiential mode the modality or relatedness of *Being*. The central tendency in the *Being* modality is towards subjectivity; that is, to allow the subject to experience itself as a "continuity of being" (Winnicott) that exists in unity with an other. In this experiential mode there are no drives, nor any drive-derived wishes and conflicts; there are only experiences of being as against not-being, with all the attending wishes, needs, and fears that pertain to it.

Two points must now be added to this phenomenological account. The first is that viewed developmentally, both modalities are in existence and operate from the beginning of life. There is increasingly more evidence that the neonate is equipped and capable of acting from the start with a sharply tuned capacity to appreciate and respond to reality based on his or her sense of separateness from the mother; but, at the same time, he or she is also capable of uniting and merging with the mother (Stern, 1985). The mother too functions in *both* experiential modes. We may thus conceptualize her "good enough" maternal capacity, her "primary maternal preoccupation," not as her ability to enter a symbiotic merger with the infant, as Mahler, Pine, and Bergman (1975) described it, or as an initial mother–baby relatedness that is pure *Being*, as defined by Winnicott (1971), but as the mother's capacity to change gears and adapt herself flexibly and appropriately to the specific experiential mode the infant is in and requires at the moment. The mother may relate to the infant in a mode or relatedness either of *Being* and merger, or of separateness and *Doing*, in accordance with the experiential mode the infant is in.

The second point is a functional one. The working assumption is that both experiential modalities are in existence and operative from the beginning of life, and that they function parallely and in continuity with each other. At any specific moment, however, only one of them will usually be dominant and ascendant. Beyond this, these experiential modes have a special meaning for adolescence. I have pointed out (Erlich, 1990, 1993) that adolescence is a developmental stage that demands the positive integration of these two experiential modes. There is, succinctly stated, no room or possibility for the development of either identity or intimacy without achieving such an integration.

What and how do these experiential modes contribute to our understanding? Subjective feelings and experiences, perceptions, and constructions of internal and external reality, such as: the phenomenological I (subject), self, identity, and object, are final products of prolonged and complex experiential processes; these processes transpire through the mediation of the experiential modes I have described. Drives and instincts, for example, are always experienced within the *Doing* mode, the modality in which the object is experienced as separate from the self. This is the experiential modality in which instinctual drama unfolds, including the sexual-instinctual upheavals of adolescence. In the modality of *Being*, self and object are experienced as a unity, with a fused, merged, inseparable existence. When the experience of *Being* is undermined and shaky, we meet with an experience of loneliness of the worst kind: the loneliness experienced in the actual presence of the object, which cannot be experienced as being, along with the self that is not experienced as being and existing (Erlich, in press).

The adolescent is connected with and related to social reality through such internal structures as ego, self, and identity. The ego, comprehended from the experiential perspective, represents the subject's experience of himself or herself in the mode of *Doing*. In this mode the experience of subjectivity temporarily withdraws to what is the experiential background, and the figurative focus shifts to the functional issues of doing and the ways and means for their achievement. The experiential focus is thus on questions of adaptation—the degree of practicality and functional efficiency of that doing that is under focus, in accordance with largely objective criteria. The goal is primarily the *task* and the need to carry it out efficiently and well, and not the "I" involved in the performance. Indeed, under such conditions, the experience of I or of selfhood seems to all but disappear and to be absorbed in carrying out the task or reaching the goal. In the mode of *Being*, on the other hand, experience centers on the united and merged being of self and other. The core of this experience is selfhood itself. The experience of the self becomes the existential dimension that *both* the subject *and* the other are committed to creating, maintaining and preserving. This experience is supported and assisted by primary thought processes, the main function of which is not to cope with external reality but to serve the expression and shaping of the subjective experience of the self (Noy, 1969).

If we turn back at this point to the questions and phenomena with which we started, it appears quite clear that patricide takes place in the mode of *Doing*. It seems equally clear that patricide is suffused with drive, intentionality, conflict, and ambivalence, and that, judged against this criterion, the reactions of adolescents to Rabin's assassination should not be understood as being in this dimension. The reactions described, by myself as well as by others, are almost totally devoid of any components of *Doing*. On the other hand, however, they seem saturated with qualities typical of the mode of *Being*, such as the spiritual experience of merging and "being-one-with"—with the adolescent or youth group, with the larger community, or with Rabin's figure and image. That is also why they should neither be regarded as experiences that would lead toward action or some direct doing, nor should they be evaluated in terms of their adaptability to objective reality. On the contrary, their meaning and significance lies in the search for fusion and merger with a larger totality and group, in and through which the self can find expression, not in action or doing, but through being part of what is happening. This is also why the phenomenon cannot and should not be explained or explored in terms of guilt feelings or disappointed expectations.

This was best expressed once again by none other than Aviv Gefen. In a BBC interview assessing reactions to Rabin's assassination, Gefen stated: "We were a bored generation; Rabin's death gave us a meaning to deal with." In other words, the issue was not competition with and ambivalence toward Rabin, the omnipotent ruler, who had blocked the adolescents' development, toward whom they had harbored unconscious destructive wishes that magically brought about his death, and for which the mourning rituals are an atonement. The opposite is the truth: the youth, through Aviv Gefen, admit to suffering of a serious problem in the mode of *Being*. They are a bored and alienated generation, suffering from meaninglessness and the absence of connectedness with ideology and values, through which it is possible to feel united, and for the sake of which it may be possible and even worthwhile to sacrifice oneself, so as to gain meaning through the fusion with the ideal other. *Rabin's death provides them with this ideal other, with whom they can merge*, and this is indeed what they do.

Here, however, we meet with yet another important point that needs to be clarified. If Rabin is not the father figure whom the adolescents "murdered," what figure does he represent, and where does its significance stem from? Here I must return to my earlier description of the scene of the embrace of Rabin and Aviv Gefen. As I perceive and interpret this scene, with all its odd closeness and affection, the emotional encounter and merger of such different generations and types, it appears to be the union, or reunion, of a grandfather and a grandson and not of a father and his son. The elderly Rabin, the representative of the founding generation or what is left of it, embraces to his heart not his son, the generation that directly continued his ways and struggles, but the next generation, the generation that follows those who followed Yitzhak

Rabin. This is why there is something strange in this union, which does not represent a straight or natural continuity, but skips over the intermediate generation. That embrace represents the mutual longing for and turning to each other of two generations separated from one another by the events of a generation, by an ideological abyss and nearly polar styles; at the same time, however, they feel a strong mutual attraction, and a wish to be close and united. This is yet another reason for its not being a case of patricide, but rather of the death of a grandfather, a grandfather that can be loved as a father cannot, whose mythical and benevolent figure looms beyond the sphere of the oedipal conflict for which the father stands.

This sort of grandfather is actually more connected to the mode of *Being* than to that of *Doing*. He represents *Being* by actually being the link that joins the grandson in with historical continuity. The symbolization of historical ties and continuity is much more evident with grandfather than with father. The phenomenon of historical and generational continuity always characterizes intergenerational relationships. But in this particular case it has a special significance, specific to Israeli society. This society, which founded and created the State and rebuilt the country, did so against the background of the Holocaust. For it, therefore, the connection with the grandparents' generation is a particularly loaded and problematic one. On one hand, a historic rift actually took place between the founders' generation and its parents, which found expression in the adolescent rebellion of youthful people against the values, culture, religion, and history of their forefathers. The founders' generation is indeed the generation that committed symbolic patricide. On the other hand, the same generation is also the one that created the conditions that enabled the Jewish people to continue its existence. The Holocaust cruelly destroyed the generation of the parents of the founders' generation, as if the terrible reality that was unleashed carried out the unconscious patricidal fantasy of the founders of the State of Israel. The emotional burden of the severed relationship with the grandfather and the abyss opened by the Holocaust served to make these dynamics of the founders' generation even more acute. The generation that grew up in the State of Israel, created after and in the wake of the Holocaust, is a generation that in many respects grew up without grandparents, without the linking chain of intergenerational continuity. The "absent grandfather," the void and dissociation related to his absence, and the difficulty in relating socially to the issue of intergenerational continuity (regardless of the actual situation in a given family), turned into an important component, perhaps even a characteristic with only partially known and understood implications, of Israeli social reality and of "Israeliness" itself.

I suggest that the longings that the adolescents felt toward Rabin can be seen as longings for grandfather, expressing the wish to unite and fuse with him, which is neither conflictual nor instinctual. Such a union imparts to the identifier the experience of continuity, and in this way, a small taste of the experience of eternity. The mourning for Rabin expresses such wishes and longings, and through them also something of the Israeli mourning for the generation of grandparents that was lost without an opportunity to better know them, to be and to identify with them.

In summary, I wish to reemphasize the dangers inherent in making use of psychoanalytic hypotheses or concepts in a manner not sufficiently aware of the finer aspects of the model and the specific characteristics of the phenomenon we wish to study and explain. Patricide, or more precisely, the murderous wishes directed at the same-sex parent, is, of course, a central theme of adolescence. Winnicott (1971) called attention to the adolescent need to murder, in his unconscious fantasy, the parent whose place he must take. "To take the place of" means only one thing in unconscious fantasy: to remove and destroy. The parent's role in this drama is quite clear: they must survive and remain alive, loyal to themselves and to their ways. No growth and development can actually take place without the adolescent's taking up his or her place in the real world. It is also absolutely clear that in this struggle there can be no substitutes for the real, actual, flesh and blood parent, who is also bodily part of the adolescent. There is no way of transferring or conferring this on someone else. Any attempt to do so, to displace or substitute, whether initiated by the adolescent or by the parent, implies the existence of a great and paralyzing fear about the parent's capacity to survive the destructive efforts of the adolescent.

The adolescents' reactions to Rabin's assassination do not contain the guilt and fear that are associated with patricide. Rather, they express wishes for merging and fusing with a totality or a whole, that is more than what there is. Rabin serves this need since he is a figure representing an entire generation that is receding from the collective national consciousness. This is particularly true for the younger generation in relation to the grandparents' generation. The wishes and longings for the grandparent find immediate outlets in the cultural modes of the adolescents, through which they can express the wish to unite and fuse, even for a fleeting moment, with something larger than themselves, with someone capable of representing a distant and lost generation, and in this way to ensure their sense of continued historical existence.

REFERENCES

Bion, W. R. (1961), *Experiences in Groups*. New York: Basic Books.

Colman, A. D. & Bexton, W. H. (1975), *Group Relations Reader.* San Rafael, CA: Grex.

Colman, A. D. & Geller, M. H. (1985), *Group Relations Reader, 2*. Springfield, VA: Goetz.

Erlich, H. S. (in press), On loneliness, narcissism and intimacy. *Amer. J. Psychoanal.*

——— (1990), Boundaries, limitations, and the wish for fusion in the treatment of adolescents. *The Psychoanalytic Study of the Child*, 45:195–213. New Haven, CT: Yale University Press.

——— (1993), Fantasy, reality and adolescence. *The Psychoanalytic Study of the Child*, 48:209–223. New Haven, CT: Yale University Press.

——— & Blatt, S. J. (1985), Narcissism and object love. *The Psychoanalytic Study of the Child*, 40:57–79. New Haven, CT: Yale University Press.

Freud, S. (1913), Totem and taboo. *Standard Edition*, 13:1–162. London: Hagarth Press, 1955.

Mahler, M., Pine, F. & Bergman, A. (1975), *The Psychological Birth of the Human Infant*. New York: Basic Books.

Noy, P. (1969), A revision of the psychoanalytic theory of the primary process. *Internat. J. Psycho-anal.*, 50:155–178.

Rapoport, T. (1996), The voice of youth—all of youth? Reactions of youths to Rabin's murder. Presented at School of Education Conference, The Hebrew University of Jerusalem.

Stern, D. N. (1985), *The Interpersonal World of the Infant*. New York: Basic Books.

Turquet, P. M. (1975), Threats to identity in the large group. In: *The Large Group*, ed. L. Kreeger. London: Constable.

Winnicott, D. W. (1971), *Playing and Reality*. New York: Basic Books.

SPECIAL SECTION ON AMBIENT GENOCIDE AND ADOLESCENCE

Introduction

MAX SUGAR, SECTION EDITOR

The word genocide, which is derived from Greek, means the destruction of a race or tribe. Although genocide has been with us since time immemorial, and is even mentioned in the Bible, it was coined in 1944. In 1946 genocide was affirmed by the United Nations as a crime under international law. Two years later the U.N. held a convention on the prevention of, and punishment for, genocide. In 1951 it was promulgated as a crime (Mant, 1978).

Why is this so important to us as psychiatrists? During the 1930s the German public was prepared by sophisticated propaganda for the killing of psychiatric patients . This included emotional films in which psychiatric patients were degraded and then used to present an argument for their own ultimate annihilation. These were produced in cooperation with doctors under Gerhard Wagner, a party member who, from 1932 on, was the leader of the National Socialist German Physicians League. The adult euthanasia program was administered by the Third Reich's work group of sanitariums and nursing homes whose headquarters in Berlin became known by the infamous code name of T-4. Subsequently, doctors, primarily psychiatrists, were paid a commision for selecting patients to be killed (Hunter, 1993). It is estimated that only one in five psychiatric inpatients survived (Meyer-Lindenberg, 1991). Medical killing included other categories as follows: patients suffering from certain specified conditions; those institutionalized for more than five years; the criminally insane; and patients who were not "German citizens." They were killed by starvation, by withholding basic treatments, or by lethal injection. On the suggestion of a psychiatrist in 1940, gassing with carbon monoxide was initiated (Hunter, 1993).

We could turn our backs on these data and consider them part of a despicable, unenlightened past. But is it only history or is there a present danger of a repetition? Genocide is a current fact: witness its appearance in the recent news media about Cambodia, Mozambique, Rwanda, Burundi, and the Balkans. We could also review history in the United States beginning with the Revolutionary War during which Whigs and Tories committed atrocities of all kinds against one another, even neighbors and friends (Brown, 1969), as well as the genocidal efforts against Native Americans.

Are physicians considered at risk for such activities? Think of Radovan Karadzic, a psychiatrist, the leader of the Serbs in Bosnia-Herzegovina, recently indicted by the World Court in the Hague for his genocidal actions. If that is too distant geographically, then we can think of the problems closer to home. Bioethicists are struggling with the question of medical rationing and euthanasia. In countries with socialized medicine, kidney dialysis and organ transplantation are not available for those over age 65. Euthanasia is legal in Holland and there is a movement to legalize it in the United States and other countries. Oregon now has rationing of medical care for the sake of the state's finances. Debates about the survival of Medicare and Medicaid are in the news frequently. This is similar to the eugenics practiced in Nazi Germany on Germans and others whereby those who were non-productive and a drain on resources, or whose quality of life had diminished markedly, were liquidated.

Therefore, the issues presented in this section need serious attention as ever-present, insidious risk problems.

Jon Shaw provides a theory of genocide on the basis of narcissism. This should help us to fathom how this horror is justified by the perpetrators and in understanding the slide away from morals and restraints. Bradley Stein takes us into the psychiatric front lines of the Balkan war with a very personal record of his efforts to provide psychiatric help to adolescents caught in a war zone. This should be helpful in dealing with such crises. Max Sugar offers a view of adolescent survivors of Nazi concentration camps and how incarceration affected their development. This information may help to recognize the effects on, and problems in treating, those growing up in a genocidal climate.

MAX SUGAR

REFERENCES

Brown, W. (1969), *The Good Americans*. New York: Morrow.
Hunter, E. (1993), The snake on the caduceus: Dimensions of medical and psychiatric responsibility in the Third Reich. *Austral. & New Zealand J. Psychiat.*, 27:149–156.
Mant, A. K. (1978), Genocide. *J. Forensic Sci. Soc.*, 18:13–17.
Meyer-Lindenberg, J. (1991), The Holocaust and German psychiatry. *Brit. J. Psychiat.*, 159:7–12.

10   NARCISSISM, IDENTITY FORMATION, AND GENOCIDE

JON A. SHAW

The world today is enmeshed in conflict. The colonial empires of the last century have unraveled. This is best seen in the fragmentation of the Russian Empire but it is pervasively evident in other parts of the world. Paradoxically, colonialism and nationalism, with its central orchestration of power, had mitigated ethnic, tribal, religious, and racial conflict between diverse groups. In a manner similar to Freud's concept of the primal horde (Freud, 1921), the killing of the father has led to increasing conflicts between siblings.

Today regional conflicts, like so many "brush fires" around the globe, ever threaten to engulf new peoples. Burundi is just beginning to recover from its most recent ethnic massacre. Since its independence from Belgium in 1962 there have been a number of horrific episodes of killing between the majority Hutu tribe and the militarily dominant Tutsi tribe. In the latest chapter in a story that will no doubt continue, approximately 800,000 mostly minority Tutsi were killed by mobs of Hutu in 100 days. The killing was discriminate, purposeful and executed with the intent to remove those who were identified with the "other tribe."

In another part of the world war trials are considering those who participated in the "ethnic cleansing" between the Bosnian Serbs and the Bosnian Muslims. In what remains of the Russian empire we have seen the Russian army systematically destroy Grozny, the capital of Chechnya with its 400,000 inhabitants. To the Russians the Chechens are synonymous with crime and banditry. While one might prefer to see these conflicts as motivated by political and economic considerations undertaken to ensure that one's own peoples are provided sufficient resources and material support, it quickly becomes apparent that irrational forces are embedded in the systematic killing that far supersedes economic and political reality.

211

The Problem of Genocide

Genocide as "the systematic killing or extermination of a whole people or nation" is not an uncommon experience in the history of man. It necessarily implies the killing of members of the same species or conspecifics. In this century we have seen the massacre of the Armenians in Constantinople, the death of six million Jews in the Holocaust, the killing of approximately three million Cambodians by the Khmer Rouge, the systematic destruction of the Tutsi or the Hutu by the other, and "ethnic cleansing" in the Balkans. While there has been a tendency to see genocidal behavior as a relatively recent phenomenon associated with the rise of states in the European sense, there is evidence from the archeological data that genocidal behavior was evident in tribal societies in the fourteenth century. A site along the Crow Creek in South Dakota revealed the remains of approximately 500 people of both sexes and all ages who were killed, scalped, decapitated, and dismembered (Krech, 1994).

How does a group of people rationalize and justify to themselves the right to massively kill others? It seems to me that genocidal behavior can be partly understood through an understanding of the relationship between aggression, narcissism, and the emotional-cognitive process of how one defines the self and the unacceptable other.

While one would like to see genocidal behavior as the product of demented or psychotic individuals it is increasingly apparent that genocide is perpetrated by largely normal leaders and their followers (Charny, 1982, 1986). Harrower (1995) noted that the Nuremberg psychiatrist who interviewed the Nazis reported that their "personalities are not unique or insane and could be duplicated in any country of the world today." In an analysis of the Rorschach data of the Nuremberg war criminals, Resnick and Nunno (1991) noted that as a group they were ambitious, cognitively rigid, action-oriented, less introspective and empathic, and less likely to cope with their affective urges through self-examination. As a group they were somewhat compulsive with mildly paranoid features. Nevertheless, the authors agreed with Harrower, that these "were average German citizens," who could be commonly found in the upper echelons of most closed bureaucratic systems.

Goldhagen (1996) struggles with the various explanations given for the Holocaust which he describes as a "central intellectual problem." He refutes the usual explanations for the Germans participating in genocidal behavior, that is: (1) *coercion*. They were unable to say no because of threats of punishments and fears of death; (2) *obedience.* They had been indoctrinated to blindly follow orders; (3) *situational pressure.* They were the victims of enormous social psychological pressure and institutional expectations; (4) *self-interest.* They were petty bureaucrats and technocrats motivated by promises of career advancement; and, (5) *bureaucratic myopia.* They never understood the horrific genocidal nature of their behavior because of their fragmentary role in the bureaucracy. Goldhagen (1996) legitimately raises the question of motivation. He writes, "People must be motivated to kill others, or else they would not do so." Goldhagen (1996) is content, however, to see the genocidal behavior embedded in German society. He believes the genocidal behavior was the product of a historically persistent and widespread profound animus toward the Jews. Ordinary Germans did not want to say "no". They were motivated by an antisemitism and a belief that Jews ought to die. This explanation fails to address the reality that genocidal behavior is a human problem. What is there about the nature of man that makes him so vulnerable to pathological belief systems such as antisemitism?

There is little doubt that mankind, whether it be Moslem, Hindu, Buddhist Christian, or Jew, is capable of beliefs which lead to the devaluation of others and a readiness to kill others for their group membership. The role of the average man in the perpetration of genocidal behavior is evident in the current epidemic of genocidal behavior. It is known that normal people can be seduced by powerful and clever authority or group influences to compromise individual judgment and even to willfully hurt other people (Asch, 1956; Milgram, 1974). The emotional and cognitive mechanisms employed are complex and yet frighteningly simple. If this were not so, genocide would be less frequent.

While hate may be evident in genocide, it is its relative absence that is so chilling to the observer. The killing goes forth without much emotion, but with absolutarian conviction and thoroughness of purpose. The aggression is lethally directed against the prey. In genocide the people killed are frequently referred to in nonhuman terms. The killing of Tutsi by the Hutu was likened to "cockroach cleansing." It is important to note that the systematic killing of the Tutsis also included those moderate Tutsis, who did not subscribe to the beliefs of the majority. History indicates that genocide invariably focuses not only on the "hated group" but also those members of one's own group who come to the support of the hated group. Thus, we can see that a Jew assassinated the Prime Minister Rabin of Israel as if he was one of the hated group of

Arabs. The assassin declared himself as serving the God of Abraham. Elaine Pagels (1995) suggests that Satan is a symbolic reflection of how we perceive ourselves and those we call the other. All too often religion, in its various forms, metaphorically defines "we" as God's people and "they" as God's enemies. Satan is used to define one's enemies, and thus a moral and religious value is placed on one's own group that is denied to the other.

It seems to this observer that the purposeful extermination of the "hated group" can be understood in the context of something which is uniquely human, the interweaving of man's aggression with his intense and enduring narcissism. First, I would like to make some comments about aggression.

The Problem of Aggression

Durant and Durant (1968), historians of philosophy, have written that the "laws of biology are the fundamental lessons of history." Konner (1993) notes that "every living creature exists in a natural state of conflict with every other creature in the environment." A number of contributions to our understanding of aggression comes from ethology. Wilson (1975) described eight kinds of aggression present in vertebrates: 1) territorial aggression, 2) dominance aggression, 3) sexual aggression, 4) parental disciplinary aggression, 5) weaning aggression, 6) moralistic aggression, 7) predatory aggression, and, 8) antipredatory aggression.

Wasman and Flynn (1962) distinguished between two subtypes of aggressive behavior in animals, that is, affective and predatory aggressive behavior. Affective aggressive behavior is characterized by autonomic arousal, threatening or defensive postures, vocalizations, and often frenzied attacks. Affective aggression may be reactive, situational, intraspecific, and not always goal directed. This type of aggression is often ritualistic, such as occurs in territorial disputes, like that of troops of Howling monkeys screaming at each other across a territorial boundary.

Predatory aggression on the other hand entails less autonomic arousal in conjunction with the stalking behavior. There is little posturing and vocalization associated with a lethally directed attack upon an interspecific prey. It is predatory aggression with stalking behavior, but with little evident affect, posturing, or vocalization, that seems to characterize much of genocidal behavior.

Genocide appears to satisfy no animal need or craving for aggression. There is no evidence of aggression in humans awaiting its inevitable discharge. Aggression, as it is described in the ethological literature is highly ritualized, having the apparent purpose of maximizing the survival of the species rather than harming and killing of conspecifics. Gratification in connection with aggression appears to be entirely absent from animal life. There is general agreement among ethologists and social scientists that there is no aggressive instinct propelling human behavior. Scott (1975) concludes that "there is no such thing as a simple instinct for fighting, in the sense of an internal driving force which has to be satisfied. There is, however, an internal physiological mechanism which has only to be stimulated to produce fighting." The fighting that occurs between conspecifics consists mainly of threatening behavior, bluff or a reaction to sexual rivalry. This stands in contrast to systematic killing that is so often characteristic of human behavior.

Psychoanalysts from the time of Freud have been well aware of the problem of aggression as it has been manifested in all its variable complexity in the analytic situation and in the observable world. Freud (1930) observed that "men are not gentle friendly creatures wishing for love, who simply defend themselves if they are attacked, but that a powerful measure of desire for aggression has to be reckoned as part of their instinctual endowment." Hobbes (1651) reflecting upon the nature of man, noted that, "if any two men desire the same thing which nevertheless they cannot both enjoy, they become enemies, and in the way to their end, endeavor to destroy or subdue one another."

The development of a concept of aggression intrinsic to man's personality and behavior is one that foments controversy. Nevertheless, one must explain aggression as a general process or be limited to describing isolated events in the psychic life of individuals. As Anna Freud (1953) observed, "There seems to be universal recognition of the fact that normal and abnormal psychological development cannot be understood without adequate explanation of the role played by the aggressive and destructive tendencies and attitudes" (p. 261). Aggression as a manifest phenomenon is omnipresent in animal and human behaviors, and would appear to reflect the continuity of behavior vis-à-vis evolution.

Much of the confusion in any discussion of aggression is the problem of definition. Joseph (1973) has observed that the term aggression is derived from the Latin, "to go forward," or "to approach," and has generally been associated with the meaning to go forward with the intent of inflicting harm. Wilson (1975), a sociobiologist, defined aggression as, "the abridgement of the rights of others, forcing him to surrender something he owns or might otherwise have attained, either by a physical act or by the threat of action" (p. 242). This is a definition that is rather specific, well-defined, and operational.

At present, most theories of human aggression are essentially predicated on a two factor model: 1) Individuals are born with a natural endowment of non-destructive aggression which may be characterized as the need to assertively explore and to act on the environment for the purpose of getting one's needs satisfied; and 2) a capacity for destructive aggression that is elaborated through developmental and learned experiences (Kohut 1977; Lichtenberg 1989; Parens 1989)

There is increasing consensus that aggression emerges predominantly out of the developmental process and that various forms of aggression are shaped and configured through identificatory pathways and the vicissitudes of object relations. Humans are unique in their relative independence from biological endowment. We come into the world as children who are relatively helpless and require many years of nurturance, protection, and education. Our dependence on learning and the social milieu for the elaboration of our character structure ensures that the aggressive motivational structures will be profoundly influenced by developmental, family, and social determinants.

Aggressive behavior appears to be a developmental trait that begins in early life and frequently continues throughout the life cycle (Shaw and Campo-Bowen, 1995). Olweus (1979) concluded that the stability of aggression is substantial, approaching that found in the domain of intelligence, and reflects an enduring reaction tendency.

As the theory of aggression has become intertwined with an adaptational and developmental perspective there has emerged an increased interest in the central role of affects at the core of aggressive behavior, such as the darker passions of anger, hostility and rage (Person, 1993). The central question confronting those interested in the problem of genocide is how the affects associated with aggression become transduced into genocidal behavior or, more importantly for our consideration, how they become woven into a motivational system. We know that the killing behavior intrinsic to genocidal behavior is but the final step in a continuum of behavior characterized by social ostracism, dehumanization, hostility, and cruelty.

While aggressive tendencies are a normal feature of the human, biologically based repertoire, the final form and character of the aggressive drive structures is determined by developmental experience, that

216

is, the quality of the earliest object relations, the structure of the ego, the capacity to regulate self-esteem, the ego ideal and the formation of the superego, and the vicissitudes of the self in its interaction with the environment.

Marcovitz (1982) suggested that four types of behaviors have to be explained in a comprehensive theory of human aggression: (1) activities toward an object such as assertiveness; (2) instrumental aggression to accomplish a goal, or aggressive behavior that occurs as a reaction to frustration, or as a response to an attack; (3) hatred, in which the aim is the destruction or humiliation of the object; and (4) sadism, the infliction of pain or humiliation on an object for the purpose of sexual excitement and gratification. It is apparent that none of these four behaviors begins to describe the systematic psychological processes intrinsic to genocide in which largely normal people systematically kill whole groups of people. It is my belief that genocide can best be understood within our contemporary understanding of narcissism.

Narcissism and Aggression

A number of authors have explored the concept of aggression as it relates more specifically to the self and the vicissitudes of narcissism (Rochlin, 1973, 1982; Eissler, 1971; Kohut, 1972). Narcissism is generally defined as a concentration of psychological interest upon the self. Narcissism implies a set of attitudes varying from simple self-regard to megalomaniacal omnipotence. While a certain amount of narcissism is normative and integral to survival, there is a propensity for one's inherent egocentricity to lead to varying degrees of overvaluation of the self.

Rochlin (1973, 1982) considered that human aggression is different from animal aggression, in that it cannot be explained either by ethological considerations or the classical psychoanalytic theory of the instincts, and that it is peculiarly related to narcissism. Humans are unique in our propensity to kill our own kind. It is estimated that over 100 million people have been killed in this century alone by aggression against ourselves. It is my thesis that genocidal behavior originates not from a natural endowment of aggression but rather from narcissistic aims.

Rochlin (1973) writes, "The conventional notion of a human 'appetite' for aggression has obscured the fact that it is narcissism which is insatiable. To satisfy its needs aggression is commissioned. It is in the service of the self that aggression has its natural task" (p. 257). He believes that narcissism is the "great menace," and that it is only the lifelong dynamic presence of narcissism that can account for the anatomy of aggression in humans. It is the difficulty in giving up ego-centric aims. Freud (1914) noted the importance of narcissism as a motivational structure in his classic paper *On Narcissism*. He postulated that the development of the ego consists in its departure from primary narcissism, and gives rise to vigorous attempts to recover the lost narcissism of childhood. The restoration of the lost narcissism, such as earlier states of perceived perfectability, ideal love, and omnipotence, may be sought through narcissistic object choices, through identification with a perceived powerful, and specially deserving group, that is, collective narcissism (Kohut, 1972), or through the search for perfectability (Rothstein, 1984).

It is when we are unable to face our anxiety regarding our biological fragility, survivability, transience and death that we may, in a compensatory manner, attempt to narcissistically create a heroic image in which there is denial of the human condition. Becker (1975) states that aggression in humans is related to our efforts to deny mortality and to secure victory over our limitations. He suggests that the problem is that man "wants a stature and a destiny that is impossible of any animal; he wants an earth that is not an earth but a heaven, and the price for this kind of fantastic ambition is to make the earth an even more eager graveyard than it naturally is" (p. 96).

While narcissism is essential for survival, it may become used as an indispensable counterpoise to our frightening irrelevance in the universe. In the face of the vastness of the globe, and the still greater vastness of the firmament to which we extend our gaze, without a healthy narcissism we would be crushed by the infinities that surround us. Becker (1968) noted the fundamental need for a "meaning" that transcends biological fragility. We must create our own meanings in the world and impart our own sense of life conviction that gives the passing years a sense of uniqueness and a special quality which differentiates ourselves from others. How else could the individual, who alone is cognizant of his or her death endure the passing of time, which brings them irretrievably closer to it. Thus narcissism serves to convert a world that is, from a psychological point of view, unlivable into an abode that was created by God expressly for God's own purpose and pleasure. Humanity's attempt to be the Olympian by reaching for the support of religion is fraught with danger and ultimately uncertainty. It never escapes the frustrations of this world, its cruelty, its imperfections and the earthly clash with one's religious vision.

It is our very humaneness and the tragedy of the human condition that gives us the potential for participating in genocide. Narcissistic aims associated with the yearning for perfectability, power over others, entitlement, and collective narcissism lead to the exploitation of others and the denial of their human rights. Charny (1986) suggests that when people are unable to face existential anxiety as a universal experience, but rather feel impelled to assert their right over others as a means of denying their own limitations, then they are likely to participate in genocide.

In the act of genocide there is the fantasy that the individual and his or her collective group have risen above the human condition, achieved a special power, and are especially deserving. Paradoxically, the narcissistic aim not only promotes the self but is associated with a search for a group within which the individual can be absorbed passively in a self-object merger, and through which he or she can recover the lost perfectibility and infantile omnipotence of childhood. Identity is invariably associated with narcissistic identification with a group ideal in which the self imagines that it is enriched by the powerful properties of the group. There is the delusion of omnipotence and triumphant grandeur. In a Kohutian sense (1977) the paradigm becomes: Even if I am alone and not all powerful, the group is all-powerful and I am part of the group, therefore, I am powerful, special and immortal.

The excessive narcissistic investment in one's collective group, and its expansion or defense in collective aggression, is one of the themes of history in which people war against their conspecifics in seemingly endless conflicts. The Nazis justified their genocide of the Jews and the Gypsies by the need to preserve racial purity. Genocidal behavior is invariably associated with the wish of the group to justify its narcissistic claims by purging dangers alledgely posed by the victims (Markusen, 1992). This is particularity evident in religious wars with rivalry between contending claims of immortality. Most genocidal behavior is predicated on religious imagery, a narcissistically shared world view of uniqueness, entitlement, superiority, and claimed immortality. Lifton (1986) has borrowed the concept of "totalism" from Erikson (1954) to describe this proclivity to think in absolute categories. Erikson (1954) defined this totalism as "a Gestalt in which an absolute boundary is emphasized; given a certain arbitrary delineation, nothing that belongs inside must be left outside, nothing that must be outside can be tolerated inside" (p. 162).

Whereas one might prefer to see genocide as a regression to a Darwinian primitive struggle in which the stronger triumphs over the weak, the behavior seems to be decidedly and uniquely human. Human aggression, directed as it is by narcissism, represents an ongoing and fundamental danger to itself and its culture. It is apparent that aggressive discharge is associated with an enhancement of narcissistic gratification and that narcissism in humans favors aggression. The attempt to understand aggression vis-à-vis a theory of narcissism, by necessity, places greater emphasis on the psychological and developmental determinants influencing personality.

I would suggest that the aggression in genocide is related to the individual's narcissistic sense of entitlement, his or her readiness for self-glorification and a need to define oneself as heroic and unique, associated with a need for disavowal of those non-heroic, unacceptable dimensions of the self that are antithetical to the heroic self. These unacceptable and rejected identity fragments we will see are projected onto the other with a double vengeance.

Identity Formation, Adolescence, and Narcissism

Virtually all of observers of development have agreed that the elaboration and consolidation of a sense of identity is a lifelong task and is one of the preeminent tasks of the adolescent period. Akhtar (1992) notes that it was Tausk who first introduced the concept of identity into the psychoanalytic literature when he described how the child has to elaborate a sense of self and constantly to find and experience himself or herself anew. The psychological birth of the infant begins with the emerging separation from the mother and an increasing individuation as the young toddler begins to move away from the mother and to develop a concept of the self, others, and the future (Mahler, Pine, and Bergman, 1975). Sandler and Rosenblatt (1962) have defined "the self representation as a more or less enduring existence of an organization or schema which is constructed out of a multitude of impressions" (p. 133). The early imprinting of identity on the infant begins when the mother, out of her unconscious need, reinforces those behaviors of the infant which create for her the child that most reflects her own unique and individual needs. The child begins to experience and perceive the self in different contexts, vis-à-vis different relationships, and elaborates self images of "who I am" and "what I am." Gender identificatory pathways are initiated and developed by the gradual working through of the oedipal tapestry. In middle childhood the self is increasingly enriched through reflected appraisals, family, and socio cultural expectations. Identity formation is greatly strengthened in the middle school years as the child moves out of the family context into peer and community relations and begins to internalize the instrumentalities of the culture, that is, the group's shared social, cultural, and religious values.

In the adolescent phase there is a new and increasing sense of urgency to the process of sculpting a sense of self, as new social and cultural expectations now demand choices and commitments which require the matching of "who I am" to what is now possible in a larger arena. Blos (1967) has suggested that the "essential task of adolescence is regression" not in the sense of a defense mechanism but as a process in which adolescents relive critical developmental experiences, conflicts, and identity fragments and, with newly emerging synthetic and integrative capacities, begin to define what they are and most importantly what they are not. It is in adolescence that the individual begins the final process of consolidating a sense of identity in which one begins to experience the self as having a sense of continuity and sameness through time that is confirmed by the self and others (Erikson, 1980). The childhood part identifications and identity fragments, some of which are contradictory and mutually exclusive now have to be honed into an integrated self. There is selective repudiation of divergent self images and assimilation of convergent childhood identifications into a new configuration as the family and sociocultural expectations requires the adolescent to make choices and commitments which leads to further self-definition. The identity which emerges is more than the sum of the childhood identifications. The adolescent has subordinated his or her childhood identifications to a new identity. Integral to this process is the elaboration and consolidation of personal values and beliefs regarding the self and one's commitment or fidelity to shared group values and beliefs. Erikson (1968) noted that identity "connotes both a persistent sameness within oneself and a persistent sharing of some kind of essential character with others" (p. 87). One's personal sense of self, and one's sense of uniqueness in a world of others is the product of this developmental and enculturation process. Erikson (1968) suggested that the concept of identity is composed of three strands: (1), a conscious awareness of oneself as having a sense of uniqueness which makes one different from others; (2), an unconscious striving for continuity of identity experiences through time; and (3), the sharing of a group ideal or belief system.

How narcissism is experienced is determined by how one defines the self, and ultimately others. It is known that groups form on the basis of similarities and establish boundaries on the basis of differences. Freud

(1921) wrote of the narcissism associated with small differences: "Closely related races keep another at arm's length: the South German cannot endure the North German, the Englishman casts every kind of aspersion upon the Scot, the Spaniard despises the Portuguese" (p. 101). Paradoxically, it is our capacity for symbolization that allows us to discriminate and identify the hated group as unacceptable in terms of its religious, ethnic, social, or political belief system. Rarely is genocide predicated only on racial or anatomical differences between groups.

Identity formation involves not only the individual defining the self in terms of what one is, but also what one is not. Each positive identity fragment is defined by negative images which may be projected out as unacceptable to the self. Excessive idealization or narcissistic investment in what one is—religious, cultural, ethnic, and political belief—in contrast to others, leads both to moral righteousness and a fragile sense of self, which Erikson has associated with "identity panic."

We have postulated that the fear that one is not all that one would like to be may lead to a wish to merge with a group ideal. This subordination to the group ideal may lead to collective narcissism. The self is then sustained by submission to group authority that confirms the individual's yearning for a special social and heroic character. The collective narcissism of Nazism sustained the individual delusion of a heroic self. The shared group ideal is maintained by the outward projection of the unacceptable identity fragments onto a scapegoat group. The scapegoat group, whether it be Jews, Bosnian Muslims, Chechnians, or Tutsi, is perceived in both rational and irrational ways. Rationally, the scapegoat group is a political and economic threat, though often significantly less so than it is perceived. Irrationally, the scapegoated group becomes the repository of all the negative images and nuances that have to be disavowed to maintain the image of the heroic and glorified self. An "as if" identity is consolidated on the basis of internalizing the identity fragments most valued by the group ideal, and the projection of the unacceptable identity fragments onto the hated group.

The persecutor has a vested interest in sustaining the negative identity of the hated group because that negative identity is the projection of the same unconscious negative identity fragment that is unacceptable to one's own persona. Thus, genocide sustains the fragile identity of the killing individual and his group in their heroic and ideal form.

The capacity to overcome the projection of the negative images of the self onto others requires that one accept the self as more simply human. The individual has to come to terms with his or her fragility and vulnerability. Genocide is averted when the individual or group begins to experience the other as like the self. To paraphrase Shylock, the Jew, in the *Merchant of Venice*, we all have the same hands, organs, senses, and passions . . . we are "fed with the same food, hurt with the same weapons, subject to the same diseases, healed by the same means, warmed and cooled by the same winter and summer. If you prick us do we not bleed? If you tickle us, do we not laugh? If you poison us do we not die? And if you wrong us, shall we not revenge?" Pretensions of group differences are based on narcissistic distortions.

The alternative to a narcissistic and exclusive definition of a heroic self is a more "inclusive identity." Instead of two groups defining the other vis-à-vis each other's projection of the unacceptable identity fragments, there has to be a redefinition of the self and the group in a wider and more totalistic human definition. We must strive to accept the reality that the negative identity fragments are part of the self. Subsequently, a more difficult task develops. The conflict must be perceived as it is, as an internal conflict, and humanity must struggle with its own limitations. This means the individual has to come to terms with his or her tragic position in the universe.

Summary

Genocide is part of the human experience. Humans are always potentially participants in genocide. Our existential dilemma is that while we are animals fated to old age, disease, and death, we yearn to deny the human condition. Our narcissistic aims lead us to create a heroic identity in which we begin to imagine ourselves omnipotent and immortal, more powerful, and deserving than those around us. We sustain the heroic self-image by merging with a group that reinforces our uniqueness by providing the identity trappings of an idealized self as we inculcate the mantle of the idealized values of the group. The negative identity fragments and images of the self are projected out onto others who are defined as non-human, undeserving, and who need to be exterminated to preserve the integrity that is essential to the collective narcissism of the killing group.

REFERENCES

Akhtar, S. (1992), *Broken Structures*. Northvale, NJ: Aronson.
Asch, S. E. (1956), Studies of independence and conformity. *Psychological Monographs*, 70:1–70.

Becker, E. (1975), *Escape from Evil*. New York: Free Press.

Berkowitz, L. (1962), *Aggression*. New York: McGraw-Hill.

Blos, P. (1967), The second individuation process of adolescence, *The Psychoanalytic Study of the Child*, 22:162–186. New York: International Universities Press.

Charny, I. W. (1986), Genocide and mass destruction. *Psychiat.*, 49:144–157.

——— (1982), *How Can We Commit the Unthinkable?* Boulder, CO: Westview Press.

Durant, W. & Durant, A. (1968), *The Lessons of History*. New York: Simon & Schuster.

Eissler, K. R. (1971), Death drive, ambivalence, and narcissism. *The Psychoanalytic Study of the Child*. 26:25–79. New Haven, CT: Yale University Press.

——— (1954), Wholeness and totality. In: *Totalitarianism*, ed. C. Friedrich. Cambridge, MA: Harvard University Press, pp. 153–168.

——— (1968), *Identity, Youth and Crisis*. New York: Norton.

——— (1980), *Identity and the Life Cycle*. New York: Norton.

Fein, H. (1995), Extermination of the gypsies. In: *Can It Happen Again*, ed. R. K. Chartock & J. Spencer. New York: Black Dog & Leventhal, pp. 129–130.

Freud, A. (1953), The bearing of the psychoanalytic theory of instinctual drives on certain aspects of human behavior. In: *Drives, Affects, Behavior*, ed. R. Loewenstein. New York: International Universities Press.

Freud S. (1914), On narcissism. *Standard Edition*, 14:73–102. London: Hogarth Press, 1957.

——— (1921), Group psychology and the analysis of the ego. *Standard Edition*, 18:69–142. London: Hogarth Press, 1955.

——— (1930), Civilization and its discontents. *Standard Edition*, 21:64–145. London: Hogarth Press, 1961.

Goldhagen, D. J. (1996), *Hitler's Willing Executioners*. New York: Alfred A. Knopf.

Harrower, M. (1995), Were Hitler's henchman mad? In: *Can It Happen Again?*, ed. R. K. Chartock & J. Spencer. New York: Black Dog & Leventhal, pp. 264–000.

Hensler, H. (1991), Narcissism as a form of a relationship. In: *Freud's On Narcissism: An Introduction*. ed. J. Sandler, E. S. Person & P. Fonagy. New Haven: Yale University Press, pp. 195–215.

Hobbes, T. (1651), *Leviathan*. New York: Collier, 1962.

Joseph, E. D. (1973), Aggression redefined: Its adaptation aspects. *Psychoanal. Quart.*, 42:197–213.

Kohut, H. (1972), Thoughts on narcissism and narcissistic rage. *Psychoanal. Study Child*, 27:360–400.

———— (1977), *The Restoration of the Self.* New York: International Universities Press.

Konner, M. L. (1993), We need enemies? The origins and consequences of rage. In: *Rage, Power, and Aggression.* ed. R. A. Glick & S. R. Roose. New Haven, CT: Yale University Press, pp. 173–193.

Krech, S. (1994), Genocide in tribal society. *Nature*, 371:14–15.

Lichtenberg, J. (1989), *Psychoanalysis and Motivation.* Hillsdale, NJ: The Analytic Press.

Lifton, R. J. (1986), *The Nazi Doctors.* New York: Basic Books.

Mahler, M. S., Pine, F. & Bergman, A. (1975), *The Psychological Birth of the Human Infant.* New York: Basic Books.

Marcovitz, E. (1982), Aggression: An overview. *Psychoanal. Inq.*, 2:11–19.

Markusen, E. (1992), Comprehending the Cambodian genocide: an application of Robert Jay Lifton's model of genocidal killing. *Psychohist. Rev.*, 20:145–169.

Mayer, M. (1995), Herr Damm. In: *Can It Happen Again.* ed. R. K. Chartock & J. Spencer. New York: Black Dog & Leventhal, pp. 157–160.

Milgram, S. (1974), *Obedience to Authority.* New York: Harper & Row.

Olweus, D. (1979), Stability of aggressive reaction patterns in males. *Psychol. Bull.*, 86:852–875.

Pagels, E. (1995), *The Origin of Satan.* New York: Random House.

Parens, H. (1989), Toward a reformulation of the psychoanalytic theory of aggression. In: *The Course of Life, Vol. 2,* ed. S. Greenspan & G. Pollock. Madison, CT: International Universities Press. pp. 83–121.

———— (1979), *The Development of Aggression in Early Childhood.* New York: Aronson.

Person, E. S. (1993), Male sexuality and power. In: *Rage, Power and Aggression,* ed. R. A. Glick & S. P. Roose. New Haven, CT: Yale University Press, pp. 29–44.

Resnick, M. N. & Nunno, V. J. (1991), The Nuremberg mind redeemed: A comprehensive analysis of the rorshachs of Nazi war criminals. *J. Personality Assess.*, 57:19–29.

Rochlin, G. (1973), *Man's aggression.* Boston, MA: Gambit.

—— (1982), Aggression reconsidered: A critique of psychoanalysis. *Psychoanal. Inq.,* 2:121–132.

Rothstein, A. (1984), *The Narcissistic Pursuit of Perfection.* New York: International Universities Press.

Sandler, J. & Rosenblatt, B. (1962), The concept of the representational world. *The Psychoanalytic Study of the Child.* 17:128–148. New York: International Universities Press.

Scott, J. P. (1958), *Aggression.* Chicago: University of Chicago Press.

Shaw, J. & Campo-Bowen, A. (1995), Aggression. In: *Conduct Disorders in Children and Adolescents,* ed. G. P. Sholevar. Washington, DC: American Psychiatric Press, pp. 45–58.

Wasman, M. & Flynn, J. P. (1962), Directed attack elicited from hypothalamus, *Arch. Neurol.,* 6:227–330.

Wilson, E. O. (1975), *Psychobiology.* Cambridge, MA: Harvard University Press.

11 WORKING WITH ADOLESCENT VICTIMS OF ETHNIC CLEANSING IN BOSNIA

BRADLEY D. STEIN

The role of child psychiatrists in assisting war victims has increased significantly since World War II. Child and adolescent psychiatrists have been increasingly active in humanitarian responses to wars and political terror in Central America (Arroyo and Eth, 1985), the Middle East (Ahmad, 1992; Apfel and Simon, 1993; Chimienti, Nasr, and Khalifeh, 1989; Klingman, Sagi and Raviv, 1993; Ziv, Kruglanski and Shulman, 1974), Africa (Shaw and Harris, 1994), and the former Yugoslavia (Zivcic, 1993). Humanitarian organizations providing aid in the former Yugoslavia recognized the adolescents' suffering, and psychosocial projects were initiated to assist these victims. As a child psychiatrist working for the International Rescue Committee (IRC), one of these humanitarian non governmental organizations (NGO), I spent most of 1994 in the former Yugoslavia. This paper will provide examples of adolescent victims of ethnic cleansing, briefly describe several psychosocial (mental health) programs, and discuss factors that may have contributed to their success.

As armed conflict increases, so does our knowledge of individual responses (Cicchetti, Toth, and Lynch, 1993; Garbarino and Kostelny, 1993; Shaw and Harris, 1994), and we are better able to design interventions to meet victim's needs (Garbarino, Kostelny, and Dubrow, 1991; Gong-Guy, Cravens, and Patterson, 1991; Richman, 1993). Children and adolescents are significantly affected by war trauma (Elbedour, ten Bensel, and Bastien, 1993) and violence (Pynoos and Nader, 1990), and require different interventions than adults (Ahmad, 1992; Chimienti et al., 1989; Cicchetti et al., 1993; Garbarino and Kostelny, 1993; Garbarino et al., 1991; Ressler, Boothby and Steinbock, 1988). Youth's rapidly changing developmental level, limited coping skills, and inability to seek services put them at higher risk than adults (Magwaza, et al.,

1993). Children and adolescent refugees face additional problems arising from displacement, and require programs prepared to address these problems (Ressler et al., 1988). Children and adolescents may also be at higher risk than adults for suffering psychological trauma due to their parents being overwhelmed by basic survival needs, being separated from their parents, or orphaned.

In Bosnia-Herzegovina, adolescents were subjected to the horrors of warfare and the trauma of becoming refugees. Many were also exposed to genocide, as residents of towns, villages, and entire regions were "cleansed" of an ethnic group by force and terror. Adolescents exposed to this process of murder, rape, and terror often found themselves far from their former homes.

Case Illustration

Tikomir is a 14-year-old boy from Vukovar, an eastern Croatian city overrun by Serbs early in the war. He lives in a refugee camp in Novi Gradska, a Croatian town near the Krajina (formerly Serb-occupied) region of Croatia. Tikomir was participating in a Croatian summer camp for refugees and was referred for "help with his behavior."

Initially Tikomir talked of Balkan history and the current conflict. Drawing a map, he explained how the problems began in 1844, and continued to the current day. Stopping, he looked at me with a serious expression. "Eighteen forty-four," he said slowly, emphasizing each syllable, "not 1944." He later discussed growing up in Vukovar with his parents and older sister. When the war began he went with all the children to the coast for safety, while his eighteen year old sister went to work in a Zagreb hospital. The shelling of Vukovar ceased after a month, and Tikomir rejoined his parents. The Serbs returned and surrounded the city, and the siege of Vukovar became imminent. Tikomir and his mother fled, first to a refugee camp, then to join his paternal grandmother in a small town in Serbia. Tikomir's father remained in Vukovar to defend the town, which has been called the Croatian Stalingrad. By time the town was finally "liberated," it had been devastated in the heaviest artillery bombardment seen in Europe since World War II (Ignatieff, 1993). Few defenders survived, and of those who did many disappeared in the Serb concentration camps. Tikomir had no news of his father since leaving Vukovar.

Tikomir and his mother joined his grandmother in a northern Serbian region populated by Hungarians and Croats. The Chetniks (Serbian paramilitary) began threatening and beating people there after several months. Occasionally there would be a stabbing, a house would burn in the middle of the night, or a Croat or Hungarian would "just disappear." Tikomir said he had "some troubles," but would say no more. As the violence worsened, most Croatian and Hungarian families fled. One evening the Chetniks broke into Tikomir's house and killed his uncle, forcing everyone to watch. The next day the family fled to a small town in Croatia, moving into the house of a Serb family which had fled Croatia for Serbia. Tikomir felt badly for his grandmother, forced to suddenly flee the only place she had ever known, but denied it being "too hard on him."

Tikomir told me he had gotten in trouble frequently since leaving Vukovar. He had never had a problem with breaking rules and getting in fights previously. Occasionally he feels sad, but overall he identifies his mood as angry. He had no neurovegetative symptoms of depression, and had few symptoms of posttraumatic stress disorder (PTSD). He hopes to be wealthy enough to have one house in Vukovar, and another in the Adriatic islands. If given three wishes, his first wish would be to return to Vukovar to "find his father." He expressed his second wish not by speaking, but by drawing a large mushroom cloud over the map of Serbia. Tikomir did not have a third wish.

Discussion of Case

This example demonstrates several unexpected yet important effects of ethnic cleansing. Despite being reported as wholesale slaughter and rape of the victims, ethnic cleansing was often more subtle and insidious. The goal was to create an ethnically pure region, not by exterminating the victims, but by forcing the victims to flee and destroying the region's ethnic community. Threats, destruction of property, kidnapping, and controlled violence against select individuals were often sufficient to frighten most people into fleeing. However, even in "ethnically cleansed" areas, a few brave or foolish individuals often remained. Ethnic cleansing was not solely Serbs attacking Muslims, but all three ethnic groups were both aggressors and victims.

Tikomir was a Croatian youth living in a relatively safe area of Croatia. Adolescents in Bosnia often had additional traumas in addition to many of the same issues as those in Croatia. It was not uncommon for Bosnian families to be of mixed ethnic background, resulting in additional confusion and pain for their offspring. One young man I met had stayed with his Muslim father in a northern Bosnian town after his father divorced his Serb mother prior to the war. After his father disappeared into a Serb concentration camp early in the conflict, this young Bosnian spent several months searching for his father before giving up and fleeing to Muslim controlled central Bosnia to find his mother. When he eventually located his mother, she refused to take him in because he was a Muslim and "she was a Serb." Eventually, he joined a paternal aunt, who protected him as they were again forced from their homes and sought refuge in a collective center in Zenica, Bosnia.

The collective centers and Bosnian towns like Zenica were often a quite different environment from the refugee camps in Croatia. Although Zenica was thought of as a safe haven, in reality it was only six miles from the front lines. Gunfire could be heard day and night, and occasionally the town was the target of Bosnian Serb shelling, receiving up to a dozen shells per day. Zenica is a large town in central Bosnia, 60 kilometers north of Sarajevo, that lost over 60,000 of its original 150,000 inhabitants during the war. However, many have been replaced by the over 30,000 displaced Muslims who arrived in Zenica after fleeing ethnic cleansing in central and northern Bosnia. The collective centers are "internal" refugee camps, often converted buildings that housed several families in one small room. They usually have no school, and no organized activity for children. Although collective centers were located throughout central Zenica, the refugees had little contact with Zenica's citizens, usually keeping to themselves.

Ethnic cleansing victims were often subjected to chronic trauma, rather than a single overwhelming one. These traumas frequently continued after victims had reached a safe area. The ethnic strife found its way into schools, villages, and even families, damaging all aspects of a civilized society. This exacerbated the psychological effects of the trauma by damaging all social structures which provide support in times of stress, an effect commonly noted in other types of disasters (Sugar, 1988). Even in ethnically homogeneous areas, refugees were often unable to establish social bonds due to frequent conflict between refugees and their host communities. The destruction of social bonds that began with ethnic cleansing continued as victims fled to safer areas, and only served to exacerbate the psychological difficulties of the victims as they moved to refugee camps in safe regions. Despite their experiences, it is worth noting that victims of the terrors in Bosnia did not always present with the classic PTSD triad of intrusive thoughts, hyperarousal, and emotional numbing. Although many were emotionally numb, few had symptoms of intrusive thoughts, and most had no hyper-arousal, although behavioral problems were quite common.

Intervention Overview

One IRC project was to develop mental health interventions for children and adolescent victims of ethnic cleansing in Zenica's collective centers. These projects had a tremendous lack of resources in central Bosnia with food, electricity, water, and housing all in short supply. Equally important, there were few mental health resources available since most psychiatrists and psychologists had fled or been killed, and there were only a handful of individuals in town with a background in mental health.

Faced with this seemingly overwhelming task, guidelines for interventions were established with IRC-Bosnia's medical director and designed to reach as many victims as possible. Interventions had to be sustainable and designed to continue after expatriate professionals left Bosnia. Finally, interventions had to be inexpensive, and they were limited to the physical and personnel resources present in Zenica.

One major hurdle in facing these tasks was the language barrier. I had not known any Serbo-Croatian prior to traveling to the former Yugoslavia, and despite my best efforts, never achieved fluency greater than the rudimentary level needed to survive daily activities. As if to demonstrate Freud's "narcissism of minor differences" (Freud, 1930) and its role in creating a psychological gap between the warring parties (Volkan, 1987), the Serbs, Croats, and Muslims had found ways to differentiate the language from each other as a way of further accentuating their separate nationalities. This only served to complicate the language barriers. Although analogous to the minor differences between American and British English, people had been ignored or even shunned for speaking the wrong language. My mastery of the language was insufficient to be able to perform any clinical work, and was not even adequate to enable me to share complicated concepts with my non-English speaking colleagues.

Fortunately, I was able to overcome this problem through the diligent efforts of an eighteen year-old Bosnian adolescent, Belma, who served as my translator and assistant. She had learned English as had many teenagers in the former Yugoslavia, augmenting what she learned in school by watching movies and listening to pop music stars. Initially, she provided word for word translation, but after several weeks, became better able to translate content, relaying what was being said. Although I was still limited by culture and not directly participating in the conversation, her insights provided many crucial contextual and nonverbal cues. She also became confident enough to be able to tell me when I was saying something inappropriate for the culture or situation. This was critical since it prevented a number of *faux pas* that would have had significant repercussions.

Still, having to work through a translator did present a number of difficulties. The most significant was the awareness of the toll that Belma's duties were taking on her. She too had gone through the war with all its horrors. Suddenly, she was exposed to daily tales of trauma and violence, often involving her peers. We tried to provide every possible support, but it was still a very difficult experience for her. Unfortunately, we were unable to find an older translator who could provide adequate translation. Despite my concern about asking her to do such difficult work, and the occasional guilt associated with my decision, it seemed to work. Not only did Belma's parents say that, despite their concerns, it was the best thing she had ever done, but in my contact with her since returning to the States she has reiterated how fortunate she felt to have had that opportunity. Still, it is important to recognize the tremendous difficulties faced by a translator who does not have the training of a mental health professional.

The Roundtable

To provide sustainable mental health services, we had to identify local individuals with some mental health expertise to serve as resources. Once identified, we could provide further information and support for them to assist others. To this end we began a mental health "roundtable," essentially an open weekly meeting of Bosnians with experience or interest in mental health. Starting with ten people, the roundtable gradually grew into a group of 20 to 30, including two refugee psychologists, one pediatrician, four school counselors, four former medical students working as psychosocial program staff in the collective centers, several teachers, and a variety of other interested individuals. The first several meetings were used to disseminate simple written information and were organized as didactics. The following meetings were frequently case consultations. People would "bring to the table" difficult cases, and the group provided suggestions and feedback. My role, after these early meetings, was to moderate and provide brief additional information when appropriate. Occasionally, I also provided written material about a particular problem. Soon, word spread of this expert group, and others in the community began to come for consultation.

Outreach

Once established, the roundtable was available for consultation to programs working with ethnic cleansing victims. IRC then began devoting more resources to supporting people working directly with ethnic cleansing victims. To reach the most people, we began holding meetings in frontline areas that had suffered the most, inviting anyone interested in working with children or adolescents. Teaching simple mental health concepts, we tried to provide simple skills and concrete tools for working with children and adolescents. In addressing behavioral problems, the focus was on providing positive and negative reinforcement. For many other problems, we focused on issues of mastery and reestablishing social supports, discussing ways to help adolescents deal with their trauma. Free-wheeling discussions covered topics such as active and supportive listening, problem solving, relaxation exercises, and group activities. Drawing, storytelling, and playacting were methods discussed that would allow adolescents to express themselves more easily.

Adults frequently had a very difficult time implementing these ideas. Adults would often not allow the youngsters to discuss their experiences, believing that talking "would just make everything worse." Adults cited as evidence the pain felt the first time children discussed their experiences. This highlighted the difficulty adults had discussing these issues due to suffering similar losses during the war. We quickly learned that the roundtable was not only going to have to serve as consultants, but would also need to offer supervision and counseling to many of those providing mental health support to adolescent victims of ethnic cleansing.

Project Example—Art Groups

The Child Mental Health Project was a psychosocial project working with children and adolescent victims of ethnic cleansing near Zenica. Having been established and run by an international NGO it was being handed over to its Bosnian staff. The Bosnian medical students staffing the project had their studies interrupted by the war, and most were little more than adolescents themselves. They had been taught basic mental health concepts, emphasizing the use of art therapy techniques. They led therapy groups for children and adolescents in the local collective centers. These monthly groups, which ranged from four to 25 participants, often lasted two to three hours. Each month the next month's activities were planned, based upon the response to the current month's activities. Frequent changes in expatriate staff led to three expatriate supervisors in nine months, preventing the program from ever really developing a long term plan. As a result of these limitations, termination with the current group of children and adolescents had not been discussed. There was also significant anxiety about continuing the project after the departure of these staff, and many of the remaining staff were struggling with their own personal issues triggered by working with ethnic cleansing victims.

Despite these difficulties, the program was quite successful in the eyes of the community. Parents felt the program had been quite helpful to their children. "Group" days were anticipated positively by parents and their children, and they became quite upset the few times a visit was canceled. In spite of the staff's limited time and training, parents and participants felt the time spent talking about the war and their collective center experience was beneficial.

In this situation, the expatriate clinical supervisor's role was providing further direction and support to the Bosnian staff. Reinstituting frequent group supervision helped the staff address their own issues regarding work with ethnic cleansing victims, as well as helping the staff with termination issues. We also tried to discern what the parents and adolescents had found to be helpful in such a limited intervention. Discussions with Bosnian staff, parents, and adolescent participants indicated that the adolescents in the groups had been spending a great deal of time together outside the groups. They also felt the groups had "given permission" for the adolescents to discuss their traumatic experiences, something many had felt they could not do previously with family or friends. Based on this information, the Bosnian staff planned to change aspects of the program when it started with a new group of adolescents. The planned participation of the parents and caretakers of the children was increased in hopes the adolescents would be more comfortable talking with their parents. An increased effort to integrate the refugees into activities for local youths was made by increasing social activities outside the groups. The transition to an independent program was eased by providing a connection with the roundtable for clinical support and supervision once the expatriate staff left Bosnia. The final important step was recognizing many of the staff's issues raised by working with the adolescents, many of whose traumas were quite similar to their own.

Project Example—Wheelchair Basketball

Another project involved collaborative work with a physical therapist aiding spinal injured adolescents and young men. In addition to losses suffered as a result of ethnic cleansing, they also had serious injuries from acts of terror or defending their homes. The local rehabilitation center physician approached the IRC and requested help with the 20 to 30 most depressed young men who were not complying with their physical rehabilitation. Many were isolated from family and friends due to the stigma of their handicap, and they often isolated themselves from each other in the rehabilitation center. In the former Yugoslavia these men would have been institutionalized for life due to their injury, and these young men fully expected to be banished from society.

Without the time or resources for individual work, we devised a group-based intervention. Educational materials were prepared for the rehabilitation center staff containing information on paraplegia, adolescent development, and mental health. A series of hour-long educational meetings was begun for the patients about spinal injuries. However, both these approaches met with limited success. The staff read the material, but did not have the energy to change their interactions with the patients. For many, it was enough to make it through the day. The patients attended the educational meetings and listened, but returned to their rooms and isolated themselves. Few had social supports inside or outside the rehabilitation center, and few opportunities to develop them.

Hoping to reinvigorate this process by increasing social interaction, we decided to start weekly wheelchair basketball games, also including some of the older paraplegics. Wheelchair basketball had never been played in the former Yugoslavia, but basketball is quite popular. After a great deal of disbelief and initial resistance from patients, rehabilitation center staff, and others, it began to catch on. Participants gradually increased in number and ability. We soon had enough for two teams with substitutes. Over several months they became confident enough to challenge international NGO's and United Nations troops to games. These games drew crowds of up to 50 people including Zenica's mayor, and were reported on Bosnian radio and television.

235

More importantly, the wheelchair basketball participants began to support each other, forming a tightly-knit group. Staff told us of all night "bull sessions," discussing wartime experiences, future hopes, and fears. They encouraged each other in physical rehabilitation and educational sessions, even searching out those missing to make sure they attended. They began making significant progress in their rehabilitation. They summoned the courage to go into town together to cafes and bars, which they had not done previously. Several became romantically involved with girls from the town, and one even found a part-time job—remarkable in a town with an unemployment rate of 90%. In summary, the wheelchair basketball provided an opportunity to form bonds which became important supports in facing other challenges.

Discussion

These examples are not what many might expect when discussing approaches to working with adolescent victims of ethnic cleansing. Some might even suggest they have no place in a serious discussion of mental health interventions. I do not mean to suggest art therapy groups that meet once a month will cure PTSD, nor will sports activities for adolescents soon replace traditional forms of therapy. Nor do I suggest these interventions cured individuals of depression, anxiety, or PTSD. Many children and adolescent victims of ethnic cleansing continue to suffer from these disorders. Yet, there appear to be clear benefits for many children and adolescents from participation in these nontraditional interventions. Although a monthly two-hour meeting is not traditional therapy, the parents and their children felt it was beneficial. They were quite upset if a day was missed due to security reasons. There was an outcry upon learning that the current program was ending and would be replaced by one serving newly arrived refugees. Although psychological traumas were never discussed at the wheelchair basketball practices, they appear to have been important in allowing the participants to address important issues not previously discussed.

Despite the nontraditional nature of these interventions, they follow a rich tradition of creative approaches to adolescent group therapy. For over thirty years group work has been used to reach adolescents, oftentimes using creative and novel approaches to engage adolescents from deprived or violent environments (O'Shea, 1972; Reiser and Kushner-Goodman, 1972; Stebbins, 1972). There have even been previous descriptions of basketball used as a focus for adolescents who were resistant to participating in more traditional group work (Rafferty and Steffek, 1977). More recently, there has been growing recognition of group treatment as an inventive solution to providing mental health services in international environments with limited psychiatric resources (Caldera, Kullgren, and Jacobsson, 1995).

A fundamental change that occurs in the face of ethnic cleansing is the destruction of a community and its social bonds. Former neighbors, friends, and even relatives turn on the victims. The fundamental belief behind ethnic cleansing is that people of different ethnic groups cannot coexist (Ignatieff, 1993). Not all ethnic cleansing victims survived the destruction of their community and social bonds. This compounds the normal turmoil of adolescence, as they abandon the patterns of childhood and develop a new identity as an adult. Adolescents with intact families and communities exposed to warfare often have a difficult time recovering, and many require extensive support from family, friends, and schools. Adolescents exposed to ethnic cleansing usually lose these supports, an additional trauma besides all they experienced in the war.

A psychosocial program's success often resulted from addressing these losses, and providing adolescents with opportunities to reestablish social bonds. Through participation in psychologically safe groups such as the art therapy groups, and working towards a common goal such as wheelchair basketball, the adolescents began to reestablish trust in peers and social bonds. Once begun in formal activities, this process continued informally outside the groups. Only with these supports were the adolescents able to discuss their experiences and draw on each other for support and validation. Only then did many of the therapeutic techniques used by volunteers and staff become effective, and the expertise of the roundtable become truly useful.

Once these social supports are in place, there appears to be an almost innate attempt by the adolescents to regain mastery over their traumatic experiences. Most of the therapeutic work was not done in groups or individual sessions, but rather in the adolescent's everyday interactions. Many have described children's attempts to gain mastery after traumatic events through play. It would appear that for many of these adolescents, their mastery began naturally, but only after establishing a strong connection with a social group.

These social supports were also important for those Bosnian adults providing mental health services to children and adolescents since most of them had also lost many of their social supports. This limited their ability to address their own thoughts and feelings about their experiences, much less facilitate this process for the children and adolescents. As noted in the discussion of the outreach efforts, one of our failures was not providing enough support and supervision for the adult Bosnian staff to facilitate their own ability to deal with their issues. The importance of meeting this need has been discussed in other areas of work with trauma victims (McCann and Pearlman, 1990), and may be the difference between success and failure for programs of this type.

Conclusions

Adolescent victims of ethnic cleansing have often been exposed to a variety of ongoing traumas, complicating the psychological trauma normally associated with exposure to warfare. Victims have experienced the destruction of their community, and so are without the social sense of belonging so important to adolescents. Given the lack of mental health resources available in a war zone, effective mental health interventions must find ways to rebuild these social supports through group activities. These provide adolescents with the opportunity to establish the social supports necessary to work through the traumas they have experienced. Although not sufficient for the most severe cases, this approach benefits a large number of victims, important in situations in which there are limited mental health resources and a high prevalence of psychological trauma.

These lessons are important as our profession works with adolescents exposed to severe trauma, and living in environments in which there is little or no social organization or support. In an era of diminishing mental health resources, learning how to establish and nurture these supports in our country will be an important contribution to helping our most vulnerable youth deal with the trauma and violence many face on a daily basis.

REFERENCES

Ahmad, A. (1992), Symptoms of posttraumatic stress disorder among displaced Kurdish children in Iraq. *Nordic J. Psychiat.*, 46:315–319.
Apfel, R. J. & Simon, B. (1993), On the value of a psychoanalytic perspective in research on children in war. In: *Research on Children in War*, ed. L. A. Leavitt & N. Fox. Hillsdale, NJ: Lawrence Erlbaum Associates, pp. 163–179.

Arroyo, W. & Eth, S. (1985), Children traumatized by Central American warfare. In: *Post-Traumatic Stress Disorder in Children*, ed. S. Eth & R. Pynoos. Washington, DC: American Psychiatric Press.

Caldera, T., Kullgren, G. & Jacobsson, L. (1995), Is treatment in groups a useful alternative for psychiatry in low income countries? *Acta Psychiat. Scand.*, 92:386–391.

Chimienti, G., Nasr, J. A. & Khalifeh, I. (1989), Children's reactions to war-related stress. Affective symptoms and behaviour problems. *Social Psychiat. & Psychiatric Epidemiol.*, 24:282–287.

Cicchetti, D., Toth, S. & Lynch, M. (1993), The developmental sequelae of child maltreatment: Implications for war-related trauma. In: *The Psychological Effects of War and Violence on Children*, ed. L.A. Leavitt & N.A. Fox. Hillsdale, NJ: Lawrence Erlbaum Associates, pp. 41–74.

Elbedour, S., ten Bensel, R. & Bastien, D. T. (1993), Ecological integrated model of children in war. Individual and social psychology. Special Section: Children and war. *Child Abuse and Neglect*, 17:805–819.

Freud, S. (1930), Civilization and its discontents. Standard Edition, 21:64–145. London; Hogarth Press, 1961.

Garbarino, J. & Kostelny, K. (1993), Children's response to war. *The Psychological Effects of War and Violence on Children*, ed. Leavitt L. A. & Fox N. A. Hillsdale, NJ: Lawrence Erlbaum Associates, pp. 23–40.

———— ———— & Dubrow, N. (1991), What children can tell us about living in danger. *Amer. Psycholog.*, 46:376–383.

Gong-Guy, E., Cravens, R. B. & Patterson, T. E. (1991), Clinical issues in mental health service delivery to refugees. *Amer. Psycholog.*, 46:642–648.

Ignatieff, M. (1993), *Blood and Belonging*. New York: Farrar, Strauss & Giroux.

Klingman, A., Sagi, A. & Raviv, A. (1993), The effect of war on Israeli children. In: *The Psychological Effects of War and Violence on children*, ed. L. A. Leavitt & N. A. Fox. Hillsdale, NJ: Lawrence Erlbaum Associates, pp. 75–92.

Magwaza, A. S., Killian, B. J., Petersen, I. & Pillay, Y. (1993), The effects of chronic violence on preschool children living in South African townships. Special Section: Children and war. *Child Abuse and Neglect*, 17:795–803.

McCann, I.L. & Pearlman, L.A. (1990), Vicarious traumatization: A framework for understanding the psychological effects of working with victims. *J. Traumatic Stress*, 3:131–149.

O'Shea, C. (1972), "Two gray cats learn how it is" in a group of black teen-agers. *Adolescents Grow in Groups*, ed I.H. Berkovitz. New York: Brunner/Mazel, pp. 134–149.

Pynoos, R. S. & Nader, K. (1990), Children's exposure to violence and traumatic death. *Psychiat. Annals*, 20:334–344.

Rafferty, F. T. & Steffek, J. C. (1977), A group approach with the hapless adolescent. *Adolescent Psychiatry*, 5:429–441. Chicago: University of Chicago Press.

Reiser, M. & Kushner-Goodman, S. (1972), A drop-in group for teenagers in a poverty area. In: *Adolescents Grow in Groups*, ed. I. H. Berkovitz. New York: Brunner/Mazel, pp. 149–153.

Ressler, E. M., Boothby, N. & Steinbock, D. J. (1988), *Unaccompanied children*. New York: Oxford University Press.

Richman, N. (1993), Children in situations of political violence. *J. Child Psychol. & Psychiat. & Allied Disciplines*, 34:1286–1302.

Shaw, J. A. & Harris, J. J. (1994), Children of war and children at war: Child victims of terrorism in Mozambique. In: *Individual and Community Responses to Trauma and Disaster*, ed. R.J. Ursano, B.G. McCaughey & C.S. Fullerton. Cambridge: Cambridge University Press, pp. 287–305.

Stebbins, D. B. (1972), "Playing it by ear," in answering the needs of a group of black teen-agers. In: *Adolescents Grow in Groups*, ed. I.H. Berkovitz. New York: Brunner/Mazel, pp. 126–134.

Sugar, M. (1988), Children and the multiple trauma in a disaster. In: *Perilous Development*, ed. E. J. Anthony & C. Chiland. New York: Wiley, pp. 429–442.

Volkan, V. D. (1987), Psychological concepts useful in the building of political foundations between nations. *J. Amer. Psychoanal. Assn.*, 35:903–935.

Ziv, A., Kruglanski, A. W. & Shulman, S. (1974), Children's psychological reactions to wartime stress. *J. Personal. Soc. Psychol.*, 30:24–30.

Zivcic, I. (1993), Emotional Reactions of Children to War Stress in Croatia. *J. Amir. Acad. Child Adolesc. Psychiat.*, 32:709–713.

12   ADOLESCENT GENOCIDE

MAX SUGAR

In the extreme condition of adolescents without parents or parent-substitutes, how does adolescent development proceed? Does it evolve as in the movie *Lord of the Flies?* Is there a developmental risk from this? Does some defense mechanism hypertrophy and protect? What happens to development when the adolescent is simultaneously in a very vulnerable and life-threatening situation for an extended period of time? When do such extreme conditions occur? The answer to that last question is in an ambience of genocide. In that case, is there anything that helps survival or development? Does some helpful person, even if ever-so-casual a contact, have an ameliorating influence? This chapter considers these questions by focusing on the Holocaust with its pervasive atmosphere of genocide since it is the best documented one to date.

Adolescent Development

It may be useful to recall briefly some facts about normative adolescence to compare with the experience of adolescent survivors. In adolescence, there are challenges and conflicts to be reworked and harmonized from previous developmental levels such as the preoedipal issues of dependency vs. autonomy, trust vs. mistrust, and the positive and negative features from the oedipal stage. From latency, there remain issues of developing industry vs. inferiority, higher levels of object relations, beginning character formation and superego development.

Normal adolescent mourning (Sugar, 1968) involves gradually giving up the infantile objects emotionally in a phasic process. In early adolescence, there is the separation-protest phase with the simultaneous wish to separate and to restore or retain the infantile objects. This is often accompanied by angry, rebellious behavior. In the disorganization phase of mid-adolescence, there is further distancing from the infantile objects, and the adolescent's ego feels, depleted, worthless, empty, and inadequate. The adolescent may appear depressed, withdrawn, or restless and often seeks new thrills or to remain isolated. There may be resurgences of the wish to restore the ties with infantile objects, but mostly there is the recognition of reality and the beginning acceptance of the emotional shift away from, and decreasing dependency on, these objects. In late adolescence, there is the reorganization phase, which includes the wish for freedom from parents' and other authorities' restrictions (Sugar, 1968). Alongside this phase is the need to explore and manage reactions to the same and the opposite sex, the need to test one's omnipotentiality and to arrive at a sense of fidelity and commitment to self and object choice.

Body image is reflected in self-image and identity, which makes it a most significant part of adolescence. When chronic illness or other conditions interfere with the expectations of adolescence, it affects identity and body image (Sugar, 1990).

For personality consolidation to occur in late adolescence, the youngster has to: (1) deal with residual trauma from childhood; (2) develop ego continuity; (3) establish one's sexual identity; and (4) resolve the second separation-individuation (Blos, 1974). This also means taking responsibility for one's actions, and not attributing them to others. By the end of adolescence character formation is evident.

Concentration Camp Experiences

Some background data may be helpful to appreciate the kind of experiences that youngsters endured in the Nazi concentration camps. Of the Nazi camp inmates, 13 million of all ages were murdered. Of these, 6,000,000 were Jews, of whom only 100,000 survived; among whom were 4,000 children and adolescents (Friedman, 1949). For Jews, before the "final solution," there were usually years of threats, restrictions, degradations, torture, and atrocities in, and before, being placed in the ghettoes. The lengthy trip from the ghettoes to the camps in cattle cars was perplexing and traumatic, with deception, little or no food or water, and no sanitary facilities.

Following incarceration, there was a series of psychological reactions beginning with depersonalization, death anxiety, apathy, and after that came a short interval of euphoria, followed by a depression that lasted from three to six months, if they survived that long (Cohen, 1953). Many died of emotional and physical exhaustion in the early stage of incarceration (Des Pres, 1976) and many committed suicide (Ryn, 1986).

The strong were kept alive to work 14 to 18 hours per day, or they were used in medical experiments. Those under 14, the aged, the pregnant, or the sick were put to death immediately, often in the presence of family members (Cohen 1953). There was no privacy at any time, and this included bathing and excretory functions. There was no change of clothes, and personal hygiene was limited.

Destruction of the victims' identity was a Nazi target. This was initiated on entrance in the concentration camp by shaving all head and body hair, and calling the prisoners only by numbers instead of names. A sense of time and hope of a future were limited by the absence of calendars and clocks. Signs stated the longevity for various groups in the extermination camps, and for Jews it was three weeks (Cohen, 1953; Des Pres, 1976). The Jewish prisoners were treated worse than those from other groups and the Polish Jews were mistreated more than the German Jews (Mattusek, 1975, p. 26).

The SS guards played sadistic games to foster loss of morale (Des Pres, 1976). Among these efforts was the provision of only two latrines per 30,000 prisoners, who could only use them twice a day at special times. No tissue paper was provided. The latrines were ditches 12 feet deep with only a railing to hold onto while squatting in full view of everybody. The prisoners were forced to urinate upon supine groups of other prisoners, or urinate into their mouths. A favorite game of the SS was to stop a prisoner on the way to the latrine and force him to do knee bends until he "exploded" (Des Pres, 1976).

The calorie intake was variable but quite low. It ranged from 533 calories per day in Dachau in the spring of 1945, to 800 per day in the last year of the war.

Many of the prisoners were ill in the camps. Those under age 20 experienced more psychological problems than did adults (Mattusek, 1975; Des Pres, 1976). The extent of the physical and emotional illness is shown in Table 1 (Mattusek, 1975; Des Pres, 1976).

Effects

What were the other effects of torture, incarceration, witnessing murder, and efforts to destroy identity? There was no heterosexual interest (Frankl, 1959; Cohen, 1953). The males were impotent and the females had amenorrhea. There was an absence of sexual jokes, but there were

TABLE 1
PHYSICAL AND MENTAL DISORDERS WHILE INCARCERATED*

Head injuries from maltreatment	48%
Epidemics	38%
Chest disorders	26%
Cardiac disorders	29%
Rheumatic Complaints	26%
Dyspeptic symptoms	26%
Sx of hunger dystrophy (cachexia, polyuria, oedema)	29%
Bacterial infections	21%
Injuries from malRx	21%
Spinal column symptoms	10%
Infections	7%
Brief febrile infection	10%
Frostbite (feet)	2%
Permanent anxiety state	28%
Depressive moods	31%
Suicidal thoughts	8%

*From Mattusek (1975)

scatological ones. Homosexuality and masturbation were widespread amongst the SS guards and the kapos (Cayrol, cited by Mattusek, 1975). The prisoners dreamt not of sex, as adolescents usually do, but of food. This is not really unique since it is similar to the reactions of infantrymen in combat for whom survival is also more important than sex.

Some adolescents banded together in groupings of two or three. Some of these became the leaders who resisted, escaped, or tried to arrange escapes, or became partisan fighters (Davidson, 1979). Adolescents who were involved with groupings were the leaders in the uprising in the Warsaw ghetto in the spring of 1943, and the escapes at Auschwitz, Buchenwald, and Treblinka. Adolescents initiated the burning of the camps at Treblinka and Sobibor, and of the blowing up of the crematorium in Auschwitz (Des Pres, 1976).

Survival

How did they survive, those who did? Luck played an important role, and some may have had more resiliency (Werner and Smith, 1982). Joining up with a group of two or three others was also vital. The prisoners had a bread-and-gift ethos which consisted of the obligation to reciprocate with something of equal importance such as a handkerchief or a piece of tissue paper (Des Pres, 1976). These supports and exchanges were most significant.

Those who kept up their personal hygiene and those who received help from others also had a greater chance to survive. Withdrawal was often a portent of suicide (Davidson, 1979; Ryn, 1986). If there was good health, that helped survival, since it meant they were useful for daily work, for 14 to 18 hours (Cohen, 1953; Des Pres, 1976). Therefore, it became a matter of great significance, and almost a daily ritual to inspect oneself, and have one's health status confirmed by others in the barracks (Levi, 1969; Des Pres, 1976; Davidson, 1979, 1985; Ryn, 1986).

With Liberation

What happened to these people with liberation in sight? When the Russians were advancing from the East, the Germans treated the prisoners as hostages and had them retreat with them in forced marches in the winter of 1944–45. The majority of the prisoners died or were shot enroute for falling behind. For example, of the 60,000 who left Auschwitz in January, 1945, only 20,000 survived.

When liberated, some of the prisoners exacted revenge by murdering their Nazi guards, just as some of the United States soldiers did when they first came into the camps (Beuchner, 1986). Some gorged themselves on food unwisely and died (Cohen, 1953).

Some learned that there was to be no fulfillment of the wish for reunion with their family, and many of these committed suicide. Those who returned to their home town found that nobody there knew, or cared, about them. The vast majority ended up in displaced persons camps for two or three years (Danieli, 1982). Those who left Europe and tried to enter Palestine were interned behind barbed wire by the British on the island of Cyprus and they reexperienced the concentration camp trauma (Friedman, 1949).

Many of these teenagers developed fatigue, loss of sexuality including the desire to masturbate (which they had regained after liberation), inability to cry, excessive sleep, detachment, and shallow emotions. There were a few cases of psychosis, many reactive depressions, conversion reactions, and hypochondriacal symptoms. About 50% to 60% of them had psychosomatic symptoms (Friedman, 1949).

The survivors felt shame and guilt about their camp experiences, their helplessness, humiliation, and losses, both family and personal. The majority left Europe and then faced a new problem of emigration to a new country with a new language and culture (Des Pres, 1976).

245

They also had the problem of deciding on a future since their education was incomplete and they lacked job skills. The teenagers had more difficulty than adults in making decisions about a job or training for it. Those adolescents who succeeded vocationally got a job just to be active and were devoted to it but changed jobs often (Mattusek, 1975, p. 156).

Adolescent Mourning

Following a parent's death, an adolescent may have academic difficulty or behavioral problems that are symptomatic of the reaction to the loss. The teenage Holocaust survivors also had the problem of being unable to mourn their losses, especially of parents. They could not mourn the actual dead since no cathartic rituals were allowed in the concentration camps and there were only unknown or mass graves, or ash heaps. Had they shown any evidence of horror, rage or grief at the executions while in the camps, their own lives would have been at risk (Grubrich-Simitis, 1979). With the family destroyed they could not proceed through normal adolescent mourning and the development of gradual emotional separation-individuation from parents (Blos, 1962; Sugar, 1968).

The three-stage normal adolescent mourning for the infantile objects, that is, the gradual decathexis (or a trial mourning) of the parents (Sugar, 1968) is a prerequisite for the development of the later ability to mourn, since that involves learning how to give up a major love object (Wolfenstein, 1966). Fleming and Altschul (1963) wrote that the loss of parents in adolescence may lead to an absence of mourning and covert denial of the reality of loss. Jacobson (1965) considered that in such cases there are continued fantasies of finding the lost parents. With these defense mechanisms the painful process of decathexis of the lost parent is avoided, and instead there develops an intensified cathexis (Wolfenstein, 1966) with overidealization. Such a teenager would not cry but would manifest an interference with affect, and isolation of feelings from thoughts.

If we assume that these developments occurred to the incarcerated adolescent facing genocide then there was a split from the usual, previous adolescent ambivalence to the parent (now departed). Affectionate feelings were retained for the overidealized parents while the hostile feelings were then displaced to others in the environment (Sterba, 1968; Klein, 1973). As a result, an adolescent arrest of development occurred at the time of parental death.

Adolescent Development For Survivors

What happens to adolescent development when facing genocide? The development of these youngsters can be summarized by comparing them with a control group of adolescents in the United States today who are in college or working as shown in Table 2. The table shows their marked variance from the normative pattern.

In conjecturing on the development achieved by these youngsters, Table 3 lists the possible completion of the tasks of late adolescence by them. The only one completed was separation from parents, but here it was forced or murderous. Some also developed friendships and if they met later, the friendship continued. Otherwise there was a paucity of the usual developmental features. Their ego functioning, ego ideals,

TABLE 2
LATE ADOLESCENCE COMPARED

	U.S.A.		NAZI	
	Working	College	Ghetto	Conc. Camp
Dependency	↓	↑	↑	↑
Learning opportunity	↓	↑	↓	↓
Capacity for self-observ.	↓	↑	↓	↓
Consolidation of charact.	↑	↓	↑	↑
Sense of independence	↑	↓	↓	↓
Autonomy	↑	↓	↓	↓
Opportunity for identification with mentors	↓	↑	↓	↓
Try out different ego ideals	↓	↑	↓	↓
Completion of sense of identity	↑	↓	↓	↓

TABLE 3
COMPLETION OF TASKS OF LATE ADOLESCENCE IN CONCENTRATION CAMPS

Tasks of Late Adolescence	Concentration Camp Incarcerated
– consolidation	No
– separating from parents	Yes
– identity formation	No
– achieving genital primacy	No
– sexual identity	No
– development of a time perspective	No
– commitment to a life goal	No
– development of intimacy	No
– development of friendships	Yes
– development of harmonizing of ego, superego and ego ideal	No

superego, adaptive, and coping skills were residuals of inculcations prior to their persecution, threats to life, and confinement. In the movie *Europa, Europa* the shifting, mixed identities of the persecuted are presented. Before incarceration these youngsters had to contend with daily questions about who they were and what they were along with fears of their identity being discovered. They developed distrust because their lives were constantly at risk. The Nazi genocide consisted of demoralization, destruction of identity, and then death. This is in contrast to the usual genocide, which is one of fear and death.

Completion of Adolescent Tasks in Concentration Camp

What were the possibilities for completion of the adolescent tasks in the concentration camp? It was a situation where it was impossible to have the usual dependence-independence struggle with parents, or to rebel, or to change ego ideals or experiment with different vocational ideas. Some lucky survivors had a delayed adolescent development by being placed in a special camp—in England for boys, and in Czechoslovakia for girls—for many months. After this, they were supported in their endeavors to learn the culture in England and to get job skills for several years. Others were able to progress developmentally after they entered psychotherapy or psychoanalysis.

It appears that these adolescents with murdered parents, massive repeated trauma, and without parental surrogates, had a developmental arrest. This was due not only to the massive trauma but also to the absence of normative adolescent mourning (Wolfenstein, 1966; Sugar, 1968) and the second separation-individuation stage (Blos, 1962).

After a disaster, adolescents often manifest hostile behavior, and an increased rate of vandalism, alcoholism, and unwed pregnancy (Sugar, 1997). Probably the Holocaust survivors who were youngsters had some of that. But we need to consider that their hostility to therapists and other helpers may have been initially a defense against retraumatization, that is, their fear of object loss. Later, this behavior appears to have been a sign of hope, following Winnicott's idea (1957) that they now felt enough trust to express anger about their losses to those closest and most helpful to them. With this displacement they were able to resume their adolescent development with rebellious, ambivalent and hostile attitudes and behavior to their helpers who were now parent-substitutes. This probably led to a different and delayed, but something-akin-to, adolescence for them. With this, I would submit that normative adolescent development and consolidation cannot occur without a continuing relationship with parents or parent-substitutes.

Summary

This chapter deals with the effects on adolescent development of living in a climate of genocide by reviewing the experiences of adolescents in Nazi concentration camps. This includes their fear, with the daily fare of threats to identity and life, degradation, physical and emotional illnesses, torture, and coping. The problems of these adolescents continued after liberation in displaced persons camps and with emigration.

It appears that there was an arrested adolescence for the vast majority of these survivors due to the massive trauma and absent parents. Due to their losses, they were unable to proceed through normative adolescent mourning and had unambivalent overidealization of parents, thus the arrested adolescence. It appears that normative adolescent development and consolidation of personality cannot be completed without a continuing relationship with parents or parent-surrogates; without parents there is no normative adolescence.

REFERENCES

Beuchner, H. A. (1986), *Dachau—The Hour of the Avenger*. Metairie, LA: Thunderbird Press.

Blos, P. (1962), *On Adolescence*. New York: Free Press.

——— (1974), The genealogy of the ego ideal. *The Psychoanalytic Study of the Child*, 29:43–48. New Haven, CT: Yale University Press.

Cohen, E. A. (1953), *Human Behavior in the Concentration Camp*. New York: Norton.

Danieli, Y. (1982), Families of survivors and the Nazi holocaust. In: ed. C. D. Spielberger, I. G. Sarason, & N. Milgram. *Stress and Anxiety,* ed., Washington, DC: Hemisphere, pp. 405–423.

Davidson, S. (1979), Massive psychic traumatization and social support. *J. Psychosom. Res.*, 23:395–402.

——— (1985), Group formation and its significance in the Nazi concentration camps. *Israel J. Psychiat. & Rel. Sci.*, 22:41–50.

Des Pres, T. (1976), *The Survivor*, New York: Oxford University Press.

Fleming, J. & Altschul, B. (1963), Activation of mourning and growth by psychoanalysis. *Internat. J. Psycho. Anal.*, 44:419–431.

Frankl, V. E. (1959), *Man's Search for Meaning*. New York: Simon & Schuster.

Friedman, P. (1949), Some aspects of concentration camp psychology. *Amer. J. Psychiat.*, 105:601–605.

Grubrich-Simitis, I. (1979), Extreme traumatization as cumulative trauma. *The Psychoanalytic Study of the Child*, 36:415–450. New Haven, CT: Yale University Press.

Jacobson, E. (1965), The return of the lost parent. In: *Drives, Affects and Behavior, Vol. 2* ed. M. Schur. New York: International Universities Press, pp. 193–211.

Klein, H. (1973), Children of the holocaust. In: *The Child in His Family*, ed. E. J. Anthony & C. Koupernick. New York: Wiley.

Levi, P. (1969), *Survival in Auschwitz*. New York: Collier.

Mattusek, P. (1975), *Internment in Concentration Camps and Its Consequences*. New York: Springer-Verlag.

Ryn, Z. (1986), Suicides in the Nazi concentration camps. *Suicide & Life-Threatening Behav.*, 16:419–433.

Sterba, E. (1968), The effects of persecution on adolescents. In: *Massive Psychic Trauma*, ed. H. Krystal. New York: International Universities Press.

Sugar, M. (1968), Normal adolescent mourning. *Amer. J. Psychother.*, 22:258–269.

――― (1990), Developmental anxieties in Adolescence. *Adolescent Psychiatry*, 17:385–403. Chicago: University of Chicago Press.

――― (1997), Adolescents and their reactions to disaster. *Adolescent Psychiatry*, 21:65–79. Hillsdale, NJ: The Analytic Press.

Werner, E. E. & Smith, R. S. (1982), *Vulnerable But Invincible*. New York: McGraw-Hill.

Winnicott, D. W. (1957), The antisocial tendency, In: *Collected Papers: Through Paediatrics to Psychoanalysis*. New York: Basic Books.

Wolfenstein, M. (1966), How is mourning possible? *The Psychoanalytic Study of the Child*, 21:93–123. New York: International Universities Press.

13 ADOLESCENT VIOLENCE—TWENTIETH CENTURY MADNESS: A CRITICAL REVIEW OF THEORIES OF CAUSATION

MICHAEL G. KALOGERAKIS

On June 10, 1968, President Lyndon Johnson signed Executive order # 11412 establishing the National Commission on the Causes and Prevention of Violence. The assassination of President John F. Kennedy galvanized public interest and government action in interpersonal violence as an aspect of the human experience that had received scant attention previously. Establishment of the Commission spurred major research interest in the subject, not only among criminologists but also among social scientists and mental health experts. Up until that time, violence was rarely a theme on the agenda of a psychiatric meeting. A perusal of the literature would have turned up a few isolated papers on the subject.

By contrast, the Commission turned out thirteen volumes in the space of a couple of years (Mulvihill and Tumin, 1969). In the three decades since, violence has established itself as an important part of the social and mental health agenda, in response to its increased prevalence in our communities, where it has reached epidemic proportions. Only very recently have there been signs that the trend may finally be abating. Violence committed by adolescents, whose rate has not been declining, has been a particularly alarming development, raising serious questions about what our society is doing to its children.

In this chapter, I propose to review briefly the major research efforts launched in the wake of the assassination and the subsequent general

This chapter was the 1997 Alexander Gralnick Award Paper at the ASAP Annual Meeting. It was dedicated to the memory of Richard C. Marohn, M.D., dear friend and colleague, with whom the author shared a long-standing interest in the violent adolescent.

and adolescent increase in crime, to examine them critically in the context of our clinical experience with violent adolescents, and to offer some personal thoughts on the matter from the perspective of a clinician and former public health official.

Few subjects stir as much emotion and controversy as adolescent violence. This is true among the general public where anxiety about its increase over the last few decades has skyrocketed; in legal circles, where the debate over whether to try juveniles as adults continues to rage; and among mental health professionals who struggle mightily with questions about etiology, prevention, and treatment.

An important development in our government's interest in violence occurred in 1985, when, for the first time ever, Surgeon General C. Everett Koop declared violence a major public health concern, placing it alongside of smoking, auto accidents, cancer and heart disease as one of the top priorities for the nation's health goals for the year 2000 (United States Public Health Service, 1990). On the international scene, where civil war, political repression and ethnic strife have devastated whole nations, UNICEF, the World Health Organization, the Médecins sans Frontières, and other international organizations have made intensive efforts to provide assistance to the victims. Throughout this time, research from the biological, social, and psychological sciences on one or another aspect of interpersonal aggression and violence has mushroomed and is beginning to provide answers to many basic questions.

Despite all this activity, we are a long way from an adequate understanding of violent behavior, let alone being in a position to control it.

Scope of the Problem

A few selected statistics governing violence will provide a graphic idea of the enormity of the problem:

1. While homicide is the twelfth leading cause of death in the general population, it was, in 1990, the second leading cause of death for 10- to 19-year-olds and the leading cause of death for African American males aged 10 to 19.
2. African American males are 11 times more likely to be killed by guns than are white male adolescents.
3. Homicide is the fourth cause of potential years of life lost, a statistic that reflects the plight of young people in particular.

4. In 1990, more 15- to 19-year-olds died from gunshot wounds than ever previously recorded in the United States. The overall firearm homicide rate increased 77% in the five years between 1985 and 1990 (Runyan and Gerken, 1989).
5. The ratio of nonfatal assaults to homicide is 100:1, based on self-reports; the actual figure is probably much higher.
6. Internationally, the United States leads all industrialized nations in homicides committed by 15 to 24-year-old males (Table 1), exceeding the second nation by more than four times.
7. Sixty percent of homicides in the United States are committed by firearms, 75% of these by handguns (Rosenberg and Mercy, 1991).
8. Less than 20% of homicides are committed during the commission of another crime such as robbery.
9. The FBI Uniform Crime Reports (1987) show that the incidence of interpersonal violence rises rapidly during adolescence, peaking between 17 and 21, before it begins to drop sharply (Figure 1).

The Nature of the Problem

As the most serious form of human aggression, violence, in its myriad forms, has been known to mankind from the beginnings of history. This has been true for the sanctioned collective violence of wars and of totalitarian regimes, but also for the proscribed or illegal interpersonal violence of our homes and streets.

Violence can be defined as behavior that inflicts or threatens to inflict physical injury or damage on other persons or the environment. As a form of human behavior, it is disordered, maladaptive, and when severe and sufficiently generalized, threatens survival of the species. It is asocial in that it represents flagrant unconcern for the general welfare of society. It is antisocial in that it arbitrarily deprives a fellow human being of his or her life or physical well-being. It is arguably suicidal in that it ultimately invites severe retaliation from the victim or the authorities.

Violence cannot be simply equated with delinquency since the vast majority of delinquent behavior is nonviolent. In addition, some adolescent violence is not part of a pattern of delinquent behavior. Nor is violence synonymous with aggression, representing as it does only the most extreme form of the latter. It follows that much research on

TABLE 1
INTERNATIONAL COMPARISON OF HOMICIDE FOR MALES BETWEEN 15 & 24 YEARS HOMICIDES PER 100,000 POPULATION

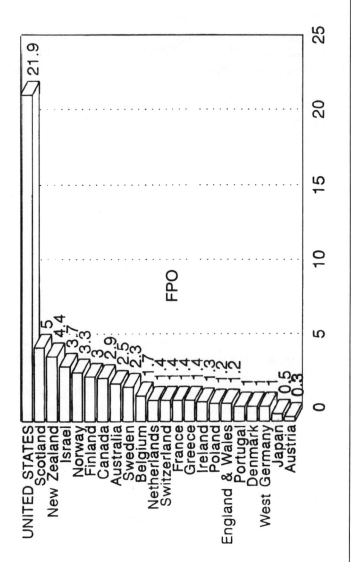

Data source: Fingerhut & Kleinman (1990).

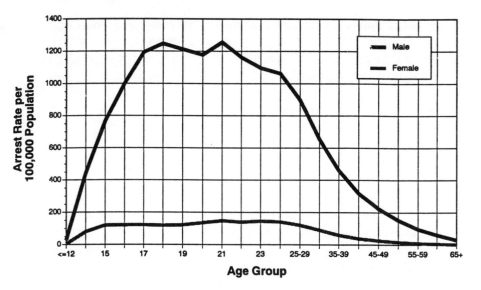

Figure 1 Violent crime. Age-specific arrest rates, United States, 1987. (*Source:* Federal Bureau of Investigation, Uniform Crime Reporting Bureau.)

aggression may have little relevance to the understanding of violence. At the same time, it is a fact that most adolescents who commit a violent act have earlier histories of aggressive behavior stretching back to preschool years. Borrowing a distinction from developmental psychobiology, Earls et al. (1993) proposed that the foundations for violence are organized in childhood and activated in adolescence. Thus, if we are to understand how violence develops, a good place to start is by examining the evolution of aggressiveness in children from its beginnings.

The Natural History of Aggression

Numerous authors, in this country and elsewhere, have reported on studies that show that aggressive behavior remains highly stable throughout childhood and into adolescence (Farrington, 1978; Olweus, 1979). Although this may suggest a biological basis for aggression, it may also be the consequence of the chronicity of the environmental conditions which foster aggression. Further, it may point to an inherent tendency for aggressive impulses to persist once they are established (e.g., adaptation to a perceived threat) and for aggressive behavior to

255

become habitual. These are questions for further research. What we can say for now is that this finding lends strong support to the validity of seeking determinants of violence early in life and following them through the developmental cycle.

BIOLOGICAL BEGINNINGS

An understanding of child development, normal and disordered, must naturally begin with what a child brings with it into this world 1) genetically, 2) prenatally, that is, as the result of intrauterine development, and 3) perinatally, or what may be associated with the trauma of birth.

These inborn variations, even those that are ostensibly within the normal range, include differences in cognitive potential, temperament, and unknown predispositions, some of which predetermine future pathology. Presumably, this is already fixed in the genetic makeup of the child and, hypothetically at least, may some day be ascertainable at birth, as our science of genetics advances. We know that a number of pathological conditions are carried in the gene structure. For those conditions, genetic makeup is destiny and cannot be overriden by environmental input or manipulation.

The door is not closed on the possibility that aggression, and perhaps violence, may some day be linked to a particular genetic abnormality that can be identified and even altered early in life. For the present, despite a brief moment in the late sixties when a genetic etiology for violence based on the presence of an XYY chromosome was proposed (Jacobs, et al., 1965), and later rejected, no researcher claims a direct connection. Here it is critical to distinguish between inborn conditions that may simply be *associated* with aggression, and others, if such can be found, that are demonstrably *causative*. Examples of inborn conditions in which aggressive behavior and even violence may be present are organic brain abnormalities, schizophrenia, and ADHD. In none of these, however, is aggression always present, so that cause and effect cannot be presumed. What remains to be clarified is the nature of the association.

The biological underpinnings of aggression have been the object of considerable attention for over three decades, beginning with animal studies conducted by zoologists such as Lorenz (1966), who studied aggressive behavior among geese, and Roberts and Kiess (1964), who studied the relationship between aggression and the hypothalamus of cats. Mulvihill and Tumin (1969) provided an early overview of what was known about the biology of aggression in humans in their report to the National Commission. They concluded that "neither genetic nor non-genetic abnormalities specifically determine violent behavior" (p. 431). They add: "there emerges one simple and indisputable fact. It is that man has the innate, inborn *capacity* [italics mine] to act aggressively and violently toward other men" and that this capacity is "modulated, shaped and conditioned by the social and cultural experiences of each individual human being" (p. 431). It would appear that, according to these authors, the actual causes of violence, including the drive or impulse to behave violently, must be sought elsewhere, not in the biological makeup.

Needless to say, this has not deterred others from pursuing a variety of potentially significant explorations. Foremost among researchers who have focused on adolescents are Lewis and her co workers (Lewis and Balla, 1976; Lewis, 1981) who directed their attention to delinquent and violent populations in hospitals and correctional facilities and reported their findings in a series of publications beginning in 1973. They identified abnormal EEGs, "soft" neurological signs, and histories or clinical pictures consistent with severe disturbances such as psychosis and epilepsy in a significant number of the youths studied. Their results and inferences have been questioned by a number of others, however, (Ratner, 1989; Benedek and Cornell, 1989), and have yet to be replicated. However this may turn out, they have established beyond any question that no evaluation of a delinquent or violent adolescent is complete unless it includes a thorough neuropsychiatric assessment.

Brennan, Mednick, and Kandel (1991) report that perinatal complications predicted persistent violent offending. In their view, the perinatal difficulties caused brain damage that led to a loss of impulse control, which in turn led to increased violence. In a recent comprehensive review, Young and his colleagues (1994) surveyed neurological, hormonal, genetic, neurochemical, and other measures. Like Ervin more than a quarter of a century earlier, they concluded that no simple relationship between biological factors and aggression had been found: ". . . there is not a single brain center, hormone, or chemical substance that controls the brain's activities during aggressive behavior" (p. 14). It is remarkable that, in an era when the biological bias in psychiatry has prevailed and biologically-oriented research has predominated, little has been added to our knowledge of the relationship between aggression and its biological roots in over a quarter of a century.

PSYCHOLOGICAL FORCES, INDIVIDUAL AND FAMILIAL

Infancy and Early Childhood

Following birth, the child's exclusive environment for at least the next three years (prior to nursery school) is most often the child's immediate or extended family. Nearly all of the impact made, therefore, has its source in the home atmosphere and the individual and collective interactions with family members. As developmental psychologists have focused increasing attention on infancy and early childhood, it has become apparent that the fundamentals of cognitive, emotional and even social development are laid down during this period and that the future personality structure is already beginning to take shape. Rutter (1980), in describing the developmental perspective as an integrating theme in psychiatry, stated it this way:

[T]he process of development constitutes the crucial link between genetic determinants and environmental variables, between sociology and individual psychology, and between physiogenic and psychogenic causes. Development thus encompasses not only the roots of behavior in prior maturation, in physical influences (both internal and external), and in the residues of earlier experiences, but also in the modulations of that behavior by the circumstances of the present [p. 1].

At life's outset, the bulk of the caretaking responsibility falls traditionally to the mother. Turning his attention to that first relationship, John Bowlby (1969), elucidated the great importance of *attachment*. An increasing number of researchers since Bowlby have directed their attention to one or another aspect of zero-to-three development, resulting in attachment theory and social cognition theory, areas of inquiry that have already produced a prodigious literature. What has been learned about the precursors or early manifestations of aggression?

It is beyond the scope of this paper to review the many potentially significant findings of this work but, in general, what has emerged is that early predictors of subsequent *maladaptation* have been identified but no factors that are specifically or reliably predictive of violence. For the moment, therefore, we are left to speculate, drawing inferences from studies of later childhood as well as retrospectively from clinical experience with adolescents themselves.

The factors that we know have a negative impact on children in the first three years that might reasonably be connected to aggression and violence can be conceptualized in the following way: (1) What is *done* to them: neglect, physical, sexual and emotional abuse, separation and abandonment; (2) What is *not provided:* nurturance, love, respect for others, limits; (3) What they *see:* disorganization and chaos, interpersonal hostility, violence; and (4) What they *hear:* hate, bigotry, stories about and sanctioning of violence.

Each of these features—and this list is far from complete—is a potential risk factor for aggression and violence. The validity of some has long since been established. We know, for example, that child abusers often were abused children themselves. Yet it is also true that some youths who were abused as children do not become violent while others who were not abused do. Emde (1990), made the point that insecure attachment can be considered a risk factor for later disorder in the child but that most infants so classified will not develop a psychiatric disorder. The explanation seems to lie in the fact that there is no simple, direct route to violence, that many intervening experiences can be determinant, and that the paths to complex human behaviors are circuitous and convoluted. Increasing recognition of this elemental fact led to the establishment recently of the discipline of developmental psychopathology, defined as "the study of the origins and course of individual patterns of behavioral maladaptation" (Sroufe and Rutter, 1984).

Social learning theory, including an emphasis on child rearing (Bandura and Walters, 1959), has been a major psychological theory of aggression for decades. Cognitive theory, which traces its origins to the beginning of the century, has more recently turned its attention to the development of aggression in childhood (Pepler and Rubin, 1991). The major thrust of these latter studies has been on cognitive functioning, with little attention to emotional factors (see especially Cairns and Cairns, 1991). Ledingham (1991), in commenting on the social-cognitive theory of aggression, states: "In general, a *cognitive-affective model* [italics mine] may prove to be a more useful model than a strictly cognitive model to explain aggression. . . . [T]o date few investigators have chosen to include measures of type, lability, and intensity of emotional response or to investigate the consequences of this for social cognition" (p. 283). I agree with this assessment and, further, believe that much of what later takes the form of aggressive behavior and even violence can be laid down very early in life, long before what has generally been assumed.

If cognition and emotion do underlie the behavior we call aggression, and we wish to trace their origins and development through the developmental cycle, the following questions may serve as a starting point:

1. What elements of cognitive development and what affective responses arising in the relationship between primary caretaker and young child seem to be related to later aggressive impulses or behavior?
2. How early do they make their appearance?
3. As they become increasingly maladaptive and ultimately symptomatic, can a regular sequence be discerned?
4. Until what age are they reversible?
5. What interventions are likely to be effective in reversing them?
6. What is the potential impact, positive and negative, of other caretakers in the household?

A glance at a composite profile of a violent adolescent drawn from the published reports of clinicians, helps to orient us as we look for relevant characteristics in infancy and early childhood. Since we are dealing with a composite, note that only some may be found in a particular case. Also, their presence does not make violent behavior inevitable. They are neither necessary nor sufficient. Table 2 indicates which features (or

TABLE 2

FEATURES COMMONLY ASSOCIATED WITH VIOLENCE-PRONE ADOLESCENTS AND THEIR PRESENCE IN THE FIRST THREE YEARS OF LIFE

	Present	As Precursors
Anger, rage, hostility	X	
Impulsivity	X	
Emotional instability	X	
Undeveloped conscience		X
Low self-esteem	X	
Disrespect for authority		X
Devaluation of life		
Alienation	X	
Immaturity	X	
Pattern of delinquency		
Gender confusion		
General aggressiveness	X	
Boundary problems		
Anxiety, fear	X	
Mental retardation (rare)	X	
Poor social judgement		X

symptoms) are likely to have made an appearance during the first three years, if only in the form of precursors. One can see that a majority of listed features may already be present, either fully or in nascent form at an early age. Whether these features become integrated as lasting elements in the developing personality or not depends on whether they are reenforced or modified by subsequent experience. When reenforcement occurs, as is so often the case because of the chronicity inherent in the life styles of the high risk families generally involved, as well as the pathogenicity of the extrafamilial environment, I believe we can speak of causation. It is possible, therefore, to ascribe etiologic significance to the period before major socialization outside the family begins. Subsequent peer influence may then be viewed as reenforcing and giving form to evolving aggression and to the development of a high risk or violence-prone personality structure.

The School Years

As the child moves past the first three years, the task of building competence socially and academically takes on increasing importance. Any obstacle encountered tends to push a child toward alternatives where success might be more easily achieved. Such obstacles in school could include inborn handicaps such as ADHD, learning disabilities, or severe understimulation at home, placing the child at a disadvantage vis-a-vis peers. Socially, any parallel handicap (e.g., excessive shyness, which can be a function of temperament), can lead to withdrawal and isolation. Even moderate failures in these areas can lead to serious self-esteem problems. Such a child is easy prey for older children bent on exploitation.

Later Childhood

Peer group and other external pressures increase significantly through the latency years and into preadolescence, at the same time that the family's hold on the child weakens. Yet it is during this period that some of the family pathology in the area of aggression and violence may be definitively transmitted, to be reenforced during adolescence. Psychoanalytic contributions, beginning with Johnson and Szurek (1952), and continuing with Sargent (1962, 1971) and Kalogerakis (1971a, 1971b), and others, have documented the intergenerational transmission, often unconscious, of violent impulses, frequently leading to tragic consequences within the family (patricide, matricide). These are the children who are likely to be seen in psychiatric facilities rather than in the juvenile justice system. Their crimes are the crimes of passion and may occur once and not again.

Latency is also the age during which the influence of television on psychosocial development has been shown to be strongest (Centerwall, 1992). Many children on a fast track are already beginning to experiment with drugs and other risky behaviors, and a pattern of delinquency may be launched.

Adolescence

The normal developmental stages of adolescence, spearheaded by the thrust to independence, carry the familiar risks of smoking, substance abuse, academic problems, including dropping out of school, running away, promiscuity, curfew issues, and the like. Problems of serious aggression are not a necessary part of this unfolding and are not apt to occur unless there is a prior individual history along the lines described, or the family is disrupted by severe interpersonal stresses at any point in the child's life, or lives in high risk circumstances economically and socially.

The actual impact made by pathogenic forces such as community violence is to some degree dependent on protective forces that may be present in a particular case. These may be 1) inborn, and include such known factors as above-average intelligence, and other less clear ego attributes such as resilience, adaptability and the like, which taken together may constitute what has been called the invulnerable child; 2) intrafamilial, such as the presence of one or more healthy secondary caretakers; and 3) extrafamilial, involving influences such as a pediatrician or nursery school teacher who may have access to the young child.

What we do not know is how effective the protection provided by these factors is. We also do not know how well the strength a child derives from a healthy home environment will protect him from future pathological forces in the community.

SOCIAL FORCES: FROM VIOLENCE-PRONENESS
TO VIOLENT ACT

For every adolescent who commits a violent act, there are probably 10 others (or 100) who are equally capable of it but never do. We have been considering the assortment of forces, individual and familial, that lead to a high risk situation. What factors determine whether an adolescent who may be presumed to be violence-prone will actually commit a violent act? Assuming a violence-prone adolescent, one or both of two internal changes must occur for violent behavior to become imminent. Either the drive to commit violence must increase beyond the threshold where it is containable, or the normally available controls must be so weakened that they no longer suffice to contain existing aggressive impulses (Kalogerakis, 1974):

$$\uparrow \text{violent impulse} + \downarrow \text{ego controls} = \text{violence}$$

The level of vulnerability already established by the combination of biological forces and early childhood experience remains the determining factor. At this point, however, social forces, notably in the impact of peers, assume an important role in moving the vulnerable child to a true violence-prone state. Once this has happened, specific interactions at a given moment in time determine whether an act of violence will actually occur. This process can be schematized as follows:

1. Vulnerabilities + Violence-promoting social forces → Violence-prone adolescent
2. Violence-prone adolescent + Facilitating factors + Trigger → Violent act

Social forces that are known to foster violence include living in a high crime area, poverty, racial, ethnic, or religious discrimination, and neighborhoods with poor or nonexistent social or mental health services. *Facilitating* factors include all external forces that increase the strength of the violent impulses or diminish the controls over them. Alcohol, drug abuse, gang affiliation, weapon availability, and criminal activity (especially the drug trade) are common examples. Television and other media violence have been shown to play a prominent role (American Psychological Association, 1993). Triggers or *precipitating factors* include a violent argument, an intolerable threat or insult, being accosted, sudden fear, a command hallucination, acute intoxication, relentless harassment, humiliation, and for criminal violence, sighting a likely victim in low risk circumstances.

What is expressed by a violent act depends on the personality make-up of the adolescent and the circumstances surrounding commission of the act. It is not difficult to recognize the differences in intent among 1) the paranoid youth obeying an auditory hallucination ordering him to kill; 2) an antisocial youth eyeing the pocketbook of an elderly passerby; or 3) a confused and agitated adolescent assaulting a sexually provocative stepmother. These varieties of violent adolescents are sufficiently distinct and the clinical picture of each remains sufficiently constant to permit a classification based on the phenomenology (Table 3). Benedek and Cornell (1989), in a study of juvenile homicide involving 72 adolescents, offer a typology that encompasses the great majority of violent youth: (1) a psychotic group, which constituted 7% of their cases, (2) a conflict group, consisting of 42%, and (3) a crime group, totaling 51%. The fact that all of their study group was composed of youths who had killed and were before the court unavoidably skewed their sample to the most violent end of the spectrum. To encompass *all* levels of violence, one should probably add a fourth group, in which no

TABLE 3
THE VIOLENT ACT: WHAT IT EXPRESSES

	Psychotic or Organic	Conflict-based	Antisocial
Conscious motive	Destruction of enemy (paranoia) Removal of impediment Random explosiveness (no specific motive)	Expression of rage Resolution of conflict Revenge Irresistible impulse	Robbery Settling a score (gang wars) Hatred (racial, ethnic) Turf issues (gangs)
Unconscious motives	Irrelevant	Redress (of wrong or humiliation) Identification with the aggressor—assertion of power	Possibly homicide, based on deeply re- pressed hate (e.g., of father or stepfather)
Degree of control	Little or none	Variable; often diminished	Unaffected in most cases
Relationship to victim	Random, arbitrary	Often known; family or acquaintance	Usually a stranger
Nature of the violence	Uncontrolled, often lethal	Impulsive, specific, occasionally homicidal	Planned, deliberate, non-specific; lethality incidental
Personality structure	Disorganized	Unstable, volatile, neurotic	Sociopathic or schizoid
Aftermath	Unaware	Remorse; relief; pos- sibly continued anger	

significant personality pathology can be detected. Such a category may of course result from the failure to do a proper diagnostic evaluation. Unfortunately, in at least some of those cases, the more likely explanation is that committing violence is easier than we would like to think, and that relatively normal individuals are capable of it, given certain circumstances. The obvious example is war. Rationalizing that the victim is not truly human (Miller and Looney, 1974) simplifies the task and may or may not require an altered state of consciousness.

Toward a Conceptual Model of Causation

Table 4 summarizes what has been presented above concerning general causative factors. Whatever formulations may be derived from the risk factors that have been identified, it is important to remember that the majority of children exposed to the ravages of the inner city and to their dysfunctional families do not go on to a life of violence (American

TABLE 4
ETIOLOGY OF ADOLESCENT VIOLENCE: A CONCEPTUAL MODEL

Internal Conditions	Family Conditions	Community Conditions
[Normal child]	[Healthy home environment]	[Health-promoting]

Anomalies:
  genetic
  prenatal
  perinatal
	Dysfunctional or pathogenic	Destabilizing

↓	↓	↓
Vulnerable child	Violence-inducing	Delinquency-promoting
↓	↓	↓
Violence-prone child +	Violent home +	Violent subculture

High-risk adolescent

+

Facilitating factors

+

Trigger

↓

VIOLENT ACT

265

Psychological Association, 1993). As already indicated, we have much to learn about protective factors that are apparently capable of neutralizing even severe pathogenicity. With this caveat in mind, let us examine potential pathways to violence in adolescence. Clinical experience and basic psychopathological principles strongly suggest that there is no single developmental route to violence. The best we can do is to trace a number of likely but not invariable pathways. The following is one such route and is based on inferences that may be drawn from the preceding review: (1) that since violence is an extreme form of human destructiveness, major warping of normal personality development is usually necessary for it to occur, and that this can begin quite early; (2) that the emotions of anger, especially in its most severe expression, rage, and hostility, are an invariable feature in the history of every violent individual, and this is probably true even when such feelings are not detectable at the time that the violence is finally committed; (3) that the object of the rage is initially a significant family figure, often the primary caretaker or her mate, but, over time, progressively undergoes generalization or displacement, until even unknowns may become potential victims; (4) that impulses develop in an increasingly malignant direction and that control over them becomes progressively defective, and this may be evident from a very early point; (5) that the value placed on human life, ultimately including one's own, undergoes progressive deterioration, until life itself is meaningless (Kalogerakis, 1971a); and (6) that all of these features are subject to reenforcement or correction throughout childhood. A different course would apply to the psychotic or neuropathically driven youth. The same is true for the occasional teenager who commits a single act of violence under extenuating circumstances. This outline seems to fit the majority of adolescents who develop a pattern of violence. It may be aptly described as the *hostile-antisocial route.*

Another, less common, pathway might be termed the *schizoid route.* Here, early development might involve an innate temperament inclined to introversion, neglect rather than abuse in the early years, experiences fostering poor social judgment, later abusive treatment, development of a submissive nature that is easily influenced by others, and, in adolescence, falling in with aggressive youths such as members of a violent gang.

What must be added to this portrayal are the elaborate and complex details of reaction and interaction as development unfolds, a matter of continuing study. Such research is needed to provide the substantive support for what at present are merely hypothetical formulations.

Prevention and Treatment

Two simple truths emerge from the foregoing discussion: that most violence is preventable and that only a multilateral approach offers any hope. Prevention of violence requires that we recognize from the outset that we are not confronted with a squeaky wheel in which it is sufficient to identify the one element in the picture that needs fixing. A more accurate metaphor is of a chain, every link of which is severely corroded. Fixing one will accomplish little, a break at any point can destroy the whole. Thus when we focus in on an individual child, we must simultaneously consider that child's total universe—immediate, intermediate, and remote. This includes its parents or other caretakers, the home setting, the immediate neighborhood, the larger subculture, the economy, the nation, government, and its policies. Prevention programs have traditionally been restricted to one or two of these levels and as a result have often failed. Outcome studies have in general been discouraging with regard to maintaining initial positive results (Coie, et al., 1991). To maintain benefits, a coordinated global effort would seem to be necessary. Such an effort, comprehensive, sustained, and adequately funded, may well be the number one challenge of governments in the next century. It will require the commitment of legislators, public health officials, social service and mental health agencies, educators, the media, the law, and clinicians. An awesome undertaking, it must be driven by the realization that lesser efforts have proven inadequate, undone by the destructive context which remained untouched.

If there is any basis for optimism, it is the knowledge that almost everything that has been identified as contributing to violent behavior can either be prevented or treated. Interventions must be relevant to the stage of development of the child after a thorough psychiatric evaluation designed to identify the hierarchy of needs that must be addressed. The assessment should include, in addition to the child, his or her family and all relevant physical, neurological, psychological and social aspects.

GENERAL PRINCIPLES

1. *Earlier is better than later*, or, primary prevention is better than secondary or tertiary. Although there are generally no good reasons for postponing intervention once a high risk situation is identified, some problems may be more easily addressed when a child is more mature.

As an example, some adolescent problems cannot be dealt with effectively until adulthood.

2. *Early intervention is family intervention*, the major emphasis being on the parents or other caretakers. This applies not only to obvious situations such as abuse and neglect, but also when parents are merely overwhelmed and confused. If we help the parents, the whole family benefits. The problem here, as with primary prevention, is access. In the preschool years, only pediatric clinics, pediatricians, and some community-based family service agencies (a good example is the Center for Family Life in Brooklyn, N.Y.) are in a position to get an inside view of a family. Training pediatricians and the family workers involved to recognize high-risk situations and to intervene effectively must be a high priority.

3. *Helping maladjustment generically will promote nonviolence.* Since, as mentioned above, research has as yet failed to turn up specific early predictors of future violence, strategies aimed at improving child-rearing techniques that have an impact on the overall adaptation of the child are appropriate and may indirectly help efforts to prevent aggression.

4. *A well-coordinated, multi-faceted approach* offers the best chance to reverse developing pathology. According to Coie, et al. (1991), approaches to intervention with aggressive children fall into five categories: behavior management, emotional control strategies, social skill training, social information processing and cognitive or emotional perspective taking. An example is the social (life) skills program promoted by the Division of Mental Health of the World health Organization (WHO, 1993). What is left out of these approaches are psychodynamically-based strategies that I believe have an important role to play in dealing with emotional and personality issues (Keith, 1984). What is essential is to choose the most appropriate intervention at the moment.

5. *Interventions need to be cost-effective, realistic, and accessible.* This may require opting for short-term approaches, targeting those aspects of the problem that are most susceptible to change in the shortest possible time. Pharmacotherapy may be very useful. Although no true antiaggression pill has yet been found, haloperidol, lithium, and the selective serotonin uptake inhibitors (SSRIs) have been used with some success. With psychotherapy, group approaches rather than individual interventions may be necessary and can be very effective. Beyond this are the many varieties of school-based programs, generally cognitive-behavioral in orientation, including the WHO life skills program. The

thrust of these programs is generic, usually concerned with the promotion of social competence.

6. *Cosmetic changes may be worse than no treatment*, since they may create the illusion that valid change has actually occurred. As an example, many of the school-based conflict resolution techniques have produced changes which, on follow-up one to two years later, have not been maintained. Quite possibly, these approaches fail because they underestimate the depth and pervasiveness of anger in a child. In the older child, once an antisocial personality structure is on its way to being established, a behavior modification approach may be naïve. However impractical, intensive psychotherapy that is psychoanalytically based is still the only therapeutic intervention that offers any hope for personality change.

7. *Broad-based community support efforts* that target community violence may have an impact on rates of delinquency and crime in a given neighborhood. Some of these efforts (Marans and Cohen, 1993; Osofsky, 1993) have achieved success by bringing together the combined approaches of social service agencies, mental health initiatives, and the local police force.

A ROLE FOR THE PSYCHIATRIST

Where, in the broad spectrum of useful interventions, is there a role for the adolescent psychiatrist? Most practitioners seldom come into contact with teenagers who are severely at risk or who have already committed violence. Such youths are rarely self-referred, but they may be brought in by a concerned family, generally when the violent behavior or threats have occurred at home. Schools may be a source of referral, usually for the psychotic or conflict group. The delinquent group are more likely to end up in court and the juvenile justice system, where they may be referred for mental health assessment.

The most important role for the psychiatrist is to conduct a thorough diagnostic evaluation, assess the level of dangerousness, and make recommendations for treatment. For this population, residential placement may be a frequent option. When the decision is to work with the youth in the community, however, intensive case management will almost certainly be required. As mentioned earlier, a small number may be appropriate candidates for individual psychodynamic psychotherapy. For this group, targeted goals may include reducing aggressivity, improving impulse control, dealing with anger, working through hostility, promoting healthier family and interpersonal relationships, and replacing destructive values with more positive ones.

Invariably, the parents will need to be included in the overall treatment plan, in which case the goals are apt to include identifying areas of misinformation and ignorance of child care principles and normal adolescent development; assessing the parents' needs and how they might best be met; providing guidelines, access to help and support; helping them to understand a maladjusted adolescent; fostering improved communications within the family; and promoting healthy life skills for all.

I would like to single out a few child-rearing items as particularly pertinent to the control of violence, from infancy on up. They are the provision of adequate nurturance, firm limit-setting in a consistent and nonhostile manner, teaching respect and consideration for others, including authorities, and appropriate management of anger. Regrettably, space does not allow for a full discussion of these needs, but it should be fairly evident that if they are successfully carried out through childhood, aggression and violence would be essentially precluded.

When participating as treatment agents, we are in our classical role as clinicians where our challenge is to treat the disease, so to speak. Those among us who would cut a wider swath have a number of additional options. By serving as a consultant to public schools or juvenile courts one can reach many more adolescents at risk for violence. Others may choose to work in residential facilities that admit such youths. Whatever the setting, the adolescent psychiatrist who is willing to work with an admittedly difficult population, is certain to be rewarded, for there are few young people who are in deeper trouble or need us more.

The Global View: Public Health Perspectives for the Twenty-First Century

It has been said that the problem of violence is "something more fundamental and ultimately more important than smallpox eradication" (Foege, 1991). This is hardly a surprising judgment if one considers the havoc that is wrought in the lives of millions wherever violence exists.

The emphasis in this chapter has been on interpersonal violence in the lives of adolescents. We know that collective, often state-supported violence around the world has taken an enormous toll—in Africa, South America, Cambodia, Ireland, Bosnia, and elsewhere. The Harvard *World Mental Health* report (Desjarlais et al., 1995), reviewing the impact of violence on societies, underscores demoralization as one of the more pernicious consequences. The authors emphasize that "therapeutic interventions must work at the cultural level as well as the psychological level to reestablish a secure moral ground for everyday life." They opine that "an undue emphasis on individual trauma may lead to the neglect or delegitimation of social harms, from the demoralization of a society to the dislocation of entire communities" (p. 134). Riots in the inner cities of the United States have been a comparatively small example of such collective violence, albeit significant for the populations involved. Tackling international violence is a monumental undertaking and many will balk when confronted with the poverty, social injustice, ethnic, racial and religious strife, and virtually nonexistent infrastructure of the societies represented.

The problem should be less daunting when we look at our domestic situation, yet we have made little progress. As indicated, we remain the most violent industrialized country in the world, and the last fifty years have seen a constant rise in the incidence of interpersonal violence, especially among our youth. We have reached levels that far surpass those of any nation in recorded history. It behooves us to ask, why in our country and why in our time? Consider the possible explanations that follow. First, though we live in the richest country in the world, we have failed to deal with the shame of our inner cities, which are literally hemorrhaging before our very eyes, as family after family and generation after generation are ravaged. Second, we not only tolerate violence, we foment it. Hate talk by talk show hosts has paralleled the vitriol of rap singers, reaching millions, and inevitably filtering down to teenagers. All too sadly, similar sentiments are not infrequently heard from some of our elected representatives. Third, incomprehensibly, citing our Constitution, we continue to produce and distribute firearms, including the most lethal weapon of all, the handgun, making them available to children of almost any age. In one study of schoolchildren, 60% said that they could easily obtain a gun if they wanted one (L.H. Research, Inc., 1993). Many authors agree that *the single most important step we could take to reduce violence is to control the availability of handguns.* As Rosenberg and Mercy (1991) remind us, the number of people who died from firearm injuries in the United States in 1986–1987 exceeded the number of casualties suffered during the entire eight and one-half years of the Vietnam War. Also, in 1985, firearm injuries cost the country some $14.4 billion. Fourth, our pre-eminent role model, the United States government, knows of no "loyal opposition." Rather, it portrays the other side of the aisle as the hated enemy, to be destroyed by any means available. Fifth, we glorify violent aggression in our contact sports, reaching millions of vulnerable children via broadcasts. Too many of our sports heroes exemplify hostile, belligerent leadership rather than the ideal embodied in the tradition of sportsmanship. Sixth, movies, video, and television provide an endless parade of violent fare, setting standards for human conduct in perhaps the most effective means ever devised. Based on estimates of the hours of TV watched and the amount of violence presented, it has been calculated that by age 18, teenagers may have watched as many as 18,000 murders and 800 suicides on television (Hechinger, 1992). Longitudinal studies have shown a correlation between levels of watching TV violence and increased aggressive behavior and violence (American Psychological Association, 1993). Fictionalized violence is not the only culprit. Local news broadcasts manage to present a distorted portrait of human life by parading seemingly endless gore and, in general, the ugly, seamier side of life.

It is patently obvious that fundamental changes are needed not only in our way of doing business in this democracy of ours, but in our cultural values and basic morality. Unless we take a good hard look at the principles that we are propagating and by which we educate our children, we shall never eradicate or even reduce violence significantly. To claim we cannot afford it is to admit moral bankruptcy. As matters stand, our inner cities are held hostage by our government, our families are held hostage by the ghetto, and our children stand as the ultimate victims, the recipients of multiple layers of unconscionable abuse which they are powerless to combat.

REFERENCES

American Psychological Association (1993), *Violence and Youth*. Washington, DC: American Psychological Association.

Baldwin, (1902), *Social and Ethical Interpretations in Mental Development*. New York: MacMillan.

Bandura, A. & Walters, R. H. (1959), *Adolescent Aggression*. New York: Ronald Press.

MICHAEL G. KALOGERAKIS

Benedek, E. P. & Cornell, D. G. (1989), *Juvenile Homicide*. Washington, DC: American Psychiatric Press.
Bowlby, J. (1969), *Attachment and Loss Vol. 1*. New York: Basic Books.
Brennan, P., Mednick, S. & Kandel, E. (1991), Congenital determinants of violent and property offending. In: *The Development and Treatment of Childhood Aggression*, ed. D. J. Pepler & K. H. Rubin. Hillsdale, NJ: Lawrence Erlbaum Associates, pp. 81–92.
Cairns, R. B. & Cairns, B. D. (1991), Social cognition and social networks: A developmental perspective. In: *The Development and Treatment of Childhood Aggression*, ed. D. J. Pepler & K. H. Rubin. Hillsdale, NJ: Lawrence Erlbaum Associates, pp. 249–278.
Centerwall, B. S. (1992), Television and violence. *J. Amer. Med. Assn.*, 267:3059–3063.
Coie, J. D., Underwood, M. & Lochman, J. E. (1991), Programmatic intervention with aggressive children in the school setting. In: *The Development and Treatment of Childhood Aggression*, ed. D. J. Pepler & K. H. Rubin. Hillsdale, NJ: Lawrence Erlbaum Associates.
Desjarlais, R., Eisenberg, L., Good, B. & Kleinman, A. (1995), *World Mental Health*. New York: Oxford University Press.
Earls, F., Cairns, R. B. & Mercy, J. A. (1993), The control of violence and the promotion of nonviolence in adolescents. In: *Promoting the Health of Adolescents*, ed. S. G. Millstein, A. C. Petersen & E. O. Nightingale. New York: Oxford University Press, pp. 285–304.
Emde, R. (1990), Preface. In: *Attachment in the Preschool Years*, ed. Greenberg, M. T., Cichetti, D. & E. M. Cummings. Chicago: University of Chicago Press.
Farrington, D. P. (1978), The family backgrounds of aggressive youths. In: *Aggression and Antisocial Behavior in Childhood and Adolescence*, ed. L. A. Hersov & M. Berger. Oxford: Pergamon.
——— (1993), Firearm mortality among children, youth and young adults. *Advance Data*, 231. Hyattsville, MD: National Center for Health Statistics.
Fingerhut, L. A. (1993), Firearm mortality among children, youth and young adults. *Advance Data*, 231. Hyattsville, MD: National Center for Health Statistics.
——— & Kleinman, J. C. (1990), International and interstate comparisons of homicide among young males. *J. Amer. Med. Assn.*, 263:3292–3295.

Foege, W. (1991), Preface. In: *Violence in America: A Public Health Approach.* New York: Oxford University Press.

Hechinger, F. M. (1992), *Fateful Choices.* New York: Carnegie Corp.

Jacobs, P. A., Brunton, M., Melville, M. M., Brittain, R. P. & McClomont, T. (1965), Aggressive behavior, mental subnormality and the XYY male. *Nature,* 208:1351–1352.

Johnson, A. & Szurek, S. (1952), The genesis of antisocial acting out in children and adults. *Psychoanal. Quart.* 21:323–343.

Kalogerakis, M. G. (1971a), Homicide in adolescents. Fantasy and deed. In: *Dynamics of Violence,* ed. J. Fawcett. Chicago: American Medical Association, pp. 93–103.

——— (1971b), The assaultive psychiatric patient. *Psychiat. Quart.,* 45:372–381.

——— (1974), The sources of individual violence. In: *Adolescent Psychiatry,* 3:323–339. New York: Basic Books.

Keith, C. R. (1984), Individual psychotherapy and psychoanalysis with the aggressive adolescent. In: *The Aggressive Adolescent,* ed. C. R. Keith. New York: Free Press, pp. 191–208.

L. H. Research, Inc. (1993), *A Survey of Experiences, Perceptions and Apprehensions About Guns Among Young People in America.* Chicago: Harvard School of Public Health.

Ledingham, J. (1991), Social cognition and aggression. In: *The Development and Treatment of Childhood Aggression,* ed. D. J. Pepler & K. H. Rubin. Hillsdale, NJ: Lawrence Erlbaum Associates, pp. 279–285.

Lewis D. O. ed. (1981), *Vulnerabilities to Delinquency.* New York: Spectrum.

——— & Balla, D. A. (1976), *Delinquency & Psychopathology.* New York: Grune & Stratton.

Lorenz, K. (1966), *On Aggression.* New York: Harcourt, Brace.

Marans, S. & Cohen, D. (1993), Children and inner-city violence. In: *Psychological Effects of War and Violence on Children,* ed. L. Leavitt & N. Fox. Hillsdale, NJ: Lawrence Erlbaum Associates, pp. 281–302.

Miller, D. & Looney, J. (1974), The prediction of adolescent homicide: episodic dyscontrol and dehumanization. *Amer. J. Psychoanal.,* 34:187–198.

Mulvihill, D. J. & Tumin, M. M. (1969), *Crimes of Violence.* Vol 12. 431. Washington, DC: U. S. Government Printing Office.

Olweus, D. (1979), Stability of aggressive reaction patterns in males. *Psychol. Bull.,* 86:852–875.

Osofsky, J. (1993), Violence in the lives of young children. Presented at Carnegie Corporation Task Force on Meeting the Needs of Young Children. New Orleans.

Pepler, D. J. & Rubin, K. H. (1991), *The Development and Treatment of Childhood Aggression.* Hillsdale, NJ: Lawrence Erlbaum Associates.

Ratner, R. A. (1989), Biological causes of delinquency. In: *Juvenile Psychiatry and the Law*, ed. R. Rosner & H. I. Schwartz, New York: Plenum, pp. 29–44.

Roberts, W. W. & Kiess, H. G. (1964), Motivational properties of hypothalamic aggression in cats. *J. Compar. Physiol. & Psychol.*, 58:187–193.

Rosenberg M. L. & Mercy, J. A. (1991), Assaultive violence. In: *Violence in America*, ed. M. L. Rosenberg & M. A. Fenley. New York: Oxford University Press, pp. 14–50.

Runyan, C. W. & Gerken, E. A. (1989), Epidemiology and prevention of adolescent injury: A review and research agenda. *J. Amer. Med. Assn.*, p 262:16 .

Rutter, M. (1980), Introduction. In: *Scientific Foundations of Developmental Psychiatry*, ed. M. Rutter. London: Heinemann.

Sargent, D. A. (1962) Children who kill—a family conspiracy. *Social Work*, 7:35–42.

———. (1971), The lethal situation: Transmission of urge to kill from parent to child. In: *Dynamics of Violence*, ed. J. Fawcett. Chicago: American Medical Association, pp. 105–113.

Sroufe, L. A. & Rutter, M. (1984), The domain of developmental psychopathology. *Child Devel.*, 55:17–29.

U.S. Department of Justice. (1987), Uniform Crime Reports. Washington, DC: U.S. Government Printing Office.

United States Public Health Service (1990), *Year 2000 Health Objectives. Healthy Youth 2000.* Washington, DC: U.S. Government Printing Office.

World Health Organization (1993), *Life Skills Education in the Schools.* Geneva: World Health Organization.

Young, J. G., Brasie, J. R., Sheitman, B. & Studnick, M. (1984), Brain mechanisms mediating aggression and violence. In: *Children and Violence*, ed. C. Chiland & J. G. Young. Northvale, NJ: Aronson, pp. 13–48.

THE AUTHORS

MORTON J. ARONSON, M.D. is Associate Clinical Professor of Psychiatry, Columbia University College of Physicians and Surgeons, and Training and Supervising Analyst, Columbia University Psychoanalytic Center.

KATY BUTLER, PH.D. is Assistant Professor of Psychiatry, Robert Wood Johnson Medical School,University of Medicine and Dentistry of New Jersey, Piscataway.

CATHERINE CHABERT, PH.D. is Professor of Psychology, University of Paris V.

SHMUEL ERLICH, PH.D. is Sigmund Freud Professor of Psychoanalysis; Director, Sigmund Freud Center, The Hebrew University of Jerusalem; and Training Analyst, Israel Psychoanalytic Institute.

AARON ESMAN, M.D. (Editor) is Professor of Clinical Psychiatry (Emeritus), Cornell University Medical College; and Faculty, New York Psychoanalytic Institute.

JULES GLENN, M.D. is Clinical Professor of Psychiatry, New York University Medical Center, and Training and Supervising Analyst (Emeritus), The Psychoanalytic Institute, New York University Medical Center.

ROBERT HENDREN, D.O. is Professor and Director, Division of Child and Adolescent Psychiatry, University of

Medicine and Dentistry of New Jersey-Robert Wood Johnson Medical School, Piscataway.

MILTON H. HOROWITZ, M.D. is Professor of Clinical Psychiatry (Emeritus), New York University Medical College; and Training and Supervising Analyst, New York Psychoanalytic Institute.

PHILIPPE JEAMMET, M.D. is Chief of Service, Child, Adolescent and Young Adult Psychiatry, Institut Mutualist Montsouris; and Professor of Child Psychiatry, University of Paris VI.

MICHAEL G KALOGERAKIS, M. D. is Clinical Professor of Psychiatry, New York University College of Medicine; and President of the International Society of Adolescent Psychiatry.

OTTO KERNBERG, M.D. is Director, Personality Disorders Institute, New York Hospital-Cornell Medical Center; Professor of Psychiatry, Cornell University Medical Center; and Training and Supervising Analyst, Columbia University Psychoanalytic Center.

DEREK MILLER, M.D. is Professor of Psychiatry, (Emeritus), Northwestern University Medical School; and Honorary President of the International Society for Adolescent Psychiatry.

VIVIAN M. RAKOFF, M.D. is Professor of Psychiatry (Emerita), Clarke Institute of Psychiatry, Department of Psychiatry, University of Toronto.

JON A. SHAW, M.D. is Professor and Director, Child and Adolescent Psychiatry, University of Miami School of Medicine, Miami, FL.

BERTRAM SLAFF, M.D. is Associate Clinical Professor of Psychiatry, Mt. Sinai School of Medicine, City University of New York; and Past President, American Society for Adolescent Psychiatry

BRADLEY D. STEIN, M.D. is Robert Wood Johnson Clinical Scholar at UCLA. His work in Bosnia occurred while he was a child psychiatry fellow at the Western Psychiatric Institute and Clinic, University of Pittsburgh School of Medicine.

MAX SUGAR, M.D. is Clinical Professor of Psychiatry, Louisiana State University Medical Center and Tulane University Medical Center, New Orleans. A past president of the American Society for Adolescent Psychiatry, he is the Editor of *Monographs of the International Society for Adolescent Psychiatry.*

CONTENTS OF VOLUMES 1–21

281

Contents of Volumes 1–21

CONTENTS OF VOLUMES 1–21

CONTENTS OF VOLUMES 1–21

Contents of Volumes 1–21

CONTENTS OF VOLUMES 1–21

CONTENTS OF VOLUMES 1–21

301

Contents of Volumes 1-21

Contents of Volumes 1–21

INDEX

313

American Psychiatric Association, 85, 88, 113, 117
American Psychological Association, 263, 265–266, 272
Amnesia, of adolescence, 10
Anal control, and eating disorders, 61
Anderson, G. M., 86, 95
Andrews, D. A., 93
Angelergues, R., 72
Anger. *See also* Impulse control disorders expressions of, 130, 266
Anomic suicide, 53–54
Anomie, 52–54
Anorexia. *See also* Eating disorders compared with melancholia, 60
as "monosymptomatic psychosis," 63–64
Antisemitism. *See* Genocide; Holocaust
Antisocial behavior
neuropsychology of, 92
social etiology of, 125–127, 135
Antisocial personality disorder, 178–182
APA. *See* American Psychiatric Association; American Psychological Association
Apfel, R. J., 227
Appelbaum, P., 128
Applegate, B., 88
Apter, A., 85, 94
Aries, P., 26
Aries, R., 42
Armstrong, T., 121
Arnsten, A. F. T., 99
Aro, H. M., 94
Arredondo, D. E., 92
Arroyo, W., 227
Artists, in psychoanalysis, 5
Art therapy groups, for wartime trauma victims, 233–235
Asbell, M. D., 99
Ascheim, S. E., 49, 52
Asch, S. E., 213
Assassination
of John F. Kennedy, 251
of Yitzhak Rabin, 213–214
adolescents' reaction to, 189–205
Assessment
of impulse control disorders, 96
of juvenile delinquents, 114, 121–122
Associated Marine Institutes, and juvenile rehabilitation, 122
As You Like It (Shakespeare), adolescents in, 35

Attachment
and aggression, development of, 258–261
delinquents' capacity for, 113–114, 122–127, 129–130, 136–137. *See also* Humanization
Attention deficit hyperactivity disorder (ADHD), 85, 88–91, 95, 98f, 99
St. Augustine, 17
Autonomy. *See also* Separation/individuation process
adolescents seeking, 63–65, 143, 152, 163

B

Bachofen, as influence on Nietzsche, 50
Baker, Josephine, self–reinvention of, 13
Baker, S., 87, 95
Baldessarini, R. J., 99
Baldwin, 259
Balla, D. A., 257
Ballenger, J. C., 86
Bandura, A., 259
Barande, I., 72
Barande, R., 72
Barkley, R., 88, 89, 90
Barnard, A., 131
Barrickman, L., 99
Bartholomew, A. A., 117
Bartko, J. J., 86
Bartle, S., 94
Bartok, J., 94
Basketball, wheelchair, for wartime trauma victims, 235–236
Bass, D., 100
Bastien, D. T., 227
Bates, J., 87
Bauer, Ida. *See* "Dora"
Baydens-Branchey, L., 95
Becker, D. F., 93
Becker, E., 218
Behavioral therapy, for impulse control disorder, 100
Being, experiential mode of, 199–203
Bekken, K., 89
Bellow, Saul, on invention in writing, 8
Benedek, E. P., 257, 264
Benedict, K., 90
Benedict, K. B., 90
Bennett, L. A., 95